Indian Media

Global Media and Communication

Adrian Athique, *Indian Media*
Noha Mellor, Khalil Rinnawi, Nabil Dajani and Muhammad Ayish,
   Arab Media
Stylianos Papathanassopoulos and Ralph Negrine, *European Media*

Indian Media
Global Approaches

ADRIAN ATHIQUE

polity

First published in 2012 by Polity Press

Polity Press
65 Bridge Street
Cambridge CB2 1UR, UK

Polity Press
350 Main Street
Malden, MA 02148, USA

ISBN-13: 978-0-7456-5332-7
ISBN-13: 978-0-7456-5333-4(pb)

A catalogue record for this book is available from the British Library.

Typeset in 11 on 13 pt Adobe Garamond
by Servis Filmsetting Ltd, Stockport, Cheshire
Printed and bound in Great Britain by the MPG Books Group

For further information on Polity, visit our website: www.politybooks.com

Contents

Introduction: A Global Approach to the Indian Media

The mass media in India represent one of the most complex fields of communication to be found anywhere in the world. This proves to be the case whether we trace this web of relationships via its technical infrastructures, its commercial organization or through the cultural formations arising from its huge and diverse audiences. As such, the most striking feature of India's media system, when viewed from an exterior perspective, is its vast size and complexity. Scale, therefore, naturally provides an overarching context to our approach. Within that context, there is sufficient depth and breadth along more or less any line of analysis for meaningful complexities to be observed and, with the necessary resources, recorded. There is not scope, however, in any one overview of the topic to capture the field at such a fine grain. Rather, it is my intention here to provide a useful introduction to the field of the Indian media, and to point towards a greater depth of information available in the present literature for those seeking to pursue particular pathways into the topic. My focus on the global also implicitly frames an international readership. For that reason, I aim to provide a skeleton of general knowledge on India that will contextualize some of the arguments presented on the operation of the Indian media. A good measure of this information may be well known to those who have first-hand knowledge of the subject matter, but I would hope those readers might appreciate the benefit of assessing a more explicitly international perspective on some of the critical debates taking place around the media in India today.

In that sense, it is notable that the primary framework for understanding the Indian media over many decades has been a national one. It is equally significant that a large part of this work has been carried out by Indian scholars over the last half of the twentieth century, and that the national story of the Indian media remains, by its very nature, a work in progress. By comparison, it is only in the twenty-first century that the 'international' academy has begun to pay serious attention to the Indian media, and a sustained demand has emerged for their inclusion in wide-ranging comparative accounts of global communication. There are a number of reasons for this shift that can be variously attributed to the commercial, political and intellectual domains. To a significant extent, the newfound interest in the Indian media reflects an era in which foreign investors began to see opportunities for investment in India, not least in the media. As economic growth accelerated in India, and the geopolitics of the world entered a new period of change, the political status of India as a global power has also become more widely recognized. For academics outside of India, it was in this climate that the long process of unwinding the eurocentricism of the social sciences finally began to make headway. There has, accordingly, been a rapid rise in the breadth and scale of publishing on the subject. Much of this work is still being undertaken by Indian scholars, both at home and in the West, but with a growing range of contributions being made from others around the world.

It could be said that the Indian media has become a newly fashionable field of interest in the contemporary 'Western' world. There is more, however, than changing perceptions at play. The media industries in India – from television to telecoms, from cinema to software, from radio to Internet – have themselves all undergone rapid change in this period. Arguably, this has been due to their relative position within a matrix of what could currently be considered the paramount concerns of sociological analysis:

(a) the transformative potential of new media technologies;
(b) the reordering of capital markets (and thus power) due to the implementation of such technologies;
(c) developments in patterns of human activity (including employment and migration); and
(d) shifts in the modes of cultural 'belonging' which can be conceived of within such a powerfully reterritorialized human sphere.

This familiar matrix has commonly been identified as the process of globalization, articulating as eternally new what Arjun Appadurai has called 'modernity at large' (1996). It remains contestable, however, to what extent we can see this phenomenon as emerging out of any single causal origin. Hence, we should be wary of reading from (a) to (d) in a lateral fashion. Not one of them is a singular determinant that can explain all of the others. Rather, it is better to understand these various components as operating within a convergent and overlapping matrix of social change.

A global approach to the Indian media necessitates an emphasis on the contiguity between those actions and the operation of an international media field. As such, we must be attentive to the dialogue conducted with the global inside of India, as well as to the influence of Indian media out in the world at large. In order to do so effectively, I will attempt to outline the case at various points for the distinctive nature of the Indian media as well as for their broad alignment with wider global trends in communications. Given the scale at which this discussion must be conducted, the dominant model of globalization will provide us with an overarching framework for characterizing the broader trends within this vast field of interactions. In that sense, what is true of the study of Indian media at the national level is also true to our approach to the largest and most ambitious object of academic analysis, our world itself. In order to undertake this 'global' approach to the Indian media, we must juxtapose models of globalization with some of the existing approaches for understanding mass communications in India. We can then compare, in broad strokes, the vast with the totality.

Technology, Scale and Distance

One of the foundational claims in support of the proposition that the modern world is unlike its predecessors is made in light of the technical capacity to collapse time and distance within a world-spanning technical apparatus. This infrastructure of machineries designed to overcome the tyranny of distance includes tangible systems of transport such as shipping, aircraft and high-speed motorized land vehicles. Just as significantly, it also includes mechanized carriers of information such as recorded works, telegraphy, broadcasting and digital information exchanges. It was the Canadian scholar Harold Innis who advanced the notion that the technical infrastructures and communicative forms of mass media were fundamentally space-binding and time-binding (1951, 1952). That is, they work to standardize spatial perception, master distance and regulate the human experience of time within their sphere of operation. Marshall McLuhan, following Innis, famously postulated in the 1960s that the mass media represented technological extensions of the human sensory system, the existence of which fundamentally altered human consciousness (1964). McLuhan also posited the notion that the advent of the electronic media had brought into being a 'global village', where each and every part of the world became interconnected by 'information highways' of mass communication (1962, 1968). For McLuhan, living in this densely connected global society, and experiencing it through new mediums like television, would inevitably transform human subjectivity.

McLuhan also claimed that the electronic media would forge a direct link with traditional 'oral' cultures, allowing 'developing' societies to leapfrog the age of print into the new electronic age. Thus, in many respects, his arguments align closely with the views of Daniel Lerner, Wilbur Schramm and others on the potentials of media systems as an accelerator of modernity in 'traditional' societies (Lerner 1958; Schramm 1964). Generally taken as the iconic account of technological determinism in media studies, McLuhan's emphasis on the effects of media technologies over and above their content is consistent with a modernist conception of mechanized progress (Williams 1974). Developed with television in mind, these ideas have been periodically applied to subsequent media technologies, particularly the networked digital information systems of the present era (Levinson 1999). Thus, the propositions of both Innis and McLuhan are in accordance with Anthony Giddens's more contemporary characterization of the technical impetus of globalization, where he notes that: 'Instantaneous electronic communication isn't just a way in which news of information is conveyed more quickly. Its existence alters the very texture of our lives' (2002: 11). Arjun Appadurai, similarly, subscribes to the view that 'electronic mediation transforms pre-existing worlds of communication and conduct' (1996: 3). For Manuel Castells, it is the rise of information technology, and global computer networking in particular, that underpins his theoretical formulation of globalization in the form of a network society (1996).

The notion of a technological catalyst for a globalized state of mind is highly significant to the Indian case – not least since the most critical developments in modern media technologies have been deployed in the subcontinent at more or less the same time that they have been deployed in industrialized societies. In India, the introduction of railways, cinema, telegraphy and broadcasting was contemporaneous with their introduction in the dominant Western world which, following the logic of McLuhan, infers a more or less instant transfer of technological change across the world, with all its attendant effects. In that sense, the technological force of globalization in India should be readily evidenced by the manner in which a nation already densely interlinked to the rest of the world by land and sea came to reposition itself in a world increasingly defined, in the first place, by print and photography and, subsequently, by moving images and data transfers. It is equally important to note that India has not only been a receiver of imported and fully formed technologies. Significant Indian contributions have been made in such fields as satellite broadcasting and computing. At the same time, the human density of India is fundamentally different from the Canadian example that informed Innis and McLuhan. In India, the sheer scale of population adds a further dimension to the process of spanning great physical distances. The capacity to bind together a billion human beings within any system of mass communication raises considerably more technological challenges than crossing ten thousand miles of terrain. For this reason, the process of technological development remains markedly uneven, with hundreds of millions of people fully integrated into half-a-dozen media systems, and hundreds of millions of others remaining largely untouched at the level of daily experience. Nonetheless, the articulation of globalization via a technological paradigm provides a useful rationale for our understanding of the modern era in which India has been brought ever closer to the wider world through increasing volumes of communication. However, this is a process that we need to understand as ongoing and not without its attendant conflicts and anxieties for reasons that necessarily escape the functions of engineering skill.

The Economic Structures of Media

While globalization is typically seen as a set of processes enabled in the first place by technology, much of the subsequent discussion has turned upon the transformation wrought by those processes upon the economic sphere. The most obvious manifestations of those changes are the increasing speed, frequency and volition of international transactions. In a more interconnected world, instantaneous communications speed up the actions of international trade to unprecedented levels. There is no doubt that the automation of commercial processes via digital technologies has provided the impetus for an upsurge in the field of global transactions over the past twenty years. Nonetheless, it is also useful to break down the overall body of transactions into different fields of activity. A proportion of them contribute to increasing volumes of trade in commodities between nations in ways that correspond to traditional understandings of international trade. Probably the most significant change in this arena has been the steady growth in the trade of intangible goods such as information, entertainment and services over and above the trade in tangible, physical goods (Coyle 1999; Leadbeater 2000). Another field of activity can be related to the capacity of communicative efficiency to establish new organizational processes that enable more complex relations of production across various international terrains. It is media technologies that facilitate the growth of more explicitly international business organizations (Castells 1996). Finally, the largest contributor to the overall volume of international transactions is the growth of financial flows seeking profit in their rapid movements between different currencies, commodities and markets (Soros 2002; Das 2004).

The role of the media within this broad field of transactions is complex. This is precisely because media technologies are, at one level, the enabling technologies for much of this activity. At another level, however, media content must also be counted as a tradable commodity in its own right. In addition, the term 'media' also encompasses the ownership and operation of institutions that provide information and entertainment services, whether commercially or on the behalf of national taxpayers. Thus, when we seek to outline the phenomenon of globalization within the media industries we are drawn to three major avenues of enquiry. First, we need to consider the role of media technologies and industries within wider economic processes (Albarran 2009; Castells 1996, 2009). Second, we need to examine both the volumes and the nature of the trade in media content around the world (Moran 2009; Thussu 2007a). Third, we are inclined to look for evidence of patterns of ownership within media institutions that either transcend national boundaries or which, regardless of their institutional origins, seek to cater to or even dominate a wide range of national markets in their operations (Flew 2007). Thus, within the diverse operations of the mass media, trends towards globalization can be evidenced in a number of different ways. Establishing a critical role for media technologies that favours international business relationships provides one set of evidence for *globalization through media*. Identifying a growing volume of international trade in media content points to the ongoing *globalization of media markets*. Finally, assessing the internationalization of capital ownership in the media business provides evidence of an emerging *global media apparatus*.

In the course of this book, I will seek to question the extent of the globalization process at work in the Indian media through all of these dimensions. The 'globalization through media' thesis directs us towards the rise of the Southern Indian city of Bangalore as a major concentration of activity oriented towards the global information technology industry (Aoyama 2003; Parthasarathy 2004). Information technologies in the form of computing applications and telecommunications are also critical to the emergence of a new industry within India over the recent past, that of providing business processing to foreign organizations (Dossani and Kenney 2009; Nadeem 2011). The expansion of India's advertising industry is also a domain in which we can see the extension of the mediasphere as serving the interests of a wider economy of consumption (Mazarella 2003). The 'globalization of media markets' thesis will direct us towards an assessment of the media flows in and out of India, where the formats of cinema and television come under particular scrutiny in terms of both the national/international origins of their content and the specific trajectories of import and export that 'stitch' India into the wider audiovisual field of globalization (Thussu 2007a; Ranganathan and Rodrigues 2010). In the last category of 'an emerging global media apparatus', we will look towards the changing patterns of ownership as well as the overall political economy of the Indian media industries (Athique 2009; Thomas 2010). This constitutes a broad theme that will be relevant across this book as a whole, as we seek to understand the complex ways in which mass communications in India have gone through distinctive periods of integration and disengagement with international investors, while also being subject to shifting policy orientations towards nationalization and liberalization within India itself.

In that sense, we should note from the outset that the seismic changes in the media over the past two decades have been consciously oriented towards private investment. They have been somewhat more cautiously oriented towards global integration, facilitated by the incremental repeal of regulations previously designed to prevent this very process from occurring. Thus, the globalization of media ownership continues to be a contested process for reasons that have been constituted historically in the Indian experience. At the same time, the importation of economic models, ideologies and organizational paradigms from around the world has been welcomed over a much longer period than the present phase of globalization, and this is also a facet of globalization that warrants some analysis. Finally, despite the obvious primacy of the global connectivity of the Indian media to our present concern, we should also note that the tripartite processes of technical enablement, cosmopolitan markets and the institutional integration of capital are at least as relevant for understanding the nature of the domestic media economy in India. In that sense, globalization has also been happening within India for a long time, and this necessarily inflects the nature of its engagement with the exterior manifestation of comparable forces.

The Cultural Dimensions of Media

The nexus between technology and finance provides us with a set of quantifiable structures by which we can assess the increasing integration between different parts of the world. They cannot by themselves, however, recount the full story of globalization, since the wholeness of the world is not only constituted by geographical distance and the distribution of resources. That is why, in making the claim that our daily experience of living in the world is undergoing radical transformation, globalization theories all attempt to link this pattern of technological connections and economic transactions with the shifting conduct of human beings. In doing so, they begin with the more or less explicit observation that human society is discontinuous and variable in its manifest forms. This is primarily evidenced in the phrase 'cultural diversity', which encapsulates the notion that human differences operate at the level of language, spiritual belief systems, socializing rituals, kinship structures, moral regulation, cultural performance and formal political organization (UNESCO 2001). With the important exception of the latter, these factors are all seen as contributing towards a sense of collective identity expressed through the notion of ethnicity. The rise of this concept during the last century marks a critical shift from understanding human differences in terms of innate racial characteristics towards a more diffuse anthropology where the reproduction of various forms of social knowledge are perceived as the major constituent in the human geography of the world.

Since ethnic social knowledge is seen as being both expressed and transmitted through an overlapping set of culturally distinct processes, there is a further implicit assumption that the present form of human difference is determined by the stability of communication. This is because established forms and patterns of social communication, along with the performative traditions of classical and popular culture, are seen as essential components of ethnic socialization (Smith 1999). As such, mass media technologies are inevitably seen as having a profound effect upon the existing order of cultural diversity. While proponents of mass communication in the developing world initially saw the overturning of traditional social orders as a necessary step in fostering scientific modernity and social progress, its critics saw the danger of cultural obliteration due to the primacy of the United States in the production of media content. By this logic, the social mores intrinsic to American film and television programming would ultimately overwrite local cultures and, over time, enforce the 'global homogenization' of culture in its own image (Schiller 1976; Tomlinson 1991). It was this defensive reading of global media flows that justified both widespread restrictions on media imports and the increasing regulatory authority of nation-states over cultural production throughout the twentieth century.

However, the notion of a strong model of media 'effects', where audiences are culturally reprogrammed by foreign ideas, has also been heavily contested. In the first phase of critique, scholars set out to demonstrate that media consumers were heavily differentiated in their responses to media content, primarily due to their own particular social circumstances (Morley 1980). For this reason, people tended to read media content in ways that made sense to them, rejecting messages that challenged their established subjective positions (Hall 1980). In the second phase of critique, the widespread acceptance of the notion that audiences were 'active' rather than 'passive' readers of content was given an international, comparative dimension which sought to record the varying ways in which audiences with different cultural identities read the same media content (Ang 1985; Liebes and Katz 1990). More fundamentally, it was noted that the very idea that the mediated projection of American culture could overwrite, say, French identity was based upon the twin assumptions that the inhabitants of those countries were themselves culturally homogeneous and that this homogeneity could be readily encapsulated via a media format (Higson 2000; Schlesinger 2000).

As media scholars became more attentive to cultural diversity – not just between, but also within, national populations – the third phase of critique sought to emphasize the inherently cosmopolitan field of popular culture in the new era of globalization that emerged at the beginning of the 1990s. The mobility of culture, through the movements of people and of media products, was seen to exemplify a new multicultural reality where all parts of the world were in constant contact (Appadurai 1996). Roland Robertson challenged the 'Americanization' thesis, using the example of the Japanese engagement with American popular culture. Robertson argued that people generally encountered foreign culture on their own terms and in their own social domain, and subsequently reworked it from an indigenous perspective, producing a hybrid product that interlaced the global with the local, leading to 'glocalization' (1994). The logical outcome of the broad-scale operation of this process was not global homogenization through an American form, but rather an acceleration in cultural-mixing, giving rise to a global 'melange' of interrelated cultures (Nederveen Pieterse 1995).

In the past decade, there has also been a growing recognition of other media exporters who contribute to the field of globalization. In recognition of the 'increasing volume and velocity of multi-directional media flows that emanate from particular cities, such as Bombay, Cairo and Hong Kong', Michael Curtin has proposed that we think of the global media not as an imperial force based in the West operating upon the rest of the world, but as a more complex matrix linking media capitals around the globe (2003: 202). This has led to the reformulation of the cultural force of globalization, following the premise that media audiences and industries inhabit a world where cultural exchange is notably uneven, but is nonetheless multi-polar and diffuse. Thus, from this perspective:

> It is simplistic to imagine an active First World simply forcing its products on a passive Third world . . . global mass culture does not so much replace local culture as coexist with it, providing a cultural lingua franca . . . the imported mass culture can also be indigenised, put to local use, given a local accent . . . there are powerful reverse currents as a number of Third World countries (Mexico, Brazil, India, Egypt) dominate their own markets and even become cultural exporters. (Shohat and Stam 1996: 149)

The Indian media emerges as a crucial point of reference within this debate because the film industry in particular has achieved a significant global presence over the course of many decades. It does not command the revenues of Hollywood, but nonetheless reaches audiences across large swathes of the developing world. Thus, the popular Indian film is often posited as the exemplar of the 'contra-flows' of media content that offset the dominance of Western media content (Thussu 2007a).

Establishing the cultural evidence for globalization in India necessarily raises broader and more subjective lines of enquiry than the technological and economic dimensions. The 'cultural imperialism' thesis retains currency, and the arrival of large volumes of Western programming over the past two decades still raises the spectre of foreign cultural influence as a symptom of globalization. As such, we must be attentive to the traces of 'Westernization' upon Indian society as exerted by media content. Simultaneously, we are also required to seek countervailing evidence of the extent to which Indian society is able to 'indigenize' Western media formats and imprint its own media productions with a distinctively Indian cultural form. As a 'contra-flow' of media content, we must also consider the cultural input of Indian media into the field of globalization. In doing all of this, however, we must keep in mind the cultural diversity of India. If it has become apparent that neither the United States nor France has a singular cultural identity when subjected to close examination, the cultural diversity of India is apparent even from the most cursory glance. All of the constituent components of an Indian 'ethnic' culture are inherently pluralized, be that language, faith, ritual, kinship, morality or performance. In that sense, we must be equally attentive to the interplay between homogenization and diversity and between hybridity and authenticity within Indian society. The cultural dimensions of globalization, from an Indian perspective, are thus very much more complicated than the general theoretical account provides for. Nonetheless, where they are absolutely in accordance is in the inherent politicization of culture in our contemporary worldview.

Historical and Neological Frameworks

Most contemporary accounts of the Indian encounter with globalization take their mark from the watershed year of 1991, when the collapse of the Soviet Bloc produced a seismic shift in international relations. In that same year, the Indian government announced its intention to follow a path of economic liberalization and, for those interested in the highly significant role of the media in this new era, this was also the year that international satellite broadcasting began transmitting over and above the old terrestrial state broadcast system. In that sense, globalization in India has generally been given a definite periodization. There is, however, a contention amongst scholars whether globalization represents a radically new set of social conditions or whether it is an extension of longer-term historical processes. In this respect, Ella Shohat and Robert Stam choose to emphasize the continuity between theories of globalization and earlier theories of modernization, seeing both as rooted in the diffusionist model of the 'imperial imaginary' of the colonial world (1996). By contrast, Arjun Appadurai argues that modernity has broken the confines of a centre-periphery model of transmission and become 'decisively at large' (1996: 3). Appadurai emphatically locates this radical transformation in the recent past, asserting that 'it is only in the past two decades or so that media and migration have become so massively globalized, that is to say, active across large and irregular transnational terrains' (1996: 9).

Appadurai therefore presents 'a theory of rupture that takes media and migration as its two major, and interconnected, diacritics', going as far as to suggest that a 'mobile and unforeseeable relationship between mass-mediated events and migratory audiences defines the core of the link between globalization and the modern' (1996: 3–4). Accordingly, Appadurai puts the electronic visual media at the heart of globalization, locating transnational media practices as both catalyst and primary evidence of a changing world. It is certainly the case that both of these phenomena have become increasingly significant for the upper middle classes of the Indian subcontinent during this period. The migration of South Asians to the West has expanded its intake well beyond the traditional elite. There are important and identifiable linkages between those patterns of migration and the dissemination of Indian media content. The expansion of the Indian domestic media environment in the past two decades articulates a cultural milieu that is entirely new to postcolonial generations, and it far outstrips the reach of previous periods of expansion during the colonial era. Similarly, the increasing internationalization of business has symbolically overturned five decades of substantially self-contained nationalist economics. Thus, for many Indians, globalization does appear to constitute an entirely new social experience, one that naturally supports the neological reading of globalization.

Taking the alternative view, Antony Hopkins, amongst others, has described the contemporary convergence of media technologies, international finance capital, geopolitics and cultural interchange as simply a continuation of related processes at play over several centuries (Hopkins 2002). From this perspective, it is argued that all of these contributing factors may have increased in sophistication over time, becoming ever more prolific and significant at a global scale, but this is primarily an increase in scale rather than a 'moment of rupture'. As such, it is argued that trade in the colonial world was also dominated by global corporations and international transactions. The British East India Company, which progressively took over the Indian subcontinent during the eighteenth century, is an iconic example of this process. Similarly, the media-migration nexus has some precedents. *The Times* of London was influential in the fostering of a transnational imaginary amongst the globally dispersed functionaries and subjects of Empire in the nineteenth century. Benedict Anderson's well-known historical research has sought to demonstrate how the spread of print media transformed the social imagination of the various peoples of South East Asia during the nineteenth century, recasting their social referents through the force of global comparisons (1991, 1998). From the historical view, therefore, the world may be more globalized now than it was thirty years ago, but the component forces of globalization have been equally strong in other epochs.

In this work, I will seek to balance these two opposing views. For the most part, I will focus on the here-and-now of the Indian media in terms of their contemporary engagement with the global. I do so in recognition that the primary concern of global media analysis is to understand the complex forces of social change in the present. However, I also firmly believe that if we are to understand the distinctive nature of the Indian media in a manner that is amenable to international comparison, we need to consider two previous phases of globalization during which the mass media played a highly significant role in articulating India's relationship with the wider world. I will therefore devote a chapter to the recent past, outlining the approaches to mass communications that India followed during the decades of international decolonization and developmental socialism prior to 1991. Before doing so, I will turn my attention further back to the period when India was fitfully integrated into an imperial global system, and was in the process of taking shape as a nation. It was in this context that the arrival of mass communications systems played a vital role in constituting the political and cultural identity of modern India. As mass media systems in India were developed and woven into the fabric of social life, they became inextricably caught up with critical debates surrounding the future society that India's inhabitants experience today.

1   Mass Media and the Making of Modern India

The colonial period in India was a lengthy and complex set of historical processes that stemmed from the expansion of international trade, increased global competition and the impact of new technologies on the international order. It was driven by the interests of multinational trading companies, military adventurers, political opportunists, patriots, entrepreneurs, religious zealots and liberal 'non-governmental' movements. It was made possible in the first instance by an acute imbalance in power between different regions of the world, and by the collapse of an older empire. In that sense, the global conditions that set the stage for two centuries of colonial rule in India are familiar to us today, even if their particular manifestations have since become matters of historical debate. What has become fundamentally different about the world since India became independent from British rule in 1947 is that the pernicious logics of social Darwinism and racial supremacy, that made the absolutist rule of one race over another formally permissible, have been toppled from legitimacy, if not vanquished entirely. The story of India's struggle for independence was absolutely central to a wider global struggle for self-determination, to the extent that Barack Obama, speaking in 2010 as the first African-American President of the United States, claimed that his own position would not be possible today without the enduring legacy of Mohandas Gandhi, the popular leader of India's independence movement (Obama 2010).

The popular image of Gandhi as a bespectacled old man in a simple loin cloth, taking on one of the world's most formidable economic and military powers, is one of the most memorable images of the twentieth century (Gold and Attenborough 1983). The photographs, newsreels and printed materials that carried Gandhi's message around the world cemented his international reputation as the *mahatma* of a non-violent campaign of resistance against foreign domination. The global mediation of Gandhi's idealist message inspired people all over the world and proved to be the match of the sophisticated propaganda machinery of the British Empire (Brown and Parel 2011). His capacity to communicate with the ordinary people of India mobilized enormous grassroots support throughout the subcontinent and, indeed, the world. At the same time, his astute understanding of the contradictions between liberalism and imperialism in British politics enabled him to mount an effective argument with India's colonial ruler in its own philosophical language. It remains true that the non-violent path to freedom could not be trodden without violence on both sides. Gandhi also had powerful backers and opponents amongst India's elite. Nonetheless, his example makes it very clear that the sophisticated use of modern communications was a critical factor in building the nationalist movement from its early days at the close of the nineteenth century. In some measure, therefore, we can productively relate the distinctive field of Indian media to the unique Indian experiences of developing substantial print and cinema industries whilst living under colonial rule.

The Colonial Press

The irony, of course, is that the development trajectory of those communication systems was in a large part a consequence of India's incorporation into the imperial system. The British East India Company, a private concern with its own military forces, grew steadily in both power and commercial ambitions throughout the seventeen hundreds and into the nineteenth century, taking sovereign rights over Indian territory. The East India Company benefited directly from the explicit backing of Britain's own national army and navy, but also from the global military and commercial communication systems that were developed hand in hand with the expansion of Britain's empire. Fuelled by the wealth and resources being extracted from its far-flung colonial territories, the British industrial revolution spurred on new technological developments which in turn extended, strengthened and coordinated those processes of extraction on an unprecedented scale. The integration of the various regions and states of India via railway transport is the most commonly cited example of this process, but the implementation of a standard postal system and the introduction of the telegraph were also critical components in the formal institution of imperialism (Thomas 2010: 44–6). Following the end of the East India Company and the assumption of direct British rule in India after 1857, the impact of these technologies and the bureaucracies that served them exerted ever greater influence over India's colonial society.

It would be wrong, however, to assume that India had not previously developed sophisticated communicative infrastructures of its own. To a significant extent, British rule after 1857 was dependent upon improving the scale and efficiency of their own communications in isolation from the 'native' public sphere that C. A. Bayly has termed the 'Indian ecumene' (1999). In that domain, the manual circulation of handwritten messages, despatch of oral emissaries and the function of commercial intermediaries between different parts of the subcontinent were necessarily limited by the vast distances, political fragmentation and linguistic diversity of the subcontinent. By contrast, the British were able to concert the actions of their rule much more efficiently via a standardized political, linguistic and technological framework. Nonetheless, as a result of its increasing interaction with and mastery of those imperial technologies, the Indian ecumene would over time ultimately overwhelm the communicative monopolies of colonial rule. The critical communications technology in that process was undeniably the printing press. The first newspaper to be printed in India emerged during the era of the East India Company. Founded by a British settler in Bengal in 1790, the *Bengal Gazette* was intended to operate as an organ for the local British settler population. Nonetheless, the *Bengal Gazette* very quickly raised the ire of the authorities in India, for largely the same reasons that the early British press also fell foul of the establishment back home (Kohli-Kandekar 2006: 22–3). The circulation of the printed interests and opinions of the British Indian population would come to represent a public petition that countermanded the absolute rule of the colonial authorities. Much like the growing power of the British press, the English press in India came to be associated with a liberal, reform-minded agenda that challenged the authorities both to justify their own actions and to respond to public demands. For that very reason, the authorities treated the press with distrust and imposed stringent licensing and registration laws for the publication of newspapers.

The most prominent of the English publications was the Bombay-based *Times of India*, founded in 1838 and remaining today one of the most read English language newspapers in the world, despite the wholesale departure of its original readership some sixty years ago. The reason for the continuing success of the *Times of India* today is the widespread prevalence of English literacy amongst Indians, a process that began to gather pace in the very years that the press was established in India. As British rule expanded further into India, both geographically and socially, in the years after 1857, the expanding bureaucracy of the Raj could not be filled by the British alone. A mixture of expediency, imperial arrogance and liberal philosophy made the British increasingly amenable to institutions of English education being made available to the Indians. For their part, educated Indians with ambitions and the necessary means could readily discern that mastery of English was to be a prerequisite for entry into the new administrative professions being created by the imperial project. Their ensuing enthusiasm for English also brought them into contact with the form and ideals of the English press, enabling them to steadily make their way into the debates over Indian politics and public life. The action of the press everywhere was, as Benedict Anderson has noted, to transform the social and geopolitical perspectives of its readers (1991). For the Indian readers of the colonial press, access to the political debates at play amongst the colonizing society transformed their political understanding of British colonialism. Even more importantly, it gave small groups of literate people across India ready access to events in other parts of Britain's Indian Empire. This inexorably gave rise to a pan-Indian public sphere that transcended the numerous localized public spheres that had previously characterized Indian public life. The press in India thus operated in a comparable fashion to Habermas's description of Europe's public sphere a century before (1989).

The emergence of an English-literate Indian middle class was a critical factor in the development of a national Indian consciousness that transcended regional differences. At the same time, however, the rise of the English press in India was no more significant than the inspiration it gave for the very rapid development of a 'native' press in a number of Indian languages such as Bengali, Gujarati and Hindi from 1818 onwards. The development of movable typefaces in standardized Indian scripts massively extended the potential readership of newspapers and books in India. It also facilitated a very different realm of discourse from the English dailies, enacting a bifurcated public sphere that continues to a certain extent even today. While the contributions of Indians to the English-language press were generally liberal and reform-minded critiques coming from an officially recognized native elite, the so-called 'vernacular press' tapped directly into a far larger set of India's middle classes, revealing in the process a much more antagonistic sentiment to the British presence (Orsini 2002). In that sense, while the English press gradually admitted selected Indians into colonial public life, the simultaneous growth of Indian language publications mobilized the social and cultural resources of India's traditional ecumene on its own terms. In this context, public debates were consciously routed through indigenous traditions, often couched in classical and spiritual terms, and frequently expressed in explicit opposition to the imposition of the British worldview in India. The meeting of the two public spheres, for those able to access both of them, was central to the literary and political renaissance that swept Bengal in the last half of the nineteenth century. It was all across India, however, that traditional discourses re-entered political debate with a new reach and vigour through the vernacular press.

For the British, the vernacular press exposed an India that they had only dimly perceived and that they rightly feared. Initially, the response of the authorities was hampered by an overall scarcity of British officials who were able to read their content directly. It was only gradually, then, that the British became aware of the expanding readership and content of these publications, and began to set 'reliable' Indian intermediaries to scrutinize their content for political agitation or anti-British sentiments (Jeffrey 2002a). By the 1870s, the already stringent rules imposed upon the Indian press in the name of public order were superseded by legislation that targeted the vernacular press specifically, and much more harshly than the English press.

> Using the broad argument of the public interest, the British appealed to the 'rule of law' and argued that public order must be maintained at all costs. It was the secret success of Imperial jurisprudence to reduce all questions of freedom of speech and expressions into questions of public order. By this token, any expression of free speech – ranging from street demonstrations and pamphlets protesting the effects of the Raj to armed revolts-were all interconnected as constituting an integrated threat to public order. . . . From 1870, the Indian Penal Code was systematically extended to cover 'constructive' threats to public order through the press . . . such a policy made a mild reformist seem like a criminal and a provocative pamphleteer like a dangerous revolutionary . . . The essence of such a policy was rooted in a total distrust of the press and what it was capable of doing. (Dhavan 2009: 89, 93)

The introduction of the Vernacular Press Act in 1878 failed to repress an exuberant field of Indian popular journalism. Under its aegis, printing presses and publications were seized, and journalists and editors were jailed, but the Indian-language publications continued to multiply across India for the remainder of the colonial period. Thus: 'Although the Vernacular Press Act (1878) was enacted to control the nationalist press, its suppression merely led to the making of a stronger more diverse vernacular press committed to the cause of freedom from British rule' (Thomas 2010: 43). As Pradip Thomas has further noted, it is far from insignificant that Indian journalists contributed a large cohort of the members of the Indian National Congress at its founding in 1885. The support of the vernacular press for the Congress was strong and enduring, as calls, first for home rule, and then for full independence, gathered in strength in the first two decades of the twentieth century. Thus, as Daya Thussu argues, an Indian press, both in English and in the Indian languages, became an integral component in the rise of anti-colonial nationalism, providing a necessary vehicle for nationalist discourse as well as serving to develop informal political constituencies amongst their readerships (2000).

Cinema Under Occupation

Despite its enormous influence over the nationalist movement, the low levels of literacy in any language amongst the masses of the Indian population imposed a practical limit upon the reach of the press. Cinema, the next manifestation of the media revolution to make its appearance, did not suffer from this constraint. The first moving picture shows had arrived in India in 1896, within months of the first shows in Europe and America, as part of the very rapid global spread of the new technology. By this time, the British Raj was at the height of its power, but anti-colonial nationalism was also growing in strength. The early years of the cinema in India were subsequently accompanied by the catalytic events (such as the abortive partition of Bengal in 1905, the Great War 1914–18, and the massacre at Amritsar in 1919) that were to lead eventually to the independence and partition of the patchwork of territories assembled under British Paramountcy in India. Against this backdrop, the cinema was initially a far from contentious ocular curiosity of Western provenance. The exhibition of film reels in India consisted of imported material from Europe and America, screened for what was a predominantly European audience in a small number of exclusive metropolitan venues. As such, the first cinema halls, commonly known as film theatres or picture palaces at that time, were constructed in the districts where the European population either resided or conducted their business affairs. The popularity of the new medium with this urban elite, and the promise of the profits to be made from theatrical exhibition, encouraged a number of Indian businessmen to build cinema halls.

As the film medium evolved rapidly in the early years of the twentieth century from a technological novelty into a widely accessible narrative form, Indian film-makers such as D. G. Phalke launched an increasingly popular indigenous film production industry. The first Indian films, notably Phalke's *Raja Harishandra* (1913), but also Calcutta-based Ganguly's *England Returned* (1913), clearly appealed to the urban Indians who went to see them. The subsequent demand for Indian productions was significant and substantial enough to provide the basis for nascent film industries to develop in British India's Bombay, Bengal and Madras presidencies. As a result, the 'number of theatres in India increased from about 150 in 1923 to about 265 in 1927' (Barnouw and Krishnaswamy 1980: 38). It was during this period of growth that the market for film exhibition steadily expanded beyond the consumption of European and American films by European and native elite audiences in the capital cities to encompass a more socially diverse audience in those cities, as well as in the lesser (*mofussil*) towns. Critically, this was also the period in which Mohandas Gandhi returned to India from South Africa (1915) and began a series of popular campaigns for social and political reform, such as the Champaran Agitation in 1918. Gandhi recognized how both imperial rule and social prejudice brought suffering to the peoples of India. By contrast with the educated elites and intellectuals who had previously dominated the independence movement, Gandhi's skill in mobilizing the common people, and his capacity to infuriate and outwit the British authorities, gained him many influential admirers. He was nominated as leader of the Indian National Congress in 1921 (Krishna 1966).

Gandhi's campaigns of non-cooperation with British rule, entailing mass defiance of British laws and the boycott of British goods, caught the world's attention through the reports of international journalists. His subsequent imprisonment by the British from 1922–4 did much to undermine their own efforts to portray Indian nationalists to the rest of the world as dangerous subversives. His message of non-violence and human dignity spread widely in a world much more densely connected by mass communication than it had been in the early years of nationalist movement. He corresponded frequently with international figures from around the world (Parel 1997). In the other direction, images and ideas from the outside world flooded into India on an unprecedented scale, including the communist ideals of Lenin and the Russian Revolution, the liberal democracy of the United States, British Fabian Socialism and the fascism of Hitler's Germany. All of these ideologies found their followers in India, who sought to adapt them to the needs of India's independence struggle, operating alongside the voices of those such as Gandhi who sought to mobilize an indigenous politics. After his release, Gandhi worked hard to reconcile the competing voices in the independence movement and periodically resumed his campaigns and agitations, culminating in the famous 'salt march' of 1930 to Dandi, where he led thousands of his followers in defiance of the British monopoly on India's salt. With the world's press in attendance, images of the British authorities violently beating unresisting activists on the march spread rapidly around the world, making Gandhi a household name as far away as the United States (Suchitra 1995).

Given the rise of anti-colonial feeling and ever more frequent public demonstrations against British rule, the Government of India in the twilight years of the British Raj had little interest in the development of a leisure industry predicated upon public assembly and accessible to the lower social orders. The government's primary interest in cinema, therefore, was in regulating the construction and programmes of cinema halls in order to prevent the inculcation of 'seditious ideas', whether they resulted from American or Indian movies. Accordingly, the censorship of films in India was instituted as early as 1918 with the Indian Cinematograph Act. Censorship of imported films primarily sought to prevent the degradation of the image of Caucasians that might arise from the exposure of the natives to Hollywood films. The British believed that Hollywood movies presented white women as promiscuous and thus threatened the moral superiority of the white race in the eyes of their colonial subjects (Arora 1995). In terms of the Indian film-makers, censorship was intended to restrict the ability of Indian film-makers to make films that sympathized with the nationalist movement (Prasad 1998: 78). Indian films were forbidden to ferment unrest, espouse nationalist sentiment or criticize colonial rule, and were frequently censored in this regard.

It is worth recognizing that this kind of paranoia surrounding new forms of mass culture, and their social impact, was also being felt at home by European elites in the wake of socialist agitation in the 1920s and 1930s. However, in the case of British India, a colonial government that was rapidly losing legitimacy had even more cause to experience trepidation about the growth of a modern public culture. When it came to the unanticipated emergence of a popular Indian cinema, it was not simply the presumed psychological effects, or the ideological efficacy of the medium, that concerned colonial officials. Rather, it was the combination of this effect with the degree of mass participation required to make the exhibition of films profitable in a market where tickets had to be priced from just a few *annas* (a fraction of a rupee). For the authorities, the rapid turnover of large crowds that was intrinsic to mass exhibition implied:

> The daily collecting of crowds in the street . . . at regular intervals before a film show and then, after being emotionally galvanized through the collective experience of film-watching, exiting together on to the streets again, [this] made the police authorities particularly concerned. The colonial government of India had long recognized crowds, especially those of religious processions and at dramatic performances, as a potentially uncontrollable threat to the political and social order. The very notion of collective gatherings, even at places of public entertainment, carried assumed connotations of riotous mobs and revolutionary masses. (Hughes 2000: 49–50)

The extension of censorship to the cinema, which quickly followed the advent of Indian film production, thus employed a similar logic to earlier British censorship of the press, theatre and other forms of communication and performance. Political themes were forbidden and 'public morality' was strictly enforced in an arbitrary fashion by a series of censorship boards dominated by British members. Accordingly, the genres which characterized Indian film-making in the colonial period were the 'mythological' and the 'social'. The former presented portrayals of Indian, particularly Hindu, narrative traditions, and the latter focused on issues of social reform (for example, the status of women and the plight of untouchables) that had risen to prominence as the process of modernization gained pace. These were themes to which the colonial authorities could not reasonably object. However, since India's nationalist leaders were espousing both cultural revival and social reform as intrinsic components in the achievement of an independent India, these subjects could not effectively be disassociated from the barely suppressed debate on India's political future. The subtext of many Indian films of the period was clearly political, and the cinema was developing a potentially far greater mass audience than the press. It was more readily available to India's illiterate majority at precisely the same time that Gandhi and others were seeking to mobilize their support for the nationalist movement. As such, the very rapid growth of the Indian film industries during the 1930s and 1940s has frequently been seen as making a significant contribution to the cementing of an Indian national consciousness (Chakravarty 1993).

For its part, the colonial government was ill-placed to proscribe the vibrant socio-cultural discourse taking place in the cinema and elsewhere without undermining its claim to cultural impartiality by intruding into Indian 'domestic' life, thus further evidencing its own illegitimacy. What it was able to do was to intervene itself in the media arena. The primary vehicles for the British in this regard, aside from the English press, were the state-owned Information Films of India and their broadcasting monopoly via All India Radio. The British-run Information Films of India produced government newsreels and documentaries that became mandatory trailers at film shows (Barnouw and Krishnaswamy 1980: 126). All India Radio, instituted in 1936, broadcast a British account of Indian and international affairs across the breadth of India. As Pradip Thomas notes, All India Radio: became 'an indispensable medium for propaganda, information gathering and dissemination. In fact, the propaganda was directed at two enemies of the Empire – the nascent Congress movement and the axis powers, Germany in particular' (2010: 46). These new state-owned media institutions were regarded by many Indians as bearers of an inherently untrustworthy subjective commentary. For those who worked for the imperial broadcasting authorities, the exciting new potentials of the medium for the benefit of unprecedented numbers of people across the vastness of India was directly hindered by their implementation as a self-interested arm of state control (Pinkerton 2008). On a small scale, the independence movement responded with pirate radio broadcasts of its own (Thomas 2010: 47). As such, the educational and political potentials of radio were quickly perceived by all of the major players. By the end of the 1930s, the independence struggle had become a war of ideas that encompassed every available medium of communication, and all forms of content, including news, education and entertainment.

Colonialism, Nationalism and Culture

The anxieties felt by the colonial authorities in India regarding the cinema reflected wider international discourses on the social effects of mass media, as well as some of the specific concerns of British rule in India. Fundamentally, the growth of mass media industries addressing an Indian 'national' public could not help but underscore the lack of cultural legitimacy intrinsic to colonial rule. The British were always keen to assert that India was not and never had been a nation, and claimed their rights to governance on the basis that the colonial state served as an arbiter between disparate ethnic, linguistic and religious communities which would otherwise descend into a state of conflict (Oomen 2000: 1). The legitimacy of British rule depended therefore on a claim of cultural impartiality, a claim that was becoming increasingly untenable in a world where nationalism, and its linking of cultural particularity and political identity, was in the ascendant. The nature of British arbitration and its doctrine of divide-and-conquer in the political arena were also in perpetual discord with Britain's economic interests in India, which required an ever-greater integration of the subcontinent. While explicit political discourse could be repressed through censorship, the supposed cultural impartiality of the Raj made it difficult to censure discussion of India's cultural heritage. As a result, the systematic repression of overt political commentary in the press forced Indian writers to express their views primarily through the domestic and spiritual domains over which the colonial government could not exert its authority. Given the cultural logic of modern nationalism, these debates inevitably became central in the formation of the Indian nationalist movements. This further cemented the link between the vernacular media and the politicization of India's cultural traditions, widening the gulf between the 'popular' media and the channels of official communications monopolized by the state.

As such, while the first generation of India's nationalist movement was heavily influenced by the English language press, it was the constituency of the vernacular press that was to expand and drive forward the independence movement in the 1920s. By focusing debates on the social and cultural components of nationhood, Indian nationalists were able to monopolize both poles of an oppositional tradition–modernity binary that was naturally exacerbated by colonial rule. Partha Chatterjee has observed that this resulted in certain particularities in the impact of modernity and the growth of the public sphere in colonial India, manifested in the conceptualization, by both colonizer and colonized alike, of distinct 'public' and 'private' domains of the nation.

> By my reading, anti-colonial nationalism creates its own domain of sovereignty within colonial society well before it begins its political battle with the imperial power. It does this by dividing the world of social institutions and practices into two domains – the material and the spiritual. The material is the domain of the 'outside', of the economy and of statecraft, of science and technology,

a domain where the West had proved its superiority and the East had succumbed. In this domain, then, Western superiority had to be acknowledged and its accomplishments carefully studied and replicated. The spiritual, on the other hand, is an 'inner' domain bearing the 'essential' marks of cultural identity. The greater one's success in imitating Western skills in the material domain, therefore, the greater the need to preserve the distinctness of one's spiritual culture. This formula is, I think, a fundamental feature of anti-colonial nationalisms in Asia and Africa. (Chatterjee 1993: 6)

Under colonial conditions, mobilizing a popular discourse centred on cultural identity provides a powerful means of challenging the illegitimacy of the state. The British Raj, as a colonial state, was predicated upon the ideological construction of the racial supremacy of the rulers and of inimical differences between its subjects. A state in this form was unable to transform itself into a nation-state since it could not, by its own premise, successfully establish a vision of 'deep horizontal comradeship' amongst its population (Anderson 1991: 7). The colonial power nonetheless controlled the institutions of state, meaning that no union of nation and state through shared cultural identity was likely to take place. As such, the growth of mass media in the late colonial period in India was taking place in a social environment where cultural activity was seen as, if not entirely antagonistic to the state, then at the very least existing largely beyond the purview of state control. For its part, the colonial regime was far from disposed to support or encourage the growth of Indian cinema, public performance or press.

The Indian Cinematograph Committee of 1927 was set up to review the conditions of cinema exhibition and film production and was intended to persuade India to restrict film imports from the United States in favour of a quota of 'Empire' films. This protectionist attempt at a global British cinema to ward off the 'corrupting' American influence was a global initiative that was put forward to Empire and Commonwealth territories around the world (Jaikumar 2006: 65–103). By this time, however, Indian films were on their way to surpassing Hollywood imports in the domestic market. As such, the Indian members of the ICC committee proposed instead that a quota be imposed for Indian-made films. The British members of the committee baulked and the report was shelved (Barnouw and Krishnaswamy 1980: 39–58; Jaikumar 2003). Nonetheless, even without such protection, Indian-made films became dominant in Indian cinema halls by the end of the decade, and 1,323 silent features were produced in India prior to the coming of sound production in 1931 (Rajadhyaksha and Willemen 1999: 32). The ICC report remains of great interest because it catches the cinema in India during the transition from being a pastime of the colonial elite in the 1910s to being India's foremost mass media by the 1940s. However, the British colonial authorities were not the only critics of the cinema and its public. In a written contribution to the ICC in 1927, Mahatma Gandhi denounced cinema as 'a sinful technology', although, writing for his journal *Harijan* in 1942, he also recognized the popularity of cinema halls, conceding that: 'If I began to organise picketing in respect of them, I should lose my caste, my Mahatmaship' (Gandhi 1942).

As Robin Jeffrey notes, Gandhi was as sceptical of the modern media as he was adroit at public relations (2009). Despite being named as 'Man of the Year' by *Time* magazine (1930), he responded to a request for a filmed interview in 1931 by saying:

> I do not like this kind of thing, but I shall reconcile myself to it, if not more than a few minutes have to be given. Although I know that this sort of enterprise will advertise you, which is your primary object, I know also that it will serve to advertise the cause which I represent – India's independence. I do not discount the value of propaganda. I have been described as the greatest propagandist in the world. I may deserve the compliment. But my propaganda is unlike the ordinary. It is that of truth which is self-propagating. Truth abhors artificiality. (Quoted in Jeffrey 2009: 175)

This distrust of artifice, commercialism and spectacle was in accord with Gandhi's longstanding commitment to austerity and simplicity in both personal and social life. His ideals of a 'return' to a traditional, pre-industrial society comprised of model villages could not be easily reconciled with an intrinsically urban, industrial medium like the cinema. For others in the nationalist movement, such as Jawaharlal Nehru, modernity was associated more positively with scientific and industrial progress and social and political reform. However, in the face of a vocal Gandhian critique within the Congress, it was also associated negatively with the intrusion of the colonial power into the public realms of politics, industry and commerce, and with the disparagement and subjugation of traditional society. As a quintessentially modern medium derived from an imported technology, cinema was thus far from a neutral practice in colonial India, either as a communicative form or as a social space. It was inevitably situated in the heated discursive contest between tradition and modernity. In thinking about the implications of the cinema hall as a public space in India, it is crucial to recognize that the cinema hall was a thoroughly modern addition to public life, not simply in terms of its technological apparatus, but also in its reordering of social space. In a context where 'respectable' women may not have appeared in public at all, and where temples, residential areas and water sources were often subject to exclusive access by certain caste, faith and class groups, the gathering together of a diverse public within a single social space appears to have represented a radical departure from existing social norms (Agrawal 1984; Srinivas 2000a).

Jeffrey further notes that Gandhi only once watched a film, and described it as a 'depressing experience and I felt like running away from the place, but could not do so. It was sheer waste of time' (Jeffrey 2009: 176). These comments reflect an intrinsic distrust of 'entertainment' that permeated the various factions of the Congress movement. For the Ghandians, social improvement began with self-improvement and disciplined gainful activity. For the socialists, the grinding poverty of much of India made entertainment a misuse of scarce resources. For the communists, the commercial cinema was an 'opiate of the masses' they sought to mobilize. For religious conservatives of all stripes, the cinema was a mesmerizing technology loaded with alien values. As such, charges were frequently made from all quarters against the cinema as an agent of capitalism, Westernization and a polluting source of foreign morality (Barnouw and Krishnaswamy 1980: 137). Undeterred, film producers such as Mehboob Khan consciously sought to express the zeitgeist of national liberation through the medium, and to employ the cinema in the reinvention of 'indigenous' cultural narratives *and* in the imaginings of social reform. Thus, the 'social film', which by the time of independence in 1947 had largely supplanted the 'mythological' and 'stunt' films of the early years, articulated both the 'need to maintain indigenous realities against the fascination for Western cultural behaviour' *as well as* a 'critique of Indian society . . . setting up an agenda for change' (Vasudevan 2000a: 133).

Nationalist politicians (whether secularist or communalist, socialist or capitalist) frequently employed rhetorical constructions of a 'traditional' India in their speeches and writings. They did so in order to forge connections between a pre-colonial past and the possibility of a postcolonial future. This 're-awakening' or 'invention' of tradition was an essential precursor for making claims for self-determination, and for gaining control of the state itself (Hobsbawm and Ranger 1983). Thus, the political standing of tradition was enhanced by its symbolic role as a site of resistance to the foreign imposition of colonial rule. However, the historicist notions that underpinned such discourses were undeniably articulated as a response to the advent of modernity. Indeed, anti-colonial nationalisms can be seen as a particularly modern form of political response, constituting a political imaginary bound by a 'shared cultural identity' centred upon the concept of indigeneity. As such, the harnessing of many diverse cultural formations to the imperatives of a Janus-faced modernity, tainted by colonialism, was an intrinsic component in the formulation of a national popular culture in India. The structuring terminology of a political and economic public domain and a socio-cultural private domain in Chatterjee's description illustrates how powerfully modernist perspectives informed nationalist discourse in India, not least on the matter of modernity itself. Indeed, it might be argued that due to their marginal position within imperialist grand narratives of progress, the inhabitants of colonial societies had no choice but to engage critically with the logic of the modern, and to do so long before the advent of Western postmodernism.

The cultural politics of Indian nationalism were necessarily complex, and their mobilization would inevitably split the independence movement in its latter years, every bit as much as the desperate and divisive manoeuvres of the colonial government. Institutionally, the inherent opposition between colonizer and colonized was reflected in the attendant division between the popular media (print, cinema) and the state organs (broadcasting, documentary). Beyond this, the domain of communications was characterized in terms of its content and function by a further split between private and public spheres of activity, powerfully marked with the binary opposition of tradition and modernity. This binary was commonly mapped on to a further opposition between Westernization and indigeneity. Under the influence of Ghandi's philosophical politics, the legitimacy of the media was also challenged by an austere model of pleasure versus self-sacrifice. As such, these powerful contradictions within political discourse on India's future were manifested in the narrative aesthetics of the Indian media. The media of necessity crossed all of these binaries, and was itself defined by them as a social institution in the eyes of politicians and the public at large. The twin attack of colonial repression and conservative critique was not enough, however, to offset the enormous growth in the scope and popularity of the mass media in India at this time. Accordingly, in the last years of empire, the press and cinema formed a large portion of the public domain where these grand themes were played out in the guise of both information and of entertainment. For all these reasons, the role of the media in India was shaped by the particular social conditions in operation. India was then, as it is now, a society in the process of massive social change. However, in order to understand the forces at play, we also need to understand them as being active across a wider global terrain, where a monopoly on technological and political progress was being wrested from the hands of the European colonial powers. An international order integrated by capitalism and by mass communications, but divided by geography, culture and race, was beginning to disintegrate. This was a world where the extremely rapid pace of change provoked many to look to the past and, in the process, change that too. Above all, this was a world being everywhere transformed by a new mass politics and the power of images.

Speaking to Diversity

In approaching the contours of the early Indian media in terms of the administrative and cultural politics of colonialism, we are able to discern certain fault lines within the public sphere that would have an enduring legacy. However, we should also be equally attentive to another highly distinctive feature of the Indian media environment, which is its inherent polyphony. The Indian subcontinent, vast in size and varied in race, religion and climate, is also host to a considerable linguistic diversity. There are a dozen major languages spoken by regional populations that are bigger than national populations in many other parts of the world. There are, in addition, some two hundred smaller languages spoken by just a few million people apiece. For the Indian press, this multi-language market inherently favoured the development of a strong regional focus in publishing. Newspaper and book production very quickly became centred upon the largest cities of India, and produced works that spoke to the constituency of the most prevalent local language. The pursuit of an accessible mass readership naturally favoured the large British presidency cities of Calcutta, Bombay and Madras, as well as the fleeting imperial capital of New Delhi.

Calcutta was the home of the Bengali language press. Madras hosted publishers of Tamil and Telugu works. Cosmopolitan Bombay was home to publishers in the major regional languages of Western India, such as Gujarati and Marathi, as well as Hindi-language works that were accessible to the much larger population of the North. Hindi-language publications were also based in Delhi, close to the seat of power in the last years of the Raj. Alongside Hindi publishing in Devanagiri script, the production of Urdu works in Arabic script reflected the common tongue and distinctive readerships of Hindus and Muslims in North India. As the major centres of European occupation, English-language publications were produced in all of these cities. Other Indian cities were also home to regional publishers in languages such as Punjabi, Malayalam, Assamese, Oriya and Kannada. As we have seen, the growth of these 'vernacular' print vehicles was essential for print materials to break out of a tiny elite readership, but the renaissance of Indian-language writing that followed was also necessarily limited by language barriers. As Francesca Orsini has noted, the leading proponents of a native Indian literature faced the ignominy of having to communicate in English as the only language that they could all understand (2002). The status of English as the link language and the language of power was highly controversial in the 1930s and remains so today. At a practical level, however, the necessity of translating and resetting materials for distribution in other parts of the country was a fairly straightforward matter. Indeed, the distances involved, as well as the strength of regional affiliation and administration, made a regional press structure logical in other ways. Works of literature were somewhat diminished by the process of translation, but the everyday operation of general and technical communication was relatively unhindered by the diversity of the linguistic field. A literacy rate of 18 per cent in any language was the real barrier (Thussu 1999: 126).

The technical side of the problem was an entirely different matter in the cinema. During the initial period of silent cinema, neither language nor literacy stood in the way of the mobility of feature films. However, the coming of sound production with the first talkie, *Alam Ara*, in 1931, provided an obstacle as much as an opportunity to Indian film-makers. While the resulting demand for films in Indian languages definitively diminished the presence of imported films to a negligible level, it also made it inevitable that Indian film production would become centred around the largest linguistic groups. The process of translating a film for a different linguistic audience was much more complicated than translation for the press. Film-makers addressed the fragmentation of the audience for Indian talkies in a number of ways: through dubbing (which was clumsy and expensive), through making films in several languages simultaneously (which was time-consuming) and by remaking successful films from one part of the country in the language of another (either formally or informally). The willingness to accommodate these conditions can be related to the specific discourses of nationalism that came to the fore in the subcontinent. While European accounts of the nation have emphasized that linguistic homogenization is a central component of, and inherent limitation to, a national consciousness, this proved to be less the case in India (for example, Gellner 1998).

The major divisions which were to emerge in the Indian nationalist movement through the 1930s and 1940s were not between linguistic communities but between secularists and communalists. The legitimacy of competing Indian nations was to be contested along religious lines, and this proved to be a more consistent factor in the imagined communities that gained political ground in late colonial India. Nationalist leaders promoting a secularist platform, such as Nehru and Azad, sought to create a multi-ethnic, multi-lingual and multi-faith nation from the territories occupied by the Raj (Azad 1959; Nehru 1961). Gandhi was not in favour of a secular India, or an 'Indian Raj', but was nonetheless publicly committed to a pluralistic spiritual society (Parel 1997). In contrast, communalists such as Golwalkar, Savarkar and Jinnah variously proposed that India's major religious communities represented separate constituencies, requiring either the establishment of separate national homelands or the submission of religious minorities to majority rule (Savarkar 1923; Jinnah 1984; Kohli 1993). Nonetheless, it is worth noting

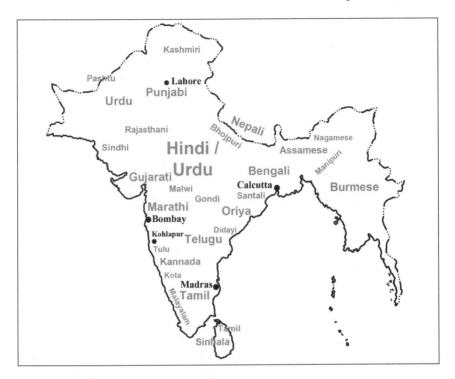

Figure 1 Linguistic Map of Colonial India, Burma and Ceylon, 1936, showing main centres of film production (author's illustration)

that even the communal nationalists sought to incorporate co-religionists on an all-India basis, regardless of their differing geographic, ethnic and linguistic backgrounds (Ahmed 1996; Sharma and Oomen 2000).

While India's linguistic diversity was to prove a secondary consideration in political discourses leading up to independence, it nonetheless exercised a profound structuring influence over the nature of the press and cinema. India had no hegemonic cultural centre. Thus, as with the press, the rise of multiple production centres making films in a number of languages intelligible to different segments of India's film-going public was a logical outcome. Prior to independence there were four main film production centres in colonial India, located in Bombay, Calcutta, Madras and Lahore. In Bombay films were produced in Hindustani, a colloquial variant of the most widely understood language of North-West India. To a lesser extent, films were also made in the local Marathi language (as were films made at Prabhat Studios in nearby Kohlapur). The Calcutta film industry in Eastern India produced Bengali-language films, while studios in Lahore made films in Punjabi. From the late

1930s, studios in Madras began to produce films in all the main South Indian languages, Tamil, Telugu, Kannada and Malayalam, as well as in Sinhala for audiences in neighbouring Ceylon (see Rajadhyaksha and Willemen 1999; Thoraval 2001). A linguistically plural internal market therefore became a distinctive feature of the Indian cinema with the coming of sound, and this would prove salient to the development of a 'national' media in the postcolonial era. The relatively short space of time between the coming of sound and independence (sixteen years), and the natural inclination of commercial film producers to cater to the largest possible market, made language a challenge, rather than an outright bar, to the growth of the cinema market. Thus, the exchange of narrative themes, visual aesthetics and personnel between the various Indian cinemas presented a counterpoint to the relative independence of the different production centres and their markets.

By the end of the 1930s, the cinema in India had established the major features of a film industry: organized studio production, an extensive system of distribution, a star system and a range of genres. The major genres were the 'mythological', centred on (primarily) Hindu religious texts, and the 'social' film, focused on issues of contemporary concern (such as urbanization, the role of women in public life, the plight of widows and 'untouchables'). There were also minor genres such as 'stunt' films, comedies and 'historicals'. The 1940s, however, witnessed a decisive upheaval in the film world that was only tangentially related to the departure of the British in 1947. There was a boom in both cinema hall construction and film production, as the Second World War had radical effects upon the Indian economy. The funding for the further expansion of Indian film production came primarily from non-institutional sources of finance outside of the existing industry. Businessmen with large sums of cash from the wartime boom that they wished to place beyond the reach of British taxation began to offer large sums to finance film-making. Before very long, these independent productions had managed to lure the major stars away from the studios, which then collapsed.

Consequently, from the 1940s onwards, the vast majority of films in India have been made as one-off productions intended to recoup all their costs in one go, as opposed to a studio system offsetting risks by producing a clutch of films at any one time. The flood of film productions, which made India amongst the top three film-producing nations of the world by 1950, resulted in extremely narrow profit margins and a strong imperative for each film to succeed with a large proportion of the mass audience. This structural change to industrial practices resulted in the formalization of the *masala* film, a super-genre (typically in the thematic mould of the 'social film') comprising of a three-hour spectacular providing something for everyone: comedy, romance, action, family drama and numerous songs. This proved to be the best way to maximize audience share in an increasingly anarchic and competitive industry. Another distinctive feature of the Indian commercial film was a profusion of musical sequences that went some way beyond the conventions of the Hollywood musical of the day. As the aesthetics of international cinema discarded the musical in the second half of the century, the enduring popularity of the Indian film song would become a well-known oddity of Indian cinema. Anomalous or not, the film song constituted a mutually advantageous synchronization between the advent of modern Indian popular music and the operation of the commercial film industry.

The development of 'native' cinemas, as found in India, was an extremely rare, if not unique, condition among colonial societies. The longer-term development of a substantive and polyglot privately owned press was a similarly unlikely achievement in a country which had yet to encounter democratic government. Their story therefore has considerable significance in how we might conceive of the relationship between media and nation, and between nation and state in general terms. As we have seen, the development of press and cinema industries across British India were both cause and symptom of the communicative integration of the subcontinent in the early part of the century. Subsequently, the intrinsic mobility of the media became indispensable to the making of modern India and its engagement with the rest of the world. Domestically, the extension of public discourse proved highly conducive to popularizing an all-India entity envisaged by the anti-colonial nationalist movement, while also revealing over time the attendant fault lines within the Indian public sphere. In this light, the early proliferation of the vernacular media in a space beyond the official discourses of the state, but very much within the articulation of the nation, has a great deal of significance in understanding the subsequent forms of the media in India.

Further Reading

Barnouw, Erik and Krishnaswamy, S. (1980) *Indian Film*, New York: Oxford University Press.

Bayly, C. A. (1999) *Empire and Information: Intelligence Gathering and Social Communication in India 1780–1870*, New Delhi: Cambridge University Press.

Chatterjee, Partha (1993) *The Nation & Its Fragments: Colonial & Postcolonial Histories*, New Delhi: Oxford University Press.

Jaikumar, Priya (2006) *Cinema at the End of Empire: A Politics of Transition in Britain and India*, Durham, NC: Duke University Press.

Orsini, Francesca (2002) *The Hindi Public Sphere 1920–1940: Language and Literature in the Age of Nationalism*, New York: Oxford University Press.

Rajagopal, Arvind (ed.) (2009) *The Indian Public Sphere: Readings in Media History*, Oxford: Oxford University Press.

2 Media Development and Mixed Messages

The British, whose legitimacy as rulers of India had been so publicly under-mined on the world stage as well as in India, announced in 1945 that they would relinquish control within three years. In the tumultuous period that followed, a bankrupt and war-weary Britain sought to extricate itself from India as quickly as possible, achieving this goal in August 1947. With inde-pendence on the horizon in the 1940s, the various political forces of India came into open conflict on the form of the new India. Muhammed Ali Jinnah's Muslim League secured an independent nation, Pakistan, for India's Muslim population in the North-West and North-East, while Gandhi's utopian ideals were thrust aside by the competing wings of the Congress Party. In the violence that followed millions were displaced, assaulted and killed, and the birth of the twin nations of Pakistan and the Indian Union was celebrated against a backdrop of suffering and great sadness. Mohandas Gandhi was himself assassinated by a Hindu extremist within a year of those momentous events. Jawaharlal Nehru became India's first Prime Minister, a post he would hold until his death in 1964.

The challenges faced by independent India were enormous. While some parts of the country had flourished during the Second World War, others had been decimated by famine. The departing British were divesting themselves of their commercial and industrial interests piecemeal, while the civil service was not only losing its erstwhile overseers but was also cut in half by the partition between India and Pakistan. The wider world was going through a partition of its own as the alliance of circumstance between the Democratic West and Communist Soviet Union came to an end, and the long Cold War began. As other colonial territories looked to India for inspiration in their own struggles for independence, the imperial world order was coming to a close. The realization of the dream of self-determination was finally at hand for the nations of Asia and Africa, but in the cold light of day the challenges of building the necessary infrastructure to lift their people out of poverty remained enormous.

Instituting the Media in Postcolonial India

Now that the anti-colonial movement had achieved its primary goal of displacing the colonial power and gaining control of the state, its next objective became the foundation of a legitimate (or at least legitimizing) nation-state. The development of an 'official' nationalism for the new India was intended to connect nation to state, and this required the unification of the previously split domains of the public-political and the private-cultural. This new goal therefore required a reversal of the earlier cultural logic of the nationalist movement, which denied the state any significant authority over the cultural domain. However, the mobilization of a unifying national identity on cultural grounds was no simple matter in itself, since India was bequeathed a territorial and institutional form that had been constructed by foreign interests, with little reference to the geography or philosophy of its own cultural practices. The debilitating classifications of the native populations engendered and fostered by colonial rule had already made the question of representation a critical one that had to be addressed. At the same time, the new state had only a tenuous hold upon the cultural legitimacy seen as essential for underpinning such a programme, and an indigenous government could not hide behind a mask of cultural impartiality as the British had done. For postcolonial India, as a nascent nation-state, the logic of cultural nationalism was at once requisite yet also threatening to its success, since the nationalist 'invention of tradition' designed to wed nation and state through a standardization of cultures was likely to be a contested, even divisive, process (Hobsbawm and Ranger 1983).

In the early tumultuous years, there was some cause to believe that the consensus forged by resistance to foreign rule might unravel entirely. Despite the carving out of Pakistan, the Indian Union continued to encompass a large number of linguistic, religious and/or ethnic imaginaries, as well as scores of nominally independent kingdoms that had remained outside of formal British control. Even after the accession of Muslim majority provinces in the North-East and North-West to Pakistan, India's Muslims still represented 10 per cent of the population. There were also millions of Indians who were adherents of Sikhism, Christianity, Jainism, Zoroastrianism and Buddhism. Millions more were classified as Adivasi, followers of pre-Aryan indigenous religious practices. Even within the Hindu majority, there were many distinct variants of practice across the boundaries of region and caste. The Indian Constitution of 1950 listed twenty-two official languages from over 800 recognized languages and dialects. Crucially, in the aftermath of independence, the only available institutions of state with which to engage in nation-building, initially at least, were those moulded by the former colonial power. One example of this was the government film unit, Information Films of India, which had been actively disparaged by the anti-colonial movement as a propaganda machine, but was nonetheless reconstituted in 1947 as the Films Division, and continued to enjoy what was effectively a monopoly over documentary production for many decades to come. Similarly, the postcolonial government maintained the state monopoly over broadcasting instituted by the British through All India Radio (Barnouw and Krishnaswamy 1980: 207–11).

As we have noted, India was already host to a diverse multi-language press and a viable film industry that had proved its popularity with a range of domestic audiences. However, while the creation of an appropriately 'national' culture may have been a key aim of the new leadership, the commercial Indian film was seen as a crass and hybrid form that was highly unsuitable for the national-building project envisaged through the government's didactic and developmentalist project of modernity (Chakravarty 1993: 55–79). The early postcolonial government included many cultural conservatives who were suspicious of the impact of 'Western' culture on Indian morals. Those on the Hindu right were equally opposed to what they saw as 'Muslim' culture, and they saw both defects in the popular film. The secular socialists were almost equally antipathetic to a commercial entertainment industry funded by the black economy and directed towards visceral escapism, romantic fantasy and vulgar aesthetics. Nonetheless, the enormous popularity of the cinema with the increasingly overcrowded urban population meant that it had to be tolerated until a better alternative could be created. Thus, the Indian government formed national academies in 1953/4 for dance, drama and music (Sangeet Natak Akademi), letters (Sahitya Akademi) and art and architecture (Lalit Kala Akademi), while increasing its powers of censorship over the film industry, placing a ban on the construction of new film theatres and, at one stage, limiting the import of raw film stock. Taxation of the industry also increased dramatically during the 1950s (see Chakravarty 1993: 63 and Armes 1987: 118).

The politicization of culture, as a site of resistance to the state, had already been well advanced during the rise of the anti-colonial movement. Given the calamitous events of 1947–8, the new government was naturally keen to put this genie back in its bottle. However, the previous independence of the cultural sphere from the state could not be simply negated by the removal of the colonial presence. The capacity for agitation and political confrontation through the popular media remained strong. As such, although freedom of speech was guaranteed in the Indian Constitution, the very first amendment was intended to curtail communications that could lead to further public disorder. As Rajeev Dhavan notes, it was a commitment to public order that guided the first Press Commission enquiry in 1950, and the subsequent retention of the entire machinery of press controls that had previously been put in place by the British (2009). By contrast, the Film Enquiry Committee, reporting in 1951, was primarily concerned with uncovering the murky financial dealings of the film industry, but went on to recommend a number of supportive measures (Barnouw and Krishnaswamy 1980: 142–50). Those recommendations, as with the ICC in 1927, were subsequently ignored and the old colonial regimes of censorship and taxation were not simply retained, but strengthened. Nonetheless, the Government of India decided against the nationalization of the popular media. Thus, there would continue to be a clear bifurcation between the 'authoritative' discourse of the nation-state and the competing articulations of popular nationalism.

Accordingly, official mistrust of the press and entertainment industries was set to continue in various guises in the new India. In part, the extreme caution exercised over any form of representation that might engender communal confrontation was well founded. Nonetheless, the continuing antagonism between the state and the popular media was also a reflection of the enormous cultural divide between the new elite and the general population. Most of India's new leaders were not only veterans of the independence struggle, but also highly educated men who had been shaped by their formal knowledge of classical Indian and European thought. Thus, in a large part, the antipathy of politicians and bureaucrats to the popular media was a symptom of cultural snobbery. This made them necessarily remote from the common people whose cultural referents were rooted in vernacular experience and framed by an entirely different engagement with both tradition and modernity. The first Minister of Information and Broadcasting, K. V. Keskar, was contemptuous of both Western and Indian popular music and removed them from the schedules of All India Radio (AIR) (Thomas 2010: 65). They were replaced with a highbrow classical revival that drove almost the entire audience to Radio Ceylon. Even Nehru himself complained that he could not understand the highly classical form of Hindi language adopted by AIR for its broadcasts (Jeffrey 2009: 172). As much as the Indian industrialists who took over the old English press were able to speak to government in that language, it was only the popular vernacular media that spoke effectively to the people on the street.

Nehru's socialist ideals committed him to the uplift of the common people who had suffered from centuries of exploitation, but, if anything, the inherent paternalism of those ideals exacerbated the communication gap between the government and the people. A marked suspicion of entertainment in general, that Nehru had shared with Gandhi, further compelled him to see the 'true' potentials of the media in largely didactic terms. In that respect,

Nehru's beliefs were consistent with the wider international approach to media technologies in countries considered to be 'undeveloped'. In their own push for industrialization, the Russian communists had employed the media primarily as a method of instruction for the purpose of technological, social and political progress. By contrast, the Imperial British had professed the need for state control of the media in order to ensure that their domestic and colonial subjects were 'bettered' by the content that they received. This 'betterment' was overwhelmingly conceived as increased literacy in the culture of the ruling elite. Both approaches were explicitly antagonistic to the populist commercial media of the United States and, even there, what was good for the goose wasn't necessarily considered suitable for 'traditional' societies (Sparks 2007: 20–37). Thus, during the 1950s and 1960s, the role of mass media in the decolonizing world was understood largely in terms of a developmental logic.

Despite their conflicting models of political economy, the communist bloc and the capitalist West were united in their adherence to the notion that social progress was to be achieved, and largely measured, through technological and scientific advance. When it came to the new nations that were freeing themselves from colonial control, there was a broad consensus through new global institutions, such as the United Nations and World Bank, that rapid programmes of industrialization would provide the necessary means for improving the living standards of their citizens. Given that the majority of those people had remained overwhelmingly agrarian, undernourished and illiterate under the selfish administrations of colonial rule, it was also widely believed that industrialization had to be preceded by massive programmes of education (Schramm 1964). Even so, it was considered that the 'gap' between the contemporary conditions of the industrial countries and the rest of the world was so vast that it would take many decades before the 'developing' world could catch up in the race towards modernity. Similarly, it was also common wisdom that the willingness and capacity to receive a modern education would require an enormous shift in the mindset of peoples who remained embedded in older, 'traditional' patterns of life (Lerner 1958). This is where mass media technologies were seen to provide a ready means of 'injecting' a modern consciousness and accelerating the process of development. Since radio, cinema and television did not require literacy, they could circumvent the literacy barrier in education and help developing countries to 'leapfrog' forward along the linear path to development that had been laid down by the experience of the Western world. Thus, it was 'believed that the mass media had a crucial role to play in fostering modern attitudes and beliefs, which were thought to be primary conditions for any significant social changes' (Sparks 2007: 3). The international orthodoxy of development communications also had a political dimension determined by the high tide of state nationalism, dictating that:

> It is generally the increasing flow of information that plants the seed of change. It is also the widened background of information that furnishes the climate for 'nation-ness' itself. By making one part of a country aware of other parts, their people, arts, customs and politics; by permitting the national leaders to talk to the people, and the people to the leaders and to each other; by keeping the national goals and the national accomplishments always before the public – thus modern communication, widely used, can help to wed together isolated communities, disparate subcultures, self-centered individuals and groups, and separate developments into a truly national development. (Schramm 1964: 44)

As such, the development mission was twofold. First of all came the pursuit of a modern industrialized economy, along with a modernized population equipped to operate it. A parallel concern was the development of a state apparatus whose hegemony over social life was recognized and to which the disparate population was loyal and committed. This project of constructing state authority over the nation also encouraged moves towards the institutionalization of the economy and, equally, over cultural production.

The State Media

Nehru was a great admirer of both British parliamentary democracy and Soviet industrialization. He therefore pursued a very rapid path towards universal suffrage in India, with elections by 1952, accompanied by a strong commitment to a planned economy dominated by the state. In a spirit of compromise that characterized all his political achievements, the central role of the state in the new Indian economy was leavened by the protection and encouragement of Indian domestic capitalism. State investments in heavy industries were therefore accompanied by massive investments in infrastructure intended to support both private and public sectors. It was believed that this emphasis on productive capacity would reverse India's dependence upon foreign imports and constitute an industrial form of Gandhian self-sufficiency. By developing productive capacity, the so-called Feldman-Mahalanobis model predicted that India would be able to accelerate the growth of domestic demand and the development process (Dasgupta 1993). In order to prepare India's human capacity for modernization, the government also instituted a vast programme of universal primary education along with a smaller number of elite tertiary institutions in science and engineering.

These included the now famous Indian Institutes of Technology (initially developed with the aid of the Soviet Union, West Germany and the United States).

Despite Nehru's overwhelming commitment to a planned economy, India's first television broadcasts were something of an accident. The electronics giant Philips, having demonstrated the technology at an industrial exhibition, donated a quantity of closed circuit television equipment to India, which was experimented with by enthusiastic engineers at All India Radio, leading to the implementation of a limited broadcast network encompassing the national capital and a few surrounding villages (Singhal et al. 1988). However, this first experiment with television was to be the sum of activity for the next decade. Television, which was then in the process of being deployed as a mass medium in the northern hemisphere, was not considered to be a viable option for India. Indeed, it was regarded by Nehru as an expensive luxury for a country where famine, illiteracy and destitution defined the existence of millions of people. Accordingly, the government's vision of the new India would instead be disseminated by expanding the radio network developed by the British further into the rural hinterlands. In addition, there was to be a mandatory imposition of Films Division productions shown as trailers at commercial film screenings in the urban centres. The content of these films was directed at extolling the virtues and achievements of development initiatives.

Nehru's antipathy towards the development of television in India was largely practical, rather than ideological – although his insistence that all of the emerging state media should eschew trivial entertainments and 'foster a scientific temper' amongst the population revealed much of the ideological programme that would define Indian broadcast media during the four decades of state monopoly (Chatterji 1991). As Ashish Rajadhyaksha has observed, the influence of the socialist planning ethos upon cultural production at a policy level was an inclination towards the promotion of state-sponsored realism, where:

> Nationalist reconstruction agendas adopted economic programmes based on the principles of scientific rationalism and its aesthetic counterpart of realism . . . Realism – or rather, various national realisms – were important in writing up the 'biography of the emerging nation-state' and creating the authoritative self-image of the nation. (Rajadhyaksha 2000a: 31–2)

The programming of All India Radio, The Films Division and the alternative government-sponsored cinema launched in the 1960s all had this agenda in common. The content of Indian state media provided an endless celebration of scientific progress and state policy, along with a kaleidoscope of what the government regarded as authentic Indian lives – heavily biased in favour of the rural India. All of this was consciously directed towards winning the loyalty of the labouring classes for the developmental socialism of the Congress Party. As Robin Jeffrey notes: 'Nehru envisaged mobile vans carrying the nation-building documentaries from village to village (as video vans did thirty years later). But, he gave no thought to radio and no consideration to the thought that audiences had to want to watch' (2009: 178). To be fair, as blind as he was to the benefits of broadcasting, Nehru was attentive to the technical potentials of telecommunications, electronics and other 'hi-tech' fields. His aim of transforming the Southern city of Bangalore into a major hub of scientific development through flagship institutions of research and education would be substantially realized in the years after his death in 1964 (D'Costa 2004; Parthasarathy 2004; Stallmeyer 2011; Stremlau 1996).

Indira Gandhi, Nehru's daughter and political successor, was an ardent follower of her father's socialist ideals, but she was much less committed to compromise. Immediately after his death, Indira became the Minister for Information and Broadcasting, and, two years later, Prime Minister. Unwilling to be a puppet of powerful brokers within the Congress, Indira quickly revealed herself to be an authoritarian centrist determined to extend her writ across the entire country (Frank 2011). Unlike her father, Indira was certainly interested in the potentials of television. As Minister for Information and Broadcasting, she commissioned the Chanda Report which made recommendations for the rapid implementation of a national television service in 1966 (Chatterji 1991). Despite the privations of an era in which many of the economic development projects had yet to bear fruit, and India was recovering from border wars with its neighbours, Indira gave a big push to television. Indian TV broadcasts were started in Bombay metro in 1972 and five other broadcast stations, or *Kendras*, were in operation by 1975. The familiar agenda of national development, integration and education naturally shaped the contours of early television programming in India, in much the same form as it had with the older state media (Rajagopal 1993). Perhaps the biggest difference from her father's approach to mass communication was that Indira's interest in the medium also extended to its utility for personal political purposes.

Faced with a highly factional Congress Party and its regional structures, not to mention the various vested interests that had worked to circumvent the implementation of political and economic reforms over many years, Indira saw the mass media as a means of connecting directly with the voting population. In that sense, her political instinct was to counter the competing powers of the establishment with a populist appeal to the masses, for whose benefit Nehruvian socialism had been conceived. This agenda would increasingly shape the form and content of the state-owned media under her premiership. Arguably, television as a medium has done more worldwide to define what it is to be middle class than any other technology or cultural form. Under Indira, however, television was consciously deployed in India in such a way as to deliberately circumvent the leisure demands of the middle classes. Indian state TV was intended instead to forge a direct address between Indira and the labouring classes, who appear to have been conceived overwhelmingly as a rural population. All of this was deeply paradoxical in a situation where only the affluent upper middle classes were actually able to afford television sets, and where broadcast capacity did not reach beyond the metropolitan areas (Rao 1999). After Delhi and Bombay, the choice of locations for the *Kendras* was Calcutta, Madras, Lucknow (in the Congress Party's political heartland), and Shringar and Amritsar, two strategic locations close to the Pakistan border. Needless to say, these environs had little resemblance to the rural India seen in their broadcast programming.

A further consideration in the extension of terrestrial television was the vast distances involved, which meant that all of the *Kendras* were essentially separate regional television stations that served different language areas. This was deeply incommensurate with Indira Ghandi's desire for a national TV system tightly controlled from New Delhi. The extent of this instinct would soon become apparent, when, in an attempt to crack down on political intrigue, fiscal corruption and labour unrest, Indira declared a state of emergency in 1975 and suspended the democratic process (Dhar 2000; Hewitt 2007). The draconian measures which were subsequently introduced to accelerate Indian 'modernization' in the absence of those logjams finally brought a definitive end to the contradictory politics of compromise pursued by Jawaharlal Nehru. The press and judiciary were muzzled more effectively than they ever were under British rule, and dissenters and political opponents were jailed. Disappointingly, many sections of the Indian press seemed only too willing to support Indira's absolute rule in the name of public order. In this environment, state media institutions such as the Films Division and All India Radio (AIR) became even more strictly regulated proponents of the official line. Thus:

> During the Emergency, the main purpose of radio and television was to project the personality of Mrs Gandhi and her son Sanjay. In that two year period AIR broadcast nearly 50,000 items about Mrs Gandhi's 'decade of achievements' and her Twenty Point Program. Station directors were left in no doubt that their role was to serve the government of the day. (Page and Crawley 2001: 52)

Against this disturbing backdrop, India's bold SITE experiment (Satellite Instructional Television Experiment) was undertaken in 1975. Partly in emulation of the groundbreaking Soviet satellite TV system – but in this instance with American technical assistance – the Indian government embarked upon a year-long exercise to bring television directly to 2,400 villages across India using NASA's ATS-6 Satellite (India Planning Commission 1981). This massive experiment was a technical watershed in testing the viability of satellite TV broadcast systems, and would spur on both American and Indian efforts in satellite technology. At the same time, SITE was also the high tide of the educational media paradigm in India. Broadcasting in four languages, the programme content of SITE was focused on educational programmes for children and instructional programmes for adults – presenting topics such as family planning, agricultural techniques, hygiene and nutrition in a manner intended to appeal to a rural – and largely illiterate – audience (Agrawal 1981; Contractor et al. 1993). The laudable didactic aims of SITE could not, however, be separated from Indira Gandhi's own political interest in direct broadcasts to the masses of rural India. Thus, on the one hand, SITE was successful enough for national television to finally get official acceptance with a new entity, *Doordarshan*, that was established following its separation from All India Radio. On the other hand, after thirty years of one-party rule, the Congress Party, the government, the state apparatus and the national media remained inseparable for Indira Gandhi. Television was to be no exception.

> Sometimes, I found that the minister [of Information and Broadcasting] was trying to say 'no, no, this is not a government organ'. Now, I have interrupted him and have said in public forums it is a government organ, and it is going to remain a government organ. We are proud that it is a government organ . . . Primarily, its function is to give the views of the government of India. (Indira Gandhi, cited in Zins 1989: 160)

Indira had nonetheless seriously misjudged the public mood. While she may have been able to face down the recalcitrant political elite and the industrialists, the people of India were too powerfully committed to the democratic ideal to be summarily returned to absolutist rule at the whim of the executive. After intense public pressure and numerous demonstrations, she called elections in 1977 to demonstrate her mandate, and was promptly expelled from office in favour of a hastily assembled coalition of disaffected politicians. It was the role played by the state-owned media in cheerleading the former Prime Minster's decrees during the Emergency that provoked India's first non-Congress government to introduce in 1978 the Prasar Bharati Bill, which was designed to formally separate the national broadcaster from direct state control. The administration did not last, however, and against initial expectations Indira was back in power within two years. Thus, the Prasar Bharati Bill would not come into effect for another twenty years – when it eventually became little more than a de facto recognition of seismic changes in global television, which made its provisions largely redundant for their original purpose.

Back in the 1980s, Indira Gandhi's return to democratic governance did not diminish her enthusiasm for TV as an organ of state policy. Colour broadcasts were launched in 1982 to coincide with the Asian Games in New Delhi and in the following years the newly proclaimed National Network was steadily extended to provide terrestrial coverage across the country. By the end of the 1980s, national television was finally a reality, with the Delhi-based broadcaster now able to use India's own INSAT 1-B to disseminate national programming across three-quarters of the vast territory of India. Despite the longstanding socialist principles that had guided media policy since the 1950s, this expansion was funded in part by opening up Doordarshan to advertising and thus making it into a profitable concern (Ohm 1999). This concession to market forces nonetheless did little to alter the basic premises of state television in India, as a 1986 report noted:

> The primary purpose of television in India is development through education, information and enlightenment, to improve the quality of life of the largest masses of people, to bring communities and societies, regions and the states together as one nation . . . The secondary purpose is entertainment per se or show-business. (in Manchanda 1998: 141)

The great paradox of India's national network in the 1980s was that the state-backed growth in technical capacity that had made it possible had also been paralleled by the steady decline of state legitimacy since the idealism of the Nehruvian era. While the European social democracies had developed national TV systems during the high tide of the political legitimacy of public institutions in the 1950s, India implemented national broadcast TV three decades later in an era when her political system, ruling elites and state institutions were widely regarded by the general population as self-serving and corrupt. Doordarshan was classed as a condescending state mouthpiece with scant regard for the desires of its audiences, and not without some cause. Furthermore, the use of the National Network to impose Hindi-language programming on non-Hindi-speaking regions was clearly resented in the South and East – despite the considerable success of Doordarshan's concession to entertainment in the form of Hindi soaps from the mid-1980s onwards. Furthermore, in spite of the considerable technological achievement of national broadcast coverage, TV ownership largely remained a preserve of the upper middle classes. Without the lure of videocassette recorders smuggled in from abroad, and the alternative content that came with them, it is likely that take-up would have been even lower (Friedberg 2000).

Throughout the four decades of state monopoly over broadcasting, the official voice of Indian state media – with its undisguised aversion to entertainment, its paternalistic attitude to its audiences and its penchant for state propaganda – remained juxtaposed by the colourful vulgarity of the Indian popular film, with its macho violence, cheap eroticism, childish humour, impossible romance and overblown sentimentality. The intractable popularity of the commercial cinema over five decades always provided a counterfoil to the state media. Throughout the years of crisis and stagnation in the late 1970s and 1980s, Indian state television broadcast a procession of aloof politicians, tame journalists, saluting soldiers, classical artistes, worthy scientists and academics, along with countless dancing children and grateful villagers. By contrast, India's biggest films were staffed with angry urban youths, corrupt officials, jaded policemen, vile gangsters, kindly prostitutes and weeping mothers. This popular circus thus provided an alternative narration of India's encounter with modernity. Taken together, the two voices of modern India provided a perfect example of the contradictions of the mixed economy era. It would take a new historical epoch to bring them into direct conversation.

A Suitable Cinema

The social conditions within which cinema in the subcontinent operated changed dramatically with the end of colonial rule. Although the cinema had enjoyed an enormous boom in popularity and in production capacity during the last years of the Raj, the division of the subcontinent exerted powerful effects upon the film industry. In Punjab, partition brought film production to a halt as the city acceded to Pakistan and key personnel and capital relocated to Bombay, where the Punjabis subsequently became an ever more significant presence in the film industry (Dwyer and Patel 2002: 82). In Bengal, partition cost the Calcutta industry a major part of its audience as Eastern Bengal became part of Pakistan, and many leading figures also made the move to Bombay. Consequently, the Bombay Hindi-language cinema was the undisputed film capital of South Asia in the early decades after independence. This period has therefore been referred to as the 'Golden Age of Hindi Cinema' (Kasbekar 1996: 402; Gokulsing and Dissanyake 1998: 16; Thoraval 2000: 49–51). Elsewhere, only South Indian cinema was developing steadily in the years after independence.

The genre that dominated this period was the 'social' film, exemplified by the work of Mehboob Khan, Raj Kapoor and Guru Dutt. These films touched on issues of social reform such as the plight of landless peasants, untouchability, the status of widows and child brides and the rights of women to employment and property. They incorporated these themes within a heavily melodramatic framework laced with uplifting songs and moral messages. Mehboob's work is known in particular for his woman-centred narratives, while Raj Kapoor was known for his portrayal of the common Indian displaced to the threatening urban landscape of India's rapidly expanding metropolis. The classic Indian hero of this period was a 'noble' and non-violent character driven by the inexorable forces of social change and impossible love. The romance between the two biggest stars, Nargis and Raj Kapoor, was national news in the fifties despite, or perhaps because of, the dubious status of film actresses as 'unrespectable women'. By the 1960s, the importance of social issues was gradually displaced by an emphasis on the romantic aspects of the films, following the huge interest shown by the public in the personal and romantic lives of the film stars.

While consciously excluded from the 'authoritative' discourse of nationhood, the fantasies produced by the commercial film industry articulated, just as consciously, nationalist themes within the super-genre of the social film. This no doubt reflected the spirit of independence, and patriotic content of this kind may also have helped to avoid further government interference in the industry. However, in this new era, the discursive mobilization of the nation was also a logical form of address to the all-India public sphere that the cinema had been contributing to for three decades. Thus, while the cinema was hampered in some ways by the lack of government recognition, it was nonetheless able to continue in its role as a popular institution, mediating the project of Indian modernity in a space at least partially independent of the state. Rajadhyaksha argues that ultimately this would give the cinema greater legitimacy as a national medium amongst the general population (2003: 35). At first glance, it would also seem logical that the national status of the Hindi cinema would have been further enhanced by the government's promotion of Hindi as the official language of India in 1950. However, resistance to the promotion of Hindi in non-Hindi-speaking areas, and the administrative reorganization of India's internal states along linguistic lines in 1956, also drove the steady growth of the non-Hindi (commonly called 'regional') cinemas of South India.

> Two developments marked the postwar decade in the Madras film world. They seemed to move in opposite directions. One was the rise of southern linguistic nationalism. It was anti-Hindi, anti-north, and extolled the glories of the ancient Dravidian languages and culture. It made Hindi a symbol of northern domination to be feared and averted. It became a highly emotional force in politics. It also became strong in the southern film world and made

extraordinarily successful use of film in its drive for power. The other phenomenon, ironically, was the successful entry of Madras into production in Hindi and its triumphant invasion of northern Hindi markets. (Barnouw and Krishnaswamy 1980: 172–3)

While studios in Madras initially provided the infrastructure for the majority of South Indian film production, the linguistic reorganization of the Indian states resulted in state governments amenable to supporting local language production. The Telugu cinema (in Andhra Pradesh), Malayalam cinema (in Kerala) and Kannada cinema (in Karnataka) were therefore developed into distinct industries. Given that linguistic identities provided a focal point for state politics in South India, close ties quickly developed between the cinema and local politics. Numerous movie stars have been chief ministers in the state governments of Tamil Nadu and Andhra Pradesh, while the Malayalam cinema has enjoyed a close relationship with the communist and left-front governments which have dominated politics in Kerala (Dickey 1993; Srinivas 2000b; Pandian 2000; Velayutham 2008). Although the Hindi cinema has remained predominant across North India throughout the postcolonial period, the Bengali film industry in Calcutta has also continued to operate, albeit within a more limited local market, and with less success in the all-India market than it enjoyed prior to independence. With no competition from television, cinema remained enormously popular and influential across India. By the end of the 1950s, India was the world's leading producer of feature films.

Given its distaste for the commercial Indian cinema and a predilection for state intervention, the government of India committed itself to the development of a 'quality' Indian cinema during the 1960s. Elsewhere in the world (but particularly in Europe), a blend of social-realism and literary *auterist* film-making had become the *cause célèbre* of non-Hollywood cinema. This 'art' cinema became the dominant motif at international film festivals throughout the world in the 1950s and 1960s. The unexpected success of Bengali director Satyajit Ray at the Cannes and Venice film festivals in 1956 and 1957 prompted the Indian government to support the production of art films as an alternative to the products of India's commercial film industries. The Film Finance Corporation (FFC) was established in 1960 to provide finance for the production of 'quality' films. The Film Institute of India was established in Pune in 1961 to develop the talent that might produce such films, and subsequently the National Film Archive of India was created and co-located in Pune in 1964 to preserve India's film heritage. Together, these institutions were intended to provide the means for a 'New Indian Cinema'. This cinema, sometimes dubbed the 'parallel' cinema, was born out of a 'realist critique of the melodramatic and distractive form of Indian popular cinema, of its excessively pitched histrionic narratives punctuated by "untidily" placed musical and comedy sequences' and 'was very much part of a cultural-political project to develop a realist and rationalist disposition in the citizen-spectator' (Vasudevan 2000a: 123). The obligations of the FFC were to 'develop the film in India into an effective instrument for the promotion of national culture, education and healthy entertainment . . . granting loans for modest but off-beat films of talented and promising people in the field' (Willemen and Rajadhyaksha 1999: 162).

By the end of the 1960s, the success of low-budget FFC-financed art films directed by Mrinal Sen (*Bhuvan Shome* 1969) and Mani Kaul (*Uski Roti* 1969) seemed to offer some promise for the art film movement. However, the lack of an alternative infrastructure for the distribution of FFC-financed films, and the continued preference for popular films amongst audiences, and hence exhibitors, meant that the vast majority of these art films received little exposure beyond film festivals. Although Satyajit Ray, on at least one occasion, publicly distanced himself from the 'New Indian Cinema' (Ray 1976: 81–99), he was nonetheless consistently presented as its figurehead and as its inspiration (Barnouw and Krishnaswamy 1980; Bannerjee 1982). This had important ramifications due to the nature of Ray's own work, because his disavowal of the 'illogical' structures of the Indian commercial film was also accompanied by a critique of the cultural hybridity of the all-India movie. To Ray, the gaudy pan-Indian address of the popular film constituted a failure to represent the realities of life in any part of the country. Thus, the vast majority of his works were very specifically located in his native Bengal, paying meticulous attention to the details of the period in which they were set. Accordingly, the influence of Ray's realist aesthetic created a certain paradox, in that it prompted the Indian government to pursue a national film-funding policy that inherently favoured intellectual and regionally specific films, whose opportunities in the all-India market were necessarily limited on both counts.

Despite the government endorsement of 'quality' films, and the theoretical dominance of realism in official and academic discourses on cinema, Indian audiences continued to demonstrate a clear preference for movies delivering fantasy and spectacle. The hybrid culture of the Indian *masala* film, a decidedly unrealistic but undeniably modern form, remained overwhelmingly India's most popular mode of mass culture. Commercial films were also influenced by European cinema and the performance traditions of the Middle East, although they drew much more heavily on the New Hollywood of the 1970s. The budget and scale of popular films increased with the advent of 'multi-starrers', such as the hugely successful *Sholay* (1975) (Dissanayake and Sahai 1992; Hariharan 1999; Kazmi 1999b: 99–115). There were also marked changes in the themes of commercial films. If the films of the 1950s had been characterized by the sympathetic portrayal of the 'common man' in rapidly urbanizing India, and the 1960s by the 'romantic' star, then the 1970s and 1980s were dominated by the rise of the vigilante genre. Many of the most popular films of the period focused on social injustice, and endorsed the violent rebellion of macho heroes from the disenfranchised classes against a corrupt establishment. Such themes were distinct from the optimism of the 1950s cinema, and this period of the commercial cinema, strongly associated with the major star of Bombay cinema in those two decades, Amitabh Bachchan, has been classified by film critics as the time of 'the angry young man' (Chakravarty 1993: 228–33; Kasbekar 1996: 406; Prasad 1998: 138–59; Kazmi 1999a; Mazumdar 2000).

The social and political context in which such films flourished was marked by a breakdown in the credibility of the state. During Indira's Emergency, it was unwise to criticize the government directly. Nonetheless, the angry, nihilistic, implicitly anti-establishment films of the period struck a chord with the public, and dominated the box office (Kazmi 1999a: 138). After the reinstatement of democracy in 1977, the popularity of such films continued well into the 1980s. In contrast, the government-sponsored project of 'quality' realism went into serious decline. The remit of the Film Finance Corporation was expanded to include a monopoly over the importation of foreign movies, and it was subsequently renamed the National Film Development Corporation (NFDC). Despite this more overt operating title, the role of the NFDC as a producer of films steadily decreased in significance throughout the 1980s (Willemen and Rajadhyaksha 1999: 162). The commercial film industry, meanwhile, continued to be a highly fragmented association of independent producers, distributors and exhibitors, financed in a large part by 'black money' interests on the wrong side of government. The lack of access to any legitimate institutional finance continued to encourage the independent financing of movies (as did the laundering effects of financing even a loss-making picture). This in turn perpetuated the over-production of films for the Indian market.

Several major shifts in the ecology of Indian cinema took place during the 1980s. The 'golden age' of Hindi cinema had passed and the production levels of the Telugu and Tamil commercial film industries in South India began to match, and then overtake, those of the Bombay industry (Willemen and Rajadhyaksha 1999: 30–1). Perhaps more significant for the longer term was the gradual growth of television ownership amongst the middle classes, coupled with the spread of the VCR. This was a combination which depleted the middle-class cinema audience, as those able to afford recorders took to watching movies at home, and a large-scale video piracy industry was quick to emerge (see Friedberg 2000; Athique 2008a). The loss of the smaller middle-class audience segment nonetheless detracted further from the social respectability of the cinema (Vasudevan 2003). In the process of catering to an audience increasingly comprised of young men from the lower classes, large parts of the film industry became locked into a cycle of mechanistic exploitation films and diminishing returns (Gopalan 2003). A contrasting outcome of the spread of playback technologies was the mass availability of cheap cassettes of film songs, which further cemented the marriage between the film industry and modern Indian popular music, becoming a major source of film-derived revenue (Pendakur and Subramanyam 1996: 83). The central role of the cinema in India's popular culture was nonetheless sustained by what was, for all intents and purposes, a closed market for domestic film-makers, along with a continuing lack of alternative forms of entertainment for the vast population of India.

A Mixed Media Economy

The long-running contest between the realist aesthetic of the state media and the commercial populism of the cinema over four decades provides a useful indication of the off-set relationship that existed between the spheres of official nationalism and popular culture in postcolonial India. At the same time, the spread of media ownership also reflected the overarching logic of the mixed economy model. The major infrastructures of broadcasting and telecommunications were monopolized by the state. The English press was in the hands of a small capitalist elite comprised of family-owned Indian business houses, and generally spoke for their interests, while the vernacular press was operated by their regional equivalents. The film industry operated on entirely free-market principles more or less outside of the 'organized' sector of the economy. All of these media institutions were, in their own idiom, sensitive to the political forces at play in Indian society. Across this spectrum, the inherent opposition between education and entertainment was a globally accepted doctrine in the 'development' era. Similarly, the tight regulation of media and communications industries was an international phenomenon under the auspices of a statist paradigm that was adhered to by all but the most liberal countries.

In that sense, the story of television in India under the dominance of the Congress Party is indicative of a mindset that was largely in keeping with the rest of the world in the 1950s and 1960s. The notion of transferring modernity into traditional societies via the 'hypodermic' action of media technologies nonetheless came to be widely challenged from the mid-1970s onwards.

Critics such as Herbert Schiller, pointed out that the reprogramming of national populations in support of technical infrastructure and institutions pioneered in the developed world constituted a new form of imperialism (1976). This was referred to as cultural imperialism, where Western models of progress were pressed upon developing countries by international bodies dominated by the industrial powers. Many cultural conservatives in India had long expressed a similar opinion, and as frustration with the progress of the development agenda set in, the consensus that underpinned the development push in its early years was rapidly eroding. In that context, despite being firmly in Indian hands, the Western origins of the major media systems continued to make them a far from neutral domain for articulating the relationships between India and the West, and between the traditional and the modern. The logic of the cultural imperialism thesis was mapped on to the existing opposition between Western and indigenous culture that already enjoyed currency in India, as well as elsewhere in the developing South (Golding and Harris 1996). The internationalism of the technological realm thus operated in clear contrast with the privileging of traditional cultures in the messages carried by the mass media. As such, attempts to determine the social significance of the Indian media in the postcolonial era continued to be powerfully structured by a binary opposition of 'modernity' and 'tradition'.

As Madhava Prasad has noted: 'The binary modernity/tradition, whether it is employed to indicate conflict or complementarity, amounts to an explanation, "a conceptual or belief system" which regulates thinking about the modern Indian social formation . . . Thus the disavowal of modernity on an ideological plane has co-existed with the contrary drive to modernization' (1998: 7–8). Prasad has concluded that the state media and the cinema worked both in open contest and in parallel to attempt, but not quite achieve, cultural hegemony over a diverse national body. Prasad believes that the socio-political formation of the postcolonial Indian state, and its insistence upon a clear separation between the traditional and the modern, had a structuring effect upon the textual structure of the Indian 'social' film, where this inconsistency was first foregrounded (1998: 6–14). By contrast, in the domain of state broadcasting, the modernist framing of a classical 'traditional' was employed in order to submerge contemporary cultural politics. The relocation of cultural performance to the distant past also served to subliminally legitimate the project of the modern, and to ensure an elite hegemony over 'development'. It was this particular mode of address that began to unravel during the crisis of the 1970s, as state-sponsored realism and the suppressed anti-state rhetoric of the 'angry young man' collided.

Ashish Rajadhyaksha also parallels the official search for a modern media spectator with the elusive goal of a normative model of Indian citizenship

(2000b). Rajadhyaksha, however, makes a more conciliatory case for positioning the cinema as a mediating institution between population and state, and for understanding the cinema in a way that permits a critical focus on the political discourses at play in movies (2003: 34–6). For Ashis Nandy, the popular cinema became crucially important precisely because it came to represent the only forum in which the idea of the nation as an ideological whole interacted with the 'slum's eye view of politics' that reflected daily life in urban India (1999: 1–19). In this conception, the cinema was uniquely compelled by the box office to enact the fantasy existence of those constrained within, or immediately threatened by, poverty and social exclusion. As a consequence, the popular cinema took on an ideological form that inversely revealed the political imperatives of the struggling lower middle class, counter-posing the elite discourse of the state media. The cinema can thus be seen to be articulating the subjectivity of what Partha Chatterjee has termed 'political society' as opposed to 'civil society' (1998).

These 'modernist' approaches to conceptualizing the Indian media are concerned primarily with the relationship of the media to both the popular audience and the state. In various ways, they seek to illustrate these relationships in reference to the demographic structure of Indian society and the political tensions at play within it. There has also been a countervailing 'traditionalist' approach in India media studies that is more concerned with identifying the 'Indian-ness' of media content, and which typically seeks to find an explanation for its popularity within the context of India's cultural traditions. Here, the two major narrative traditions of Hinduism, the *Ramayana* and *Mahabharata*, have been seen by various commentators to function directly as governing structures for Indian film narratives (Booth 1995; Freitag 2001; Lal 1999; Lutze 1985; Mishra 1985, 2002). Others see the epics as providing at least a significant component of the repertoire of Indian cinema (Chakravarty 1993; Gokulsing and Dissanyake 1998; Inden 1999). Thus, the Hindu epics are seen as forming a subtext implied by the naming of characters, narrative codes and iconography, even within films where the explicit focus is upon contemporary issues. Moti Gokulsing and Wimal Dissanayake describe such appropriations as not simply subconscious reiterations, but also active appropriations, since the 'central ideology underpinning the two epics is of preserving the existing social order and its privileged values', and that 'there is also a significant way in which the Indian popular cinema legitimises its existence through a reinscription of its values onto those of the two epics' (1998: 18).

Gregory Booth sees this incorporation as the central appeal of the popular cinema, claiming that 'beneath the Westernized gloss of the commercial cinema, and despite its manipulative capitalist tendencies . . . it is the continued use of these traditional elements that explains the ongoing popularity of

Hindi films' (1995: 171). However, an explanation centred on pan-Indian meta-narratives arguably serves to downplay the numerous multicultural and international influences upon the Indian film, not to mention the cultural diversity of Hinduism itself. It is upon this basis that Ashis Nandy (2002) has argued that the search for cultural explanation in modern India should be focused on India's diverse folk traditions as opposed to either secularism or a monolithic classicism. Ravi Vasudevan also makes a distinction between 'culturalist' explanations of Indian cinema which emphasize either the classical traditions or the folk traditions (2000b: 9). Interestingly, such a distinction echoes the elite-popular oppositions that also structure modernist approaches, suggesting that both avenues of interrogation (the modern and the traditional) necessarily entail an investigation of the balance between democracy and orthodoxy.

Accordingly, while the ownership, regulation and structure of the mass media in India reflected the compromises of the mixed economy, the form and content of mass communication inevitably transmitted a number of highly mixed messages to the population. Within the range of available media, Indians sought to negotiate the contradictions not only between tradition and modernity, but also between bureaucratic centralization and assertive regional politics, between highbrow and popular performance, between state authority and democratic participation, and between international cooperation and cultural imperialism. These issues were not just pressing for India, but were keenly felt in other developing societies around the world and vociferously debated within the United Nations, and amongst the Non-Aligned Movement where India was a leading voice. Despite this keen awareness of the contradictions of development, going forward with the rest of the world was widely accepted as the only option, and so whatever their differences about the legitimacy of media technologies for education or entertainment, the state and popular media both sought to modernize the Indian population in different ways. They also consistently invoked a national ethos, even where they differed in their cultural politics, and the long-term durability of this ideal in the public domain is indicative of their success. In this respect, the Indian mass media delivered on many of the goals of Schramm's model of development communication, albeit not without encountering diverse opposition, making numerous political concessions and revealing the necessary limitations of the top-down model of transmission envisioned by the architects of modernization.

Further Reading

Chakravarty, Sumita (1993) *National Identity in Popular Indian Cinema 1947–1987*, Austin, TX: University of Texas Press.

Chatterji, P. C. (1991) *Broadcasting In India*, New Delhi: Sage.

Nair, K. S. and White, Shirley (eds) (1993) *Perspectives on Development Communication*, Thousand Oaks, CA: Sage.

Prasad, M. Madhava (1998) *Ideology of the Hindi Film: A Historical Construction*, New Delhi: Oxford University Press.

Schramm, Wilbur (1964) *Mass Media and National Development: The Role of Information in Developing Societies*, Stanford, CA: Stanford University Press.

Sparks, Colin (2007) *Globalization, Development and the Mass Media*, London: Sage.

Rajadhyaksha, Ashish and Willeman, Paul (eds) (1999 edn) *Encyclopaedia of Indian Cinema*, London: BFI.

3   Liberalization, Diversity and the Age of Television

The third phase of globalization in which the mass media has played a critical role is the contemporary period, commonly referred to in India as the era of 'liberalization'. At the economic level, this has been a period characterized by the push towards a consumerist society with the aim of sustaining more rapid economic growth. The need for reforms became pressing in 1991, in light of the wider economic realities that followed the collapse of the socialist world economy, along with an acute balance of payments crisis. The liberalization agenda has been pursued through policy shifts seeking to deregulate certain domains that were previously heavily controlled by the state through a licensing system, the so-called 'license Raj'. As such, earlier policies favouring state industries and market controls have been steadily modified to produce an environment more conducive to private investment, including foreign investment. As such, there has been a substantive, if not sweeping, re-evaluation of the longstanding policy of import substitution in favour of a more 'globalized' import-export approach. Beyond the technicalities, however, the popular image of the contemporary era is that of a switch from a socialist to a free-market society. One of the most visible symptoms of the deregulation era in Indian society has been the progressive opening up of the media sector. In the same year that the broader political and economic picture appeared to change decisively, transnational satellite television began broadcasting into India.

The deregulation of Indian television that followed instigated the very rapid growth of private entertainment-based television stations that drew heavily on international television formats as well as the back catalogue of the commercial film industry. Contemporaneous developments have included a revival in the film industries, and broad expansion in the fields of press and radio, along with the sunrise industries of information technology and mobile telephony (Greenspan 2004; Jeffrey 2000; Kohli-Khandekar 2006; Rajadhyaksha 2003; Thomas 2010; Thussu 2008). This sizeable expansion of the realms of commercial communication has also been closely linked to a significant expansion in the field of advertising and marketing (Mazarella 2003; Ranganathan 2010). The commercial application of new media technologies, curtailment of state monopoly and the swift arrival of large, vertically integrated media combines from abroad have transformed the Indian media environment. In this light, it is entirely fitting that the mass media have vocally celebrated the new regulatory outlook, becoming an exemplar and cheerleader for the liberalization economy.

Invasion from the Skies

As we have seen, for the first four decades after independence the media industries in India provided an illustration both of the mixed economy model established by the Congress Party, and of the federal structure of the country. On the one hand, the Indian film industries supplied different language groups across the country with populist fare at the cinema. On the other hand, the realms of radio and television were state monopolies that remained under tight central control. Nation-building agendas and didactic methodologies dictated the wider purpose and content of television broadcasting in India, giving the national broadcaster Doordarshan a justified reputation as a state mouthpiece with an aversion to entertainment. Indian government technicians had been quick to recognize during the 1970s that the advent of the satellite era would resolve most of the technical obstacles to an Indian national TV network. However, satellite broadcasting was also destined to fatally undermine the entire system of state monopoly through which Indian television had been conceived. This was, again, part of a wider international phenomenon, where the increase in satellite infrastructure opened up commercial opportunities for private enterprise. The potentials of satellite television broadcasting were many. In the first place, they circumvented the tight national controls on the terrestrial broadcast spectrum and facilitated vast coverage without the very considerable expense of building terrestrial transmitters. In addition, the wide footprint of geostationary satellites made extraterrestrial broadcasting an inherently transnational affair.

There was an established precedent for circumventing the state television monopoly in India. Faced with the didactic programming of Doordarshan, India's urban middle class had been steadily forming small-scale illegal neighbourhood cable TV systems since the 1980s. These intensely localized networks broadcast programming drawn from handmade productions as well as commercially pirated and foreign-sourced videocassettes (Kohli-Khandekar 2006: 68–70). This alternative, localized and unofficial television culture was to prove crucial when its global apposite revolutionized broadcasting across the subcontinent in May 1991. This was the moment at which Li Ka Shing's STAR TV began using the ASIASAT to broadcast across South Asia from its uplink station in Hong Kong (Butcher 2003). This was also a moment when the worldwide demand for transnational TV news outlets was massively enhanced in the immediate aftermath of the telegenic war fought in the Persian Gulf at the beginning of the year. The launch of the five-channel STAR package just weeks after the conclusion of the ground assault was extremely well placed to capitalize upon the satellite TV craze under way amongst India's affluent English-speaking elite (Thussu 2005). Freed from the paternalism of Doordarshan, this influential group was finally able to consume the 'international' content of entertainment and news sourced directly from the anglophone world. Ironically, five decades after colonial rule, the BBC became a source of TV news that won favour over the Indian National Network.

Nonetheless, despite numbering some 14.6 million households, this initial take-up was still a very small audience in proportional terms, less than 5 per cent of the total television audience (Thussu 2007b: 595). However, the rapid substitution by canny neighbourhood cable operators of pirated video films for pirated satellite broadcasts quickly led to a much larger illegal market for imported television across urban India (Umchanda 1998: 145). By 1993, a large proportion of India's more modest upper middle classes could access a growing range of international TV channels for as little as one US dollar per month. A phenomenon quickly emerged in urban India where neighbour-hood-specific illegal cable networks provided a wide range of international channels along with the latest Indian films and live cricket matches to their subscribers, interspersed with intensely local events such as weddings and religious festivals within the neighbourhood itself. All of this was plastered with the advertisements of local businesses (Mishra 1999). This grassroots TV world had simply exploded beyond the cherished national ambitions of Doordarshan, going both local and global simultaneously. As such:

> Between the extra-territorial satellite system and the state broadcasting net-works a new industry grew up, which was effectively the gatekeeper for the satellite channels and to a growing extent for the terrestrial broadcaster as well. Wholly indigenous, the cable industry developed by providing an affordable distribution channel for transnational and global broadcasters. (Page and Crawley 2005: 129)

With no effective legislative or technical defence against what was known as the 'invasion from the skies', the cultural influence of foreign media (which had been so effectively restricted for three decades) was a major source of concern for India's officials. Both of the major wings of Indian politics, the Hindutva right and the secular socialist left, along with the nationalist mainstream, had sufficient cause to oppose the 'invasion from the skies' (Umchanda 1998; Chacko 2002). The popularity of commercial Western television content provided a very direct challenge to the conjoined programmes of development, cultural maintenance and state authority to which television in India had been committed. As Indrajit Bannerjee has noted, the negative response to satellite television across Asia was in accord with 'most debates on the cultural implications of globalization and the extensive global media and cultural flows that characterize the world today' (2002: 520). Many of those debates continue to centre upon the equation of capitalism, Euro-American culture and imperialist ambition (Chadha and Kavoori 2000; Sinclair and Harrison 2004). The acquisition of STAR by Rupert Murdoch's News Corporation raised the stakes considerably. As such, it was the Western provenance of 'international' television that came to the fore, and the concerns amongst the elite about the impact of cultural imperialism in this new form were very real (Butcher 2003).

Effectively opposing a satellite broadcaster uplinking from another territory was another matter entirely. Since the Indian government was unable to restrict access to foreign media content transmitted via satellite, it quickly became more amenable to the idea of privately owned television in India. It was clearly untenable for the Government of India to continue preventing the implementation of indigenous commercial television where this was seen to be advantageous to foreign-owned networks operating beyond any state regulation. In a context where the Congress Party was reconsidering its overall economic and ideological position in a 'post-socialist' world, the domain of broadcasting was a natural candidate for deregulation. As Dipankar Sinha records, a landmark ruling was subsequently made in the Supreme Court in 1995, finding the Doordarshan monopoly to be unconstitutional (2005: 147–8). In 1997, the Prasar Bharati (Broadcasting Authority of India) Bill, which had been originated in the interlude between Congress governments in 1978, was finally enacted, making Doordarshan an autonomous public body along the lines of the British BBC. Shortly afterwards, the Broadcasting Bill of 1998 gave private Indian broadcasters up-linking rights from within India and legitimated broadcasters with 80 per cent Indian ownership and a substantial quota of Indian-made programming. Tax exemptions and subsidies were also made available for domestic media production. Thus, in the years following the entry of STAR into the Indian market, the state monopoly on television in India was abruptly terminated, opening the field for the rapid expansion of commercial Indian television stations. If one thing was going to survive the demise of the socialist dream, it was India's longstanding commitment to import substitution. Thus, as Chadha and Kavoori note:

> While these steps have sometimes been interpreted as signalling a shift towards the liberalization of India's state-controlled electronic media, in reality, these initiatives have a protectionist goal, which is to encourage and support the

emergence of a national media production industry that can effectively compete with Western broadcasters and limit the inflow of their products into the Indian market. (2000: 420–1)

As the regulatory reorganization unfolded in the first half of the 1990s, Doordarshan, along with other national broadcasters in the region, had little choice but to accept that its days of market exclusivity were over as far as the upper middle classes were concerned. Nonetheless, despite the capacity of the cable pirates to spread satellite TV well beyond those able to actually afford it, the reliance on English-language programming by multinationals like STAR was always going to restrict international satellite TV to a niche audience. In this sense, Hollywood's loss of the Indian cinema market to local-language producers in the 1930s had already proved the efficacy of the world's most complex language barrier. STAR's preferred solution of dubbing international programming in Hindi, the most prevalent language of North India, was a short-term and unimaginative solution to this problem. This was to become highly significant, because despite its head start and very considerable resources, STAR TV was slow to recognize the twofold problem of expanding the satellite TV demographic: India's lower middle classes would not be content for long with the novelty world of US television, while its elite audience much preferred their foreign programmes in English. Both groups clearly found *Baywatch* in Hindi an absurdity. Looking on, Subhash Chandra, the imaginative chairman of an Indian toothpaste tube manufacturer, was quick to realize that locally produced content would be the key to success in Indian television. What Chandra understood instinctively was the pent-up demand for a middlebrow, indigenous television aesthetic of the kind that Doordarshan had never pursued or wanted, and that international recyclers of content did not adequately understand. Put simply, what was needed was a vulgar Indian popular culture, an aesthetic that was readily available to Chandra through the expansive cultural capital enjoyed by the Indian film industries.

The launch of Chandra's Hindi-language ZEE TV was to be one of the great business successes of the Indian 1990s. Making deals with the film world, Chandra was able to rely heavily on the back catalogue of the prodigious Indian cinemas. ZEE TV was thus able to appeal to the 90 per cent of the Indian television audience that identified popular films as their preferred content (McMillin 2002; Thussu 2005). While state television had failed to produce any notable celebrity figures during four decades of broadcasting, the public obsession with the lives of Indian film stars remained without parallel. As such, the importation of the Bollywood A-list into a new range of talk shows, gossip spots and celebrity panels was an obvious move towards a new popular form of television. Further, the distinctive song-and-dance sequences of the Indian film would come of age once more in the realm of television. The lip-syncing of film stars in glamorous costumes and locations provided a readymade MTV for television and free advertising for the cinema (Asthana 2003; Juluri 2002, 2003). The production of Indian variants of the TV quiz show format introduced a cheap and massively popular form of programming to the market, and the final ingredient was the introduction of new Hindi soaps that mixed Bollywood and Hollywood clichés to enormous effect. It was this programming mix in the family of ZEE TV channels that drove a massive expansion of television ownership into the middle classes during the 1990s, reaching four times as many households as STAR and transforming the cultural make-up of the satellite audience. Thus, the story of ZEE TV:

> demonstrates how national media can indigenize global products by developing derivatives of programmes broadcast on international television. This process works at different levels – in employing metropolitan broadcast language codes and conventions and in adapting programme formats, such as game and chat shows, unknown in India before globalization. Zee's success is based on a mixture of Hindi film and film-based programming, serials, music countdowns and quiz contests, aimed at a younger audience. (Thussu 1999: 127)

Rupert Murdoch responded, characteristically, to the rise of ZEE by buying up a massive stake in the company. This highly competitive partnership proved strangely successful. STAR's international infrastructure and channels along with ZEE's popular local content provided the definitive formula for the new world of Indian television. At first glance, it would seem logical to look at the pairing of ZEE and STAR, up until their subsequent divorce in 1999, as a match-up between international media capital and a local concern providing market access. After all, this has remained the modus operandi of doing business in India, liberalization era or not. However, this may provide a misleading impression in the specific case of satellite television. At the outset STAR did not need any government permissions to do business in India, and it seems equally clear that it was ZEE's own international ambitions as much as anything that provided impetus for the STAR-ZEE partnership. While ZEE could have found the necessary funds for expansion elsewhere, what partnership with STAR really gave ZEE was access to international markets. This allowed ZEE to draw a quarter of its revenues from émigré Indians in lucrative Western markets, who were prepared to pay a premium for modern Indian television. The launch of ZEE UK and ZEE US in 1995 thus became a critical component of Chandra's operations, bringing in a quarter of subscription revenues (Dudrah 2002a; 2005; Thussu 2005). What STAR gained in return from ZEE was the capacity to understand the programming demands of a broader Indian viewership. As such, following the termination of the partnership with ZEE, STAR immediately diversified into Hindi-language programming and began to commission volumes of Indian-made content for its schedules.

The subcontracting of the majority of content production instigated the rapid development of a highly competitive industry in television programming that consisted of over six thousand production houses by the mid-2000s, with a turnover of some 22 billion rupees (Kohli-Khandekar 2006: 89). By the time that STAR and ZEE went their own ways at the end of the decade, the entire sphere of television in India had been transformed beyond recognition. The Prasar Bharati Bill had finally sanctioned the separation of Doordarshan and its National Network from the Ministry of Information and Broadcasting, and committed it to a commercially viable broadcasting model. In order to protect the advertising revenues that it had previously enjoyed in this new competitive environment, Doordarshan underwent its own reinvention as a multi-channel, and far more commercially oriented, service (Ohm 1999; Thomas 2005: 101–6; Rodrigues 2010). However, the rapid change from state monopoly towards a commercial television environment and the tripartite division of Indian broadcasting between Doordarshan, STAR and ZEE was not to be the extent of India's television revolution. The entry of Japan's Sony Entertainment Television in 1995 further increased the intensive competition for ratings at the all-India level but, in fact, another equally significant shift in the dynamics of the broadcast environment was also under way.

Monopoly to Polyphony

Hot on the heels of the multinationals and the big Hindi networks, the deregulation of television also opened the way for the rapid emergence of regional language broadcasters across India. Just as sound pictures had led to multiple production centres and distinct vernacular markets for cinema, the freeing of television from the Hindi-centric policies of state broadcasting paved the way for the emergence of large regional players in Indian television. The Tamil-language channels Sun TV and JJTV both used the complex map of private cable networks to go on air in 1993. Within two years, AsiaNet, Eenadu TV, Udaya TV and others launched to provide services in the other major South Indian languages (Malayalam, Telugu and Kannada). Their massive popularity in their local markets mirrored the meteoric rise of regional language cinemas in South India in the 1960s, and led to a further wave of local competitors. Similarly, there were close links between regional language broadcasters and the major regional political parties along similar lines to their earlier partnership with the cinema. It was rapidly apparent that commercial television in India was not only to be national, international and intensely local – it was also to acquire a distinctly regional dimension. As Divya McMillin predicted in 2001:

> Regional private networks play a crucial role in local imaginings and, in the long run, may rise in tremendous political power through their manipulation and reflection of regional identity. These networks, rather than the transnational Star TV and ZEE TV, will rise as strong contenders to Doordarshan – not as one entity against Doordarshan but as many, independently, against one. (2001: 64)

The popularity of regional television was quick to provoke a response from the big national players. As the state broadcaster, Doordarshan had always produced some regional-language programming, albeit via scheduling that made it subordinate to Hindi and with a framing that was markedly centrist rather than regional. However, in this new competitive environment, and undoubtedly mindful of the increasing regionalization of India's political landscape throughout the 1990s, Doordarshan launched a number of regional language channels between 1993 and 1997. Rather than relying on the regional *kendras* alone, Doordarshan used the state-owned INSAT 1D satellite to make its ten new 'ethnic' language channels available across the breadth of the country, alongside its 'national' Hindi broadcasts. This proved to be hugely significant for a nation where internal migration has increased steadily for more than a century. South Indian migrants in New Delhi were now able to watch television in their own language as much as their relatives back home were able to do via the private cable networks. ZEE TV also extended its interests into regional language broadcasting, most notably in North Indian languages such as Punjabi, Bengali and Marathi.

The early debates about the advent of satellite television were largely couched in terms of an intrinsic opposition between the national and the global. This was conceived of in terms of two poles that were respectively seen as National-Hindi-Hindu and International-Christian-English. Before long, however, the imperatives for these two formations to respectively deregulate and indigenize their broadcasting gave rise to a far more complex nexus between regional, national and global cultural formations. The televisual field operated across this increasingly inter-referential spectrum of expression. As much as international TV formats were adapted for the Indian market, and the Indian cinema was reinvented for television, a broader range of vernaculars within India impinged upon the national-global encounter and produced a television environment that was characterized most of all by its polyphony.

As with the Indian press, there are substantial differences in the manner of address and the programming mix adopted by the regional broadcasters and the national ones, and between the Hindi, English and vernacular platforms. The nature of the interface between cable and satellite systems means that these overlapping voices are available simultaneously for contrast and comparison over a hundred channels of television. The three languages policy in education (regional-Hindi-English) over past decades, along with economic migration, has substantially increased the multi-lingual capacity of audiences, allowing them to draw together the disparate voices of Indian television in accordance with the particular context of their own interests, be that entertainment or information.

In that respect, what is also notable about the television revolution in India is the popularity of television news with the public. By the end of the 1990s, half-a-dozen private Indian news channels had emerged, radically transforming the nature of TV news. Under the guise of its imperative to 'inform' and 'educate', Doordarshan had long provided an itemized listing of the official government line on various matters in the form of news. Since 1991, CNN and the BBC had carried the voice of the UK/US international news duopoly. It was the emerging field of private news providers in India, however, that first introduced crime reporting, on-the-spot reporting of localized news items, man-in-the-street responses and other stock-in-trade aspects of contemporary television news (Mehta 2006). Since government legislation required a majority Indian ownership for news broadcasters, STAR commissioned New Delhi Television (NDTV) to provide English-language local news for STAR. ZEE responded with the first dedicated news channel, ZEE News, deploying a more populist format in Hindi. Major Indian press houses also entered the TV news market. The India Today Group launched Aaj Tak in Hindi and Headlines Today in English. The Sahara Group launched another news channel, Sahara Samay. In 2003, STAR and NDTV parted company. NDTV subsequently became a major independent player in the South Asian news market, broadcasting in both Hindi and English, while targeting satellite subscribers around the world. In 2006, NDTV expanded its international agenda by launching its own dedicated overseas channel in Indonesia (Mehta 2006). Following a similar pattern to its engagement and divorce with ZEE, STAR went on to launch its own Hindi-language STAR News.

The emergence of a competitive field of television news providers in the private sector was significant in displacing the previous cross-media status quo of Doordarshan/All India Radio and the major newspapers. In the process, television news was given an entirely new voice, which as Daya Thussu has observed, has tended to reflect a business-oriented perspective that celebrates the free market and favours further deregulation (2007b). STAR

News, in keeping with the broader agenda of News Corporation, combines a similarly pro-market message with celebrity gossip and political scandal in a fast-paced format typical of the global phenomenon of 'infotainment'.

> The focus of news is on fashion shows and on urban fads and frolics. Inevitably, a segment of news from the film industry is included in the daily package. The celebrity culture and what has been called the 'Page 3' world – gossip-laden reportage of the life and times of the metropolitan party-goers, their affairs and glitzy lifestyles – dominates coverage . . . When not covering stories about celebrities, Star News focuses on political sleaze and scandal, exposing bureaucratic mismanagement and corruption in public sector units and small private enterprises, but rarely, if ever, the large corporate groups. (Thussu 2007b.: 604)

According to Thussu, the intensely competitive nature of commercial news broadcasting has prompted the other news channels to emulate the STAR News style, resulting in a 'tabloid' news arena that is increasingly dominated by sound-bites and sensationalism. In keeping with the major constituencies of liberalization, the content of television news has also taken a conspicuously metropolitan tone in its subject matter. Rural affairs are left to Doordarshan, while foreign affairs are left in a large part to the English-language channels. As such, there is much found wanting in the present form of television news, particularly from the perspective of the established traditions of journalism, where similar commercial pressures are nonetheless also being felt. However, no one is seriously proposing a return to a state monopoly on news broadcasting. While many Indians recognize that there is a quality gap between television news and printed news, the private channels remain immensely popular in the big cities. The long-running exposés of political corruption tap into the common wisdom of the middle classes. Celebrity titillation provides the young with a cloak of glamour for changing material aspirations. But, more than this, the present melange of official pronouncements, commercial lobbying, prurient society columns and novelty items across news broadcasting is yet another manifestation of the polyphony that now characterizes Indian broadcasting (Mughda and Cottle 2008; Mehta 2007).

Nalin Mehta also provides a useful example of the impact of an enlarged news media on interstate relations through his analysis of media coverage of the India-Pakistan summit at Agra in 2000 (2006). By the time of the summit there were half-a-dozen competing private news networks popular with audiences on both sides of the border. Mehta takes note of the markedly different messages that were sent out by Pakistani President Musharraf in his interviews with Pakistan's state television (PTV), Doordarshan and the leading private news channels, Aaj Tak and NDTV. The arena opened up between the opposing state broadcasters by private television allowed Musharraf to tailor his address for these newly constituted cross-border audiences. Thus, there has been an implicit recognition of the different political constituencies and positioning associated with the different media outlets. The access gained by private television to officials from both countries and their presentation of competing viewpoints on critical issues, would have been unthinkable back in the state monopoly era. As such, commercial television is becoming a crucial component of the political environment in the South Asian region. Given the disjunctures between the political and linguistic geography of the subcontinent, the action of non-state broadcasters across the region infers a larger South Asian media sphere. Bengali broadcasters, for example, are effectively transnational broadcasters since their biggest audiences are to be found in neighbouring Bangladesh. Similarly, the Tamil language channels in the South reach Tamil-speaking audiences in Sri Lanka. Thus, the linguistically driven regionalization of Indian TV has simultaneously created transnational television audiences within the region (Burch 2002; Page and Crawley 2001; Sonwalker 2001).

Within the space of two decades, commercial providers have recast the role of TV for an era where transmission signals and content are simultaneously globalized, transnational and subnational. It has become a pressing task for scholars of television in South Asia to investigate how the complex media sphere formulated by the overlapping footprints of television interlaces so many publics within, and beyond, the national space. In that sense, what defines the era of polyphony for Indian television viewers today is that they are no longer presented with a homogenized India that is described for them. In the twenty-first century, with many sources of programming rather than only one, the project of a single national television audience is no longer viable. There are instead multiple shifting coalitions of spectatorship within the televisual field. The growing complexity of television now reaches across Asia, and it is able to do so precisely because of the eclipse of the statist paradigm. There is a loss here, perhaps, but also a potential gain, since India is undeniably the heavyweight in the emerging transnational media sphere in South Asia. It is a matter of no small importance, therefore, that the greatest allegiance of contemporary Indian television is to television itself. As a counterpoint to the old nationalist broadcast models, we may need to apply this lesson to understanding the wider phenomenon of global television.

The Field of Liberalization

Proponents of the free market can only take heart that the widely disparaged failure of the National Network to capture the public imagination was followed by an era that saw the privatization of television drive India's emergence as a regional giant in transnational broadcasting. The scale of growth has been breathtaking, with the audience for television in India expanding from around 30 million in the 1980s to some 500 million in 2008 (Rodrigues 2010: 3). Taking a more cautious tone, we might note that the technical capacity behind India's television revolution is very much a legacy of the technological efforts made during India's socialist past (Parthasarati 2010). The fact remains, however, that in its long-running attempt to be everything that the popular cinema was not, Doordarshan failed to become popular (Roy 2008). As such, Indian television today has eschewed developmental pedagogy in favour of the brash aesthetics of Indian cinema and the seductive fashions of international TV formats (Moran and Keane 2003). It is neither truly indigenous nor truly international and could arguably be seen to represent everything that its erstwhile regulators sought to avoid. At the same time, the pivotal role played by contemporary television in promoting the aspirations at the heart of India's 'New Economic Policy' appears to have won government sanction.

For this reason, it makes sense to see the present state of television not simply as an outcome, but rather as a major contributor to the field of liberalization in India. The expanding commercial media have been instrumental over the past two decades in transmitting a wider narrative through which India has been variously described as 'rising', 'shining', 'poised' and 'unbound'. As key beneficiaries of deregulation, the media have consistently mobilized support for an expanding regime of economic liberalization. The major regulatory features of this programme have been the curtailment of currency controls, the reduction of import tariffs, the progressive loosening of restrictions on foreign investment and the end of state monopolies across numerous sectors of the economy (McCartney 2009). As a result, India has attracted significant inflows of foreign investment and is increasingly returning to its historically significant role in international trade. It is against this backdrop that the Indian media sector has grown exponentially. This growth has been driven in a large part by the advertising revenues being spent on cultivating the enlarged middle classes that are now seen as the cornerstone of this 'emerging market' for capital goods and information services. Thus, the tilt towards a 'New Economy' constitutes an official endorsement of the rising patterns of consumption associated with an 'aspirational' middle class. It is the urban middle class, forged amongst an environment of international brands and an increasingly globalized workplace, that is now being offered as a model of social progress (Fernandes 2004). This entails a very different model of development from the previous era of wide-scale state intervention, self-sufficiency programmes, rural 'authenticity' and the primacy of heavy industry.

As a witness to the disastrous example of breakneck liberalization in Russia during the 1990s, the Indian government opted to implement these sweeping changes incrementally. A gradually decreasing mandatory regime for Indian ownership in various sectors was designed to ensure that Indian concerns enjoyed preferential market access until they became sufficiently established to engage with their international counterparts on their own terms. Thus, it is only after two decades that majority foreign ownership has been permitted in the media sector, itself the clear forerunner in the field of liberalization. To a certain extent, this approach towards supporting the development of Indian commerce while simultaneously accessing foreign expertise is consistent with some of the longer-term goals of the early independence period. Where there has been a more distinct ideological change is in the willingness of the state to allow Indian capital to accumulate without hindrance, making India's 'big business' much, much bigger than it was. Even more radical than this, however, is the implicit instruction for the urban middle classes to actively pursue a 'developed' lifestyle without being restrained by the development needs of the rural hinterland and the poor. This is a very significant change for a society where consumerism has been actively disparaged for several decades in the name of social cohesion, and where it still remains out of reach for the majority of the population.

As such, there are very pressing questions about the widening gap in economic development under the aegis of liberalization. We can readily contrast an urban middle class enjoying 450 channels of television, glitzy new shopping malls and rapidly increasing car ownership against the widespread exclusion of the rural poor, lower castes and minorities from the fruits of the New Economic Policy. Outside of the metropolitan hubs where private-sector investment has been concentrated, Indians are having to contend with rapid inflation in the price of basic foods, housing shortages, disparities in education, collapsing public healthcare and underemployment. There is also a notable geographic division here, as investment displays a tendency to concentrate in the big cities of the West and South where there is already a significant economic base. The rural hinterland and the East of India have yet to see the benefits of liberalization outweigh decreasing public investments in infrastructure and human capacity. The business-friendly national press have been happy to characterize this division in terms of the ideological intransigence of Bengal's left-wing state government and the general 'backwardness' of states such as Bihar and Jharkand. However, a sustained hard-line communist insurgency across much of Eastern India throughout the liberalization era has proved impossible to ignore (Chakrabarty and Kujur 2009). The challenge of balancing the uneven development of such a vast and diverse country remains considerable for the Indian government, and as it grows in size the private sector should arguably contribute more to that process.

Much of the formal regime, along with many of the social symptoms, of liberalization in India will be familiar to others around the world. Liberalization as a doctrine established its hegemony across the world to such an extent in the period 1991–2007 that it has often been mistakenly equated with globalization itself. This is a reflection of the extent to which the economic tenets of liberalization were adopted by the world's core international bodies, such as the International Monetary Fund, World Bank, World Trade Organization and by various arms of the United Nations (Stiglitz 2003). Functionally, liberalization is a process that seeks to encourage the withdrawal of the state from the economy. This withdrawal entails both the privatization of state-owned companies and the reform or repeal of any legislation designed to 'distort' the market in the name of public interest. Primarily, liberalization reflects a worldview that sees the nationalization of institutions as suppressing their capacity to create wealth for individuals (Hayek 1944). It also sees the reduction of profit motives and regulatory protection as reducing the motivation of employees. This all harms the competition that is inherent to a free market. Economic malaise is thus typically associated with the proliferation of state regulation as a major cause of inefficiency (Friedman 1993). Theoretically, liberalization constitutes a rejection of both socialist and nationalist economics in favour of a 'neo-classical' model of a unified capitalist market operating on the laws of profit alone (Turner 2011). Technically, it has also been associated with a 'monetarist' economic model that focuses on the supply side of capitalism and posits a public of rational consumers whose demand is dictated by reasonable self-interest. Ideologically, liberalization is deeply opposed to the state exercising power over private commerce through the political process or otherwise. Taken broadly, we can see the exposition of liberalization in India during the 1990s and 2000s as being consistent with its international influences, particularly in the Western world.

A consistent dichotomy during the rollback of nationalist economics around the world has been a resurgence in the fortunes of cultural nationalism as a political force. Indeed, it has been one of the great ironies of liberalization that the leading proponents of neo-liberal economics have also been heavily in favour of a social and cultural conservatism enforced by the state. In part, we can see this as symptomatic of a state retreat in the economic domain being compensated by the further encroachment of the state into the social domain. The state, after all, has to regulate something. We can also see that the increasingly intensive competition between national economies for supranational investors, along with the growth of economic migration, has fuelled insecurity and xenophobia, which, in turn, boosts the appeal of cultural and ethnic politics. India, in this regard, has not been immune to the cohabitation between economic liberalization and cultural militancy (Oza 2006). The interlacing of media expansion and economic liberalization during the 1990s was also coterminous with the first full term of a non-Congress government from 1998 to 2004. This transformation of the political order was long in the making, but it was the meteoric rise of the BJP and the resilience of powerful regional parties as independent power brokers that largely determined Indian national politics in the liberalization era. The roots of the BJP lie in the militant Hindu majority politics of the RSS, founded in 1925 and long opposed to secular, socialist politics of the Congress (Savarkar 1923; Kohli 1993; Hansen and Jaffrelot 2000). At one level, the many constituent parts of the Hindutva movement, such as Maharashtra's Shiv Sena, have expressed a cultural chauvinism deeply opposed to 'foreign' culture, both Western and Muslim (Eckert 2003). In that sense, the 'invasion from the skies' and the internationally inspired content of the new commercial media were both frequent targets of jingoistic sentiments in the early 1990s.

At the same time, however, the BJP proved itself to be far more 'media-savvy' than its Congress opponents. Observing the religious fervour unleashed by the television mega-serials of the *Ramayana* and *Mahabharata* during the 1980s, BJP strategists were alert to the utility of mass media for promoting the ideology of *Hindutva* (Hindu-ness) (Rajagopal 2001). The use of proselytizing cassettes, video and particularly close links with the Hindi-language press were central planks of this strategy. As the Hindi press tripled in size, the BJP also grew very rapidly from a marginal party to become India's dominant political force (Jeffrey 2002b). The series of political campaigns mobilized by the BJP around Hindu–Muslim flashpoints, such as the Ayodhya dispute, were designed to maximize media attention and put communal sentiments at the centre of public discussion. The high stakes strategy of inflaming, rather than suppressing, India's communal divisions fed directly into the new media environment of competitive sensationalism and provocative commentary that followed deregulation (Manchanda 2002). The BJP was also able to harness a conservative backlash against the growing presence of Western culture and commerce in Indian cities, stoking a defensive Indian patriotism that became increasingly assertive about a more 'martial' approach to international relations.

Paradoxically, once the BJP-led coalition had secured government under Bihal Vajpayee, it subsequently pursued policies that favoured a closer relationship with the United States and the acceleration of the liberalization programme being demanded by the business lobby (McGuire and Copland 2007). The BJP was also assiduous in cultivating the media, successfully forging a consensus with segments of the film industry, press and television, as well as throwing its weight behind the international ambitions of the software industry. Thus, the circuit of communication during the 1990s was deeply infused with emotive jingoism, alongside increasingly vocal aspirations to become a major player within the economic and political paradigm of globalization. Such contradictions were to be expected in a context where the public sphere was greatly increased in both depth and scope. Alongside the discourses of Hindutva and its global agenda in the media mainstream, the strong relationships between regional political parties and the regional media further consolidated their influence on public debate. Outside of the linguistic, ethnic and theocratic movements, caste-based parties in North India also sought to develop their own public constituencies via the mass media. In opposition until 2004, the Congress Party was compelled to construct a new relationship with the commercial media in recognition of this new era of coalition-based politics.

A transformation in the political culture of India is by no means the full extent to which the field of liberalization needs to be understood in cultural terms. At one level, the simultaneous clash and realignment of Indian politics and aesthetics with a Western media technology and its cultural forms has been consistent with earlier encounters. The longstanding opposition of cultural authenticity versus modernization also interacts with the energies unleashed by liberalization in ways that underscore the consistent power of both militant parochial forces and the effusive hybridity of Indian popular culture. The attendant shift in cultural authority from the state into a pluralist domain has been highly significant in forging the spirit of the age. Thus, it is in the mass media that the forces of globalization and liberalization are increasingly experienced and contested. How the competing urges of internationalism and parochialism play out may well be determined by the impact of history's greatest baby boom upon the cultural values of the subcontinent in this decade and the next. It is for their benefit that the overarching ideal type of the new middle classes as the hegemonic social group is made evident in the content of television (Fernandes 2004; Scrase and Ganguly-Scrase 2010). Questions, of course, remain as to the extent that television in its present form can further broaden its appeal while delivering this particular ideological programme. The past carries weight, and the diverse terrain of India's cultural geography inexorably exerts its own influence proportionate to the impact of global forces. In this respect, the regionalization of Indian television retraces the contours of the 'old' media landscape of press and cinema. This would appear to suggest that the liberalized media model is being adapted to the cultural diversity of India, with particular reference to the different scales of social imagination fostered through local, regional, national and international media practices.

The Age of Television

As I have outlined here, the story of television in India – at least, in the manner in which it is now commonly told – is a story of a shift from two very different worlds. The pivotal moment in this narrative is the dawning of the so-called liberalization era in 1991, which is widely seen as marking the transition from an era of statist monopoly defined by elitist autocracy and aesthetic realism to an era of popular entertainment, cosmopolitan internationalism and consumerist fantasy. This, then, is the new era of polyphony; a time for individualism, and for the expression of a list of desires that were long suppressed in the name of national integration, including desires for regional expression, consumer durables, unruly politics and audiovisual banality of a suitably 'international' standard. This telling of the tale undoubtedly simplifies the story somewhat, and we might be better advised to see these changes across a broader period from the mid-1980s onwards. Nonetheless, this fable is a very important historical lesson for understanding the nature, purpose and future of television in Asia. Over the period of the television revolution in India, the Western world has been very much concerned with the transformative potentials of computer networks. However, we should – as Graeme Turner has noted – remain wary of any pronouncements of a post-TV era (2009). In India, it could be argued that the era of television has only now come into being, since the era of state monopoly from 1959–91 largely corresponded with a lengthy extension of the government newsreel by other means. From this perspective, the rapid leap made by Indian television from the long era of monopoly into competitive multi-channel, multi-format, transnational broadcasting is even more striking.

After dragging its heels over the role of television in a country with so many pressing social and economic challenges to overcome, India spent two decades failing to construct a national television address that could be readily accepted by a diverse population. Contrary to the scientific focus of developmentalism as an ideology, it was by no means the technical obstacles that undermined India's great national television project, but rather an extraordinary failure of social imagination on the part of her decision-makers. While the statistics produced during the era of monopoly told a story of the gradual extension of geographic coverage in an exact parallel of the discussion of Indian railways and with little resemblance to anything actually conceived of as an audience, the era of polyphony has been very much focused on the bums-on-seats ethos of commercial broadcasting. Indeed, the very essence of the television era is apparent in this discursive shift from geographic to demographic conceptions of the audience. It is in urban India that this transformation has been most readily apparent. In 1990, visitors to India were unlikely to see a television broadcast unless they had very affluent hosts or stayed in a five-star hotel. Televisions, where you did see them, seemed to be used almost entirely for watching popular films on videocassettes. Ten years later, however, you wouldn't expect to take a ten-dollar hotel room without getting access to at least fifty channels of colour TV. The crucial point here is not the comfort of the habitual tourist, but rather the fact that fifteen years ago, India felt cut off from the rest of the world, while today television pours information in constantly from every other part of the globe (albeit through an anglophone filter). India has conducted a strategic engagement with the present phase of globalization, and for the average citizen the proof positive of this is that India is now part of the world of global TV.

This electronic abundance shouldn't be too readily celebrated, however. It is fair to say that rural India and the labouring masses of the country are almost entirely absent from the new world of Indian television. The audience that preoccupied India's state planners and the screens of state television for so long now appears to be of little if no interest to a commercial television system devoted to middle-class aspirations. Doordarshan is largely left to cater to the average Indian, and despite the familiar rhetoric, commentators have noted that even the state broadcaster has been driven by commercial imperatives to focus on winning back the urban middle-class audience (for example, Ohm 1999). Of course, a lack of representation does not mean that the less privileged will not enjoy the glitter of the everyday TV soaps, but a representation gap cannot but add to the existing gaps in both social expectations and economic fortunes between urban and rural India, between East and West, and between castes and communities. In their own distinctive ways, both Hindutva politics and the longstanding social structures masked by socialism have facilitated a television universe that is Hindu and upper-caste in character. As such, the era of polyphony is linguistically and region-ally diverse but not socially diverse in the widest sense. The religious and ethnic minorities, the poor, the old and the politically old-fashioned are all under-represented in the casting of Indian television. You are far more likely to see foreigners on your screen.

Commentators have argued that the era of polyphony has been technologi-cally determined by satellite television and ideologically determined by the triumph of liberal capitalism (Chatterjee 2004; Fernandes 2000). There is truth in both claims. However, the longer story of broadcasting in India also demonstrates with consistency that even when you are in firm possession of both medium and message, a willing audience is required. Fundamentally, this is why the era of high-handed, monopolistic state broadcasting in the region is over. The audience for the television revolution was born during the 1970s and 1980s, when the moral authority of autocratic statist nationalism reached its nadir. Since then, a growing suspicion of the governing elites, a sense of entitlement stemming from the democratic experiment and the desire to actually reap the promised fruits of development have transformed the relationship of the Indian state with its public. From a liberal pluralist perspective, the state monopoly over public broadcasting was a necessary victim of successful nation-building, rather than being symptomatic of its failure. Certainly, in contrast with the European case, few Indian commentators have lamented the displacement of the Doordarshan monopoly. Perhaps this is why, in the larger scheme of things, the worthy, illiterate Asian peasant of developmental discourse has been so comprehensively overwritten by the increasingly cosmopolitan 'emerging consumer' of the Asian century. They are both media fictions, but the impact of such imagined communities upon media policy and content should not be underestimated.

Further Reading

Page, David and Crawley, William (2001) *Satellites Over South Asia: Broadcasting Culture and the Public Interest*, New Delhi: Sage.

Juluri, Vamsee (2003) *Becoming A Global Audience: Longing and Belonging in Indian Music Television*, New Delhi: Peter Lang.

Jeffrey, Robin (2000) *India's Newspaper Revolution*, London: C. Hurst & Co.

McCartney, Matthew (2009) *Political Economy, Liberalisation and Growth in India 1991–2008*, London and New York: Routledge.

Mehta, Nalin (2007) *India on Television: How Satellite News Has Changed the Way We Think and Act*, New Delhi: HarperCollins.

Rajagopal, Arvind (2001) *Politics After Television: Hindu Nationalism and the Reshaping of the Public in India*, New Delhi: Sage.

Ranganathan, Maya and Rodrigues, Usha (2010) *Indian Media in a Globalised World*, New Delhi: Sage.

4   The Global Dynamics of Indian
         Media Piracy

The first decade of the twenty-first century has seen an increasing level of academic and commercial interest in Asian media and, by extension, in the mediation of Asia. Within this context, the migration of Western media content into India initially provided a focal point for the discussion of mediated cultural exchange, and thus of globalization, within the subcontinent. However, the liberalization era has also seen an acceleration in the *dispersal* of Indian media content worldwide. These export activities form a highly significant part of the wider pattern of media migrations out of and within Asia as a whole. As transnational media flows multiply within the region, from Korea to Karachi, it has become increasingly apparent that the dispersal and exchange of media content is becoming a prevalent feature of everyday life in the region (Holden and Scrase 2006; Thussu 2007a; Kim 2008). The international presence of Indian movies is highly significant because it is inextricably bound up with the major tropes of globalization, that is: innovations in communications technologies, mass migration and the mobility of multinational capital and consumerism. Nonetheless, the contemporary focus of globalization theories should not obscure the fact that photomechanical feature films have been inherently mobile cultural artefacts for almost a century prior to the current period of media proliferation. India has historically been an exporter of films and this is highly relevant to understanding the global nature of Indian cinema today.

The Disorganized Industry and the Informal Economy

India makes more films than any other country in the world, and has done so for five decades. Add to this the ubiquitous umbrella term 'Bollywood', with which Indian cinema has been increasingly associated, and it is easy to conjure up an image of an industrial juggernaut where a handful of mega-studios churn out films and media moguls exact huge profits from exhibition, sell-through and ancillary rights. Such an image would be highly misleading. In the first place India has not one, but several, major film industries serving different audiences at home and abroad. Second, the most striking difference between the Indian film world and Hollywood is the relative lack of formal organization to be found in Indian film-making. The film business in India remains characterized by intense fragmentation, since 'Unlike the U.S. film industry where supply is controlled by a handful of oligopolistic corporations with monopoly power, hundreds of Indian producers compete for markets' (Pendakur 2003: 35). The informality of capital and the dispersal of assets in the product chain of Indian cinema belies a very sophisticated system of production and dissemination which, through its collective efforts, manages to produce the largest output of films anywhere in the world and deliver those films to one of the world's largest and most diverse audiences.

The largely informal relations between the different sectors does, however, also lead to conflicts over the spreading of risks in an industry where only 10 per cent of films will break even. A distributor may finance a film (usually on the basis of the featured stars) and then use this financial leverage to dictate creative terms to the film director via the producer. In turn, theatre owners in important metropolitan locations may charge exorbitant rents to the distributor for the use of the facility to show the finished film. The feedback of box-office data and profits back up the chain is extremely unreliable, as the heavy burden of punitive entertainment taxes has encouraged the widespread underestimation of ticket sales and profits. Furthermore, in order to avoid being placed at a relative disadvantage by players in other sectors of the industry, and to overcome shortages in working capital:

> producers have historically resorted to raising money from private investors who come primarily from construction, jewelry and associated trades . . . they are often willing to pay usurious rates of interest (36%–40%) to an investor. Not only are there such high returns in lending money to film producers, but unaccounted money can be put to use in an industry where stars and others usually get paid in cash and receipts are only issued for a fraction of the total amount involved . . . It is not surprising then to find pirates, thieves, criminals and underworlds dons attempting their hand in the film industry. (Pendakur 2003: 51–3)

In the context of the Hindi film industry in Mumbai, it has been estimated that 40 per cent of films made in the 1990s were financed by 'dubious money' (Koppikar 1997: 31). This 'dubious money' may not all originate in organized crime per se, since both illegal funds that arise from criminal activities and capital that has avoided taxation are considered 'black money' in India. Distinctions between the two are notoriously hard to trace amongst the cash payments that dominate not only the film industry but the economic life of the city itself (Appadurai 2000: 633; Aiyar 2005). Nonetheless, as Smruti Koppikar relates, the decision of a major underworld figure, Dawood Ibrahim, then based in Dubai, to begin financing films in the 1980s saw formerly obscure small businessmen and well-known video pirates become film producers in their own right, launching big film projects with major stars (Koppikar 1997: 31). In recent years, extensive coverage in the press has been given to the reliance of large parts of the industry on these forms of finance, as well as to lurid tales of extortion, blackmail and murder (for example, Srivastava 2003).

One such tale, which usefully brings together the strands of piracy, murder and commercial and technological innovation within India's informal entertainment economy, is the story of the 'Cassette King', Gulshan Kumar (see Liang 2006). As is well known, film songs have been central to the Indian cinema experience since the coming of sound production in 1931. With the introduction of audiocassettes to India in the 1970s, the sell-through of film soundtracks was probably the closest thing to a guaranteed investment in the volatile entertainment industry. However, the established audio companies in India, given to selling small quantities of vinyl recordings to affluent consumers in the major cities, were much too slow in responding to the implications of cheaper and more portable playback technologies. Thus, the established music companies were swiftly beaten to the point of sale by Gulshan Kumar. Kumar's strategy was twofold. In the first place, he exploited a loophole in the copyright regulations, which allowed him to record near-perfect imitations of copyright film song recordings (and their packaging) as 'cover versions' without paying any royalties. He then marketed his 'T Series' cassettes by pioneering a nationwide distribution network, operating in the informal economy where local wholesalers and pavement traders flooded the country with cheaply produced cassettes. Kumar's Super Cassette Industries offered buyback schemes to reduce risks to its retailers, dropped the price of recorded music within the reach of the masses and, furthermore, penetrated even the smallest towns, where the established music companies had never bothered to trade.

By the early 1990s, Gulshan Kumar was rich, and a household name. Revenues from film music became so lucrative that cassette manufacturers were able to begin directly bankrolling the production of films, thus feeding finance back into the industry whose intellectual property they had so effectively plundered. More significant, however, than direct financing to any assessment of the balance of deficit and benefit through audio piracy is that the cassette operators had successfully pioneered an expansion of the market into areas that the official distributors had lacked the means, or the will, to exploit effectively. Subsequently, there was a gradual normalization of those markets through agreements by producers on the pre-sale of audio rights and a price war that brought recorded music within the reach of many more consumers. There was no such happy ending, however, for the 'Cassette

King' who was brutally murdered in 1997, allegedly for failing to adequately provide for his own protection with the Mumbai underworld (see Koppikar 1997).

The nexus between the film industry and the black economy over many years has been both cause and consequence of the industry's difficult relationship with the Indian government. A lack of access to legitimate funds caused by the government's denial of official industry status, punitive levels of taxation and rising production costs all helped to push the industry further into the underworld throughout the 1980s. Accordingly, the announcement by Sushma Swaraj (then Union Information & Broadcasting Minister in the BJP-led government) in 1998 that the film industry was finally to be given official status could be seen as an attempt to break this spiral and trigger a radical overhaul of the way that the industry functions. This change in tack by the government was prefigured by the simultaneous deregulation of India's state media and the entry of foreign capital into India's media market. It was also spurred by a recognition of the growing profile of Indian films overseas and the perceived benefits of this to India in terms of the projection of a positive image on the world stage. This belated official encouragement was nonetheless part of a carrot-and-stick approach as the authorities also began to launch unprecedented investigations into the finances of the industry. As part of these investigations, wire-tapping led to the arrest of film financier Bharat Shah. It was alleged that his film *Chori Chori Chupke Chupke*:

> was funded by slush money funnelled in from mafia-style criminal syndicates ... The police used as evidence two audio tapes recording conversations between Shah and underworld don, Chotta Shakeel. In the tape, Shah and Shakeel allegedly discussed an extortion racket involving a businessman. The tapes are also said to implicate Shah in illegal foreign currency transactions. (BBC Online 30 September 2003)

In 2003, Shah was found guilty, along with producer Nasim Rizvi and his assistant Abdul Rahim Allah Baksh, of 'withholding information from the police about links between the Indian film industry and the mafia' (Srivastava 2003). The case brought about a wave of protests from industry personnel, amidst a growing list of film personalities requiring official police protection (*Indian Express* 19 December 2000; BBC Online 30 July 2002; Gangadhar 2005). The stakes were made further apparent when film producer Rakesh Roshan was subject to a shooting attack after 'avoiding' a series of calls from the underworld. As Marie Beattie relates:

> Bombay's powerful underworld – which has long played sugar daddy to Bollywood's Big Names – has lately been turning very, very nasty. Stars, directors and producers live with the constant fear of threats, extortion and even

> murder . . . it seems to be payback time, with the mafia eager to control lucrative overseas distribution rights and to bully the top stars into acting in the productions they're backing. (Beattie 2002)

The imperatives given here for the underworld to defend its turf within the film industry indicate not only the continuing presence of black money in the production sector, but also the extent to which overseas markets have become crucial for the profitability of the industry. Overseas markets for Indian films were financially marginal prior to the 1990s and thus classified as one combined territory. Overseas audiences were therefore rarely considered in the planning of any film (Rajadhyaksha 2003: 29). However, the changes in foreign exchange and import-export regulations in the liberalization era have made foreign audiences a much more accessible source of legitimate income than they were in the past. Hence, a much more significant box office for Indian films in key Western markets, along with growing profits from ancillary products (such as overseas music and broadcast rights), have made the export sector an attractive revenue stream for the leading players (Thussu 2000; Rajadhyaksha 2003; Padmanabhan 2005). Export markets are now a major source of income, 'divided along 13 territories, 10 in Asia and the Middle East, and three which cover Britain and Europe, North America, and Australia' (Dudrah 2002a: 28). In the space of a decade, overseas distribution rights have rocketed from next to nothing to almost 30 per cent of returns for a 'Bollywood' spectacular, transforming in the process not only the business model but also the worldview of the Indian cinema and its protagonists (see Inden 1999; Deshpande 2005). As such, the dynamics of film exports are central to understanding the intersection between the Hindi film industry in Mumbai and organized crime.

Playback Formats and the Global Dispersal of Indian Films

The presence of the underworld in the export sector reaches back over several decades, having arisen at a time when export restrictions and regulations stood between the products of the Indian cinema and enthusiastic audiences outside the country. After the coming of videocassettes, in particular, in order to exploit these markets, the connections of the informal economy were employed. Indeed, it is doubtful if the Indian film would have anything like the global presence it now has without such operations. The impact of the videocassette on the distribution of Indian films, with its inherent portability, its domestic use and its ability where necessary to circumvent national and legal boundaries, was the technological catalyst which heralded a new period of internationalization for Indian films. Prior to the advent of VCR technology in the late 1970s, Indian films had already been exported across Asia, Africa and the Middle East. Significant growth in export profits, however, was held back by the prohibitive cost of producing and circulating film prints, stringent import taxes (to which returning prints were subject) and currency controls, as well as political barriers erected by hostile governments. The government of Pakistan, for example, moved to ban the importation of Indian films, first in West Pakistan in 1952 and subsequently in largely Bengali East Pakistan in 1962 (Rajadhyaksha and Willemen 1999: 23–4). These impediments to the spread of Indian film culture were suddenly weakened, however, by VCR technology, which, by the early 1980s, had revolutionized the nature of global film distribution (Levy 1989; O'Regan 1991).

The VCR facilitated a quantum shift in the relationship between the Indian cinema and audiences abroad. In the first place, it allowed a highly fragmented industry located in the so-called 'developing world', and in what was then still a significantly 'controlled' economy, to operate at a global scale despite a lack of available capital for investment in developing its off-shore markets. The VCR enabled Indian films to circumvent government canal agencies, censors and tariffs, and to establish a reliable supply network worldwide without first acquiring the 'critical mass' upon which Hollywood's global operations have relied historically (that is, vertically integrated major studios organized in the MPAA cartel). In contrast to the block-booking and mass monopoly practices through which the US industry established itself during the photochemical era, the pattern of distribution achieved by Indian films through playback media over the last twenty-five years can be seen as exemplary of the effective targeting of a dispersed (mostly) niche audience through demand-driven film distribution, undertaken along a chain of relatively small entrepreneurs. In this sense, the Indian film provides a compelling example of what can be achieved when a technological innovation is successfully conjoined with the economic ideology of the free market in order to provide an 'on-demand' service to consumers.

Seen retrospectively, it can easily be argued that the ability of VCR technology to match viewers with content heralded the end of the broadcasting paradigm and the rise of the niche audience as the dominant model of media reception. However, at the same time, the loss of control over the processes of replication inherent to the technology also precipitated the crisis of playback piracy that continues to grip the world's media industries. In India's domestic market, the impact of piracy in the early 1980s was considered serious enough to prompt predictions of the end of Indian cinema. Ultimately, this did not happen, most likely due to the prohibitive expense of VCR equipment for the majority of the film-going public, although it certainly dented the upper middle-class audience considerably (Boyd et al. 1989: 137). Nonetheless, it has taken two decades, and considerable efforts, to reduce 'losses' from piracy within India itself to a conservatively estimated 14 per cent (KPMG-CII, 2005: 50). A major issue here has been the relatively weak status of industry organizations due to lack of official industry status and the large number of producers, distributors and exhibitors with competing interests. A further issue has been the regional nature of Indian film production (and the economy generally). Street traders in Bangalore, for example, do not trade in copies of Kannada films so as not to attract the ire of the local industry – but they openly trade in titles produced by other Indian and international industries. The situation is even worse outside of India, where the vast majority of Indian films being consumed continue to be unlicensed copies from which the producers gain no returns.

Prior to the video revolution, the export of photographic film prints through slow-moving, officially regulated channels largely functioned as the cultural arm of international relations (as in the case of exports to the Soviet Union from the 1950s). By contrast, the diffuse networks of media piracy that sprang up around the circulation of Indian films on videocassettes were operated on solidly capitalist principles. The Gulf States became a substantial video market for Indian features from the outset, not only for domestic consumption by local residents and substantial numbers of South Asian guest workers, but also as a transit point for films on the way to many other parts of the world (Pendakur 1990: 241). There were a number of reasons for this, not least that the government ban on Indian film imports in Pakistan made viewers there leap at this chance to obtain the prohibited product (O'Regan 1991; Friedberg 2000: 444). Given their relative proximity and their economic links to both India and Pakistan, the Gulf States – and in particular the city of Dubai – were a natural base for serving this unofficial market. As such, the flow of pirated film prints to Dubai from India had been well established by the 1960s (Seagrave 2003: 79). The spread of the VCR, however, allowed the mass reproduction of each smuggled print. Since the 1980s, the illegal circulation of Indian films on playback formats has become so common in Pakistan that the continuing ban is now virtually meaningless, with Indian films widely available on cassettes, digital disks and even cable television (Purewal 2003: 550–1).

In other instances, where the barriers to the penetration of Indian films were primarily due to the economies of scale inherent to cinematic exhibition rather than political concerns, the videocassette was also to have a dramatic effect. In Britain, for example, there was a relatively small market during the 1970s for theatrical showings of Indian films to South Asian migrants in the major cities, often at matinee showings. After the arrival of the VCR, this practice fell into immediate decline as a much larger market for domestic viewing across Britain developed overnight (Dudrah 2002a: 25). Occasional viewing of old and worn prints of dated films at inconvenient times was a practice easily displaced by access to a clutch of the latest releases for consumption in the comforts of the home environment at a fraction of the cost. The ability of the pirates to exploit this worldwide niche, and to develop a system of informal distribution that touched the remote corners of the globe, was notable and draws some useful parallels with Gulshan Kumar's simultaneous pioneering of audio sales through pavement vendors back in India. Indian films consequently became ubiquitous in the bazaars of the 'developing' world and in the grocery stores of South Asian communities in the West, while remaining virtually non-existent in official shops and outlets (see Brosius 2005; Athique 2006). Some of the profits from these huge and dispersed illegal operations doubtless found their way back to the industry in India by one means or another, notably through production finance and salaries for stars, but it seems equally certain that the lions' share of returns were lost to the 'entrepreneurs' that made up the various links in the delivery chain.

The nature of Indian cinema's export markets had a place in setting the piracy paradigm. India's biggest natural export market, Pakistan, maintains a ban on Indian films for political reasons and does not, in any case, recognize Indian intellectual property, making legitimate export impossible (Khan 2005a). For a long time the niche markets of South Asian migrants in developed countries were too small to be of interest, either to mainstream distributors active in those territories or to copyright enforcement agencies (Ray 2000: 184). The other markets where Indian films were popular across Africa, Asia and the Middle East were (and in many cases still are) all markets where piracy of media products was rampant and where even Hollywood producers have great difficulties in protecting their products. These were typically markets in developing countries where official film exchanges were subject to stringent restrictions by national governments which, paradoxically, lacked resources or enthusiasm for the prevention of piracy. So, as much as the policy regime in India was for a long time unfavourable to export activity, the conditions in the receiving countries were, for one reason or another, highly favourable to piracy. It is important to recognize, however, that without the pirates it would have been difficult to have adequately developed these export markets in the first place. Bottlenecks put in place by a series of governments prior to the 1990s – whose state-socialist film policy centred on displacing rather than facilitating the commercial industry – were a serious impediment to legitimate commercial distributors. Strict foreign currency controls acted as a disincentive by raising the cost of financing overseas operations and preventing the repatriation of significant profits. Furthermore, the structural fragmentation of the industry did not provide for efficient collaboration, or sufficient capital, for pursuing overseas markets after the fashion of the Hollywood studios. Instead, the longstanding reliance of the industry on underworld finance naturally predisposed that smugglers, and later duplicators, would take charge of the foreign markets.

One thing that has been demonstrated very effectively by the global networks supplying Indian films is the capacity of informal economy to build new markets and to foster increased levels of habitual consumption. In the West, a new generation of South Asians was brought up and exposed to a diet of Indian films on (mostly pirated) videocassette. In recent years this cohort has rejuvenated, and even expanded, the legitimate theatrical exhibition market (Dudrah 2002a: 25). Indian films now frequently reach the top ten at the UK box office, with film exhibitions operating alongside over 4,000 video outlets (Dudrah 2002a: 22; Geetha 2003: 31). Similarly, in the US: 'Pirated videocassettes rented and sold through South Asian-owned video stores proliferated in the 1980s in the metropolitan centers' (Pendakur 2003: 27). Nonetheless, in recent years, several Indian films have still managed to draw large enough crowds to scale the reaches of the box-office listing in the gigantic US theatrical market (Rajadhyaksha 2003: 114–15). In 2006, Indian films were expected to gross $100m in the US theatrical market – three times what Hollywood makes in India (Bamzai 2006: 37).

In part, this renaissance for theatrical exhibition has been made possible by the spread in the West of multiplexes and 'multiculturalism' amenable to niche products. Nonetheless, over the longer period it is the contribution made by video piracy that has been decisive in fostering the global familiarity of Indian cinema. The new digital formats that have now replaced videocassettes, VCD and DVD are further fuelling worldwide film piracy. This is due to their even greater portability and the fact that the mass reproduction of video disks is quicker than the old cassette technology, requires less plant investment, is cheaper and (usually) of higher quality. There are also some positives for consumers – for example, the access to cheaper subtitling technologies facilitated by digital technologies is helping to bridge the language gap between Hindi cinemas and non-Hindi-speaking audiences, particularly in the important second-generation diaspora. If Indian producers are to realize their increasingly globalized ambitions, it has now become an imperative for the industry that it more efficiently capitalizes its offshore playback markets through official sales. Accordingly, some of the major Indian media producers are now keen to attend to the 'problem' of piracy in order to begin receiving more of the profits from the global popularity of their product. For their part, the pirates seem equally determined to hold on to the very significant share of the export earnings that they have enjoyed over the last three decades. It is the technological and economic vectors commonly seen as defining globalization that are shaping the terrain upon which this contest is being played out.

Getting Organized

Since the mid-1990s, the film business in India has been in the throes of major changes brought about by the liberalization of the economy and by the commercial application of new digital technologies. The arrival of large, integrated media combines from abroad has prompted a review of the anarchic conditions of mass independent production, which have existed since the 1940s. Since multinationals such as Fox and Sony have only been partially successful in expanding the market for dubbed US imports in theatres, these new players have now begun to provide some finance for local film productions alongside their investments in television programming. Official industry status for the film business has also seen growing investments from India's corporate sector. For producers able to access them, these new sources of institutional finance have strengthened their hand considerably. With a corporate ethos in mind, some of the major film producers have been making serious efforts to coordinate their activities as production houses with the marketing and distribution of their films. Within this shifting environment, one of the leading production companies, Yash Raj Films, has chosen to focus its energies on export markets and to take on the pirates. The creation of director-turned-producer Yash Chopra, Yash Raj Films instigated its own distribution arm in the 1990s and was quick to recognize the changing dynamic with overseas markets. Yash Raj opened its own offices in London and New York in 1997 and 1998 (Dwyer 2000: 12). A string of films produced by the label from 1995 onwards have enjoyed considerable success in these countries, with Chopra claiming that the UK market was now the 'number one' market for their work (BAFTA 2006). Their investment in these markets has also made them particularly sensitive to the prevalence of playback piracy.

Yash Raj Films have instigated increasingly frequent raids and legal proceedings against the pirate trade and publicize these activities on their website, following a policy of 'naming and shaming' outlets that they have prosecuted for stocking counterfeit Yash Raj titles. This serves 'as a warning that the Indian film and music industry intends to aggressively prosecute companies and individuals that engage in piracy' (Yash Raj Films 2004a). In recent years, Yash Raj has been involved in raids in the USA, the UK, the

Netherlands and Australia, seizing hundreds of thousands of illegal DVDs (Yash Raj Films 2004a/b, 2005, 2006; BBC News Online 15 March 2005, 27 May 2005; Athique 2006). The reason that a handful of Western markets are being targeted so heavily by these anti-piracy operations is not only the high per unit and per capita returns they offer to producers in light of the exchange rate and retail price, but also because they possess copyright enforcement regimes under which pirates can be prosecuted effectively. Comparatively speaking, it still remains incredibly difficult to prosecute intellectual property rights in the African and Asian markets that are long-standing destinations for Indian film exports. By contrast, as part of the American-led effort to further control intellectual property worldwide, all of the anglophone countries have strengthened their intellectual property laws in recent years. Fortuitously, the entry of their own media companies into India, their willingness to attract increasing numbers of offshore Indian productions, and the considerable success of Indian films in their own theatrical markets in recent years, have all prompted countries such as the UK, the US and Australia to take a tougher stance on the piracy of Indian films. Extra impetus, critical mass even, has come along with the associations being made by industry lobbyists and government between media piracy and terrorism (Hindu Business Line 25 November 2003; Valenti 2003; Film Distributors Association UK 2005).

Not all Indian producers, however, possess the clout of Yash Raj Films when it comes to clamping down on the pirating of their products. As such, the British Phonographic Industry (BPI) estimates that as many as 70 per cent of Indian movie DVDs in the UK are pirate copies, making it a much bigger problem for Indian producers than for their Anglo-American counterparts (Gibson 2005).

> David Martin, the BPI's anti-piracy director, said it was becoming increasingly difficult for authorities to stem the tide of pirated films, typically manufactured in Pakistan, Malaysia and China where copyright laws are lax. They are then imported by both large criminal networks and small time operators. 'Millions of units are turning up in the UK, South Africa, Canada and the US. Our intelligence tells us that on any given Pakistan Airways flight from Karachi there'll be 30 to 40 bringing in DVDs, effectively acting as mules,' he said. 'They will bring in spindles of up to 2,000 DVDs in each case, which they can buy in Pakistan for £1 each. From wholesalers in London they sell for £7 to £8 so the profit margins are tremendous.' (Gibson 2005)

According to Willem Van Adrichem, the Dubai-based regional coordinator for the International Federation of Phonographic Industry (IFPI): 'We have indications that there are very close contacts between organizations in

India and Pakistan who exchange the masters and bring them to Pakistan' (in Badam 2005: 47). This is an indication of the extent to which the rapid speed of the piracy operations is the result of leaks from within the industry itself. The leaking of film masters appears to be a much bigger problem than is generally recognized for all of the world's major film industries. Similarly, in the Indian case, films 'are often pirated from the actual prints or masters' and 'counterfeiting from the original DVDs occurs later' (Badam 2005: 46). As Subhra Gupta relates: 'the pirates are frightfully organized and keep tabs on the movement of original film prints, the market is flooded with dupes (duplicates) within a day' (2001). The distribution system for pirated films throughout India is also sophisticated, extensive and entrenched in the urban environment, to the extent that the industry has been forced to recognize a greatly diminished theatrical window, meaning bigger releases and shorter theatrical runs with a greater emphasis on the premium, metropolitan markets ('A centres'). In recent years, new players in distribution have also been implementing combined digital distribution and projection systems in order to maintain tighter control over their content (Kohli-Khandekar 2006: 126–8).

There have also been very significant changes in the regulatory environment for intellectual property in India. As Pradip Thomas has noted, successive changes to copyright laws over the 1990s increased the scope and severity of intellectual property violations in India (1999). These changes were specifically intended to make India compliant with the regime of the World Intellectual Property Organization (WIPO). A raft of more recent legislation, covering areas from design patents, information technology, telecommunications and biotechnology to cultural goods and services, during the past decade, has served to demonstrate 'the extent to which a global "proprietary" agenda has become a significant aspect of India's social and economic futures' (Thomas 2010: 119). In order to ensure access to global markets for its own knowledge-intensive industries in technology and science, India has been obliged to legislate a domestic environment where the patents of foreign companies are more extensive in scope and receive much more stringent legal protection. In the process, a number of bilateral partnerships have been agreed with developed countries to guarantee the enforcement of intellectual property rights. This trade-off is an important component of India's integration into the present regime of global trade. However, it also has important ramifications for the media industries since, under these obligations, media content is treated as just another commodity of commercialized information. This means that India is obliged to pursue a much tougher line on the illegal replication and distribution of films, music, television and software. Indubitably, there are obvious benefits for local producers of media content who have subsequently been able to mobilize police actions against pirate media vendors, as well as forging alliances with the trade bodies in the United States who increasingly regulate the global trade in cultural goods.

Greater cooperation within the Indian film industries themselves, along with the extended legal frameworks that have emerged from the international Trade in Intellectual Property and Services (TRIPS) agreements, has further supported enforcement initiatives intended to tackle domestic piracy at the level of retail (see Correa 2007; Desai 2005). However, the endemic nature of media piracy in India outstrips the police resources that can be made available and, from the actions that have taken place to date, prosecutions are held back by an overloaded judicial system According to Gauri Lakhanpal, in 2006, there were 'more than 1,500 MPA – [Motion Picture Association] initiated and supported film piracy cases pending resolution in Indian courts' (2006). In any case, a clampdown in India alone, or even in concert with deterrent operations in the West, will not be enough to unravel global piracy networks given the extensive involvement of third countries (Khan 2005b; Prabhakar 2006). In 2003, India's Commerce and Industry Minister, Satyabarata Mokherjee, publicly urged Malaysia to clamp down on the piracy of Indian media products (BBC Online 2 December 2003). Really effective cooperation with Pakistan in this area is much more critical, but, given the ongoing geopolitical situation, this remains contingent upon a much wider range of outstanding bilateral issues. Nonetheless, under similar pressures from the Western world, the Pakistan government conducted raids on six illegal replication plants in Karachi in May 2005, discovering 400,000 pirated disks and 10,000 masters, the bulk of this material being Indian movies (Badam 2005: 47).

There are some signs, however, that the pirates may already be moving ahead of the 'safe haven' operating model by outsourcing reproduction to duplicators in the receiving markets. According to the British Phonographic Industry (BPI), whose primary focus in the UK is on large-scale distributors and duplicators, rather than retailers: 'A clampdown by Customs and Excise in the last years, coupled with the declining cost and increasing quality of DVD burning equipment, means that DVDs – like fake CDs – are now increasingly made in the UK' (BPI 2005). In September 2005, A raid by the BPI led to the seizure of 'GBP 400,000 worth of counterfeit stock and equipment capable of producing 50,000 fakes a day' from a suburban house in London's Southall. According to the BPI, 'the sheer size of the factory – which included 24 multi DVD burners, three photocopiers, three computers, a labelling machine and thousands of blank CDs and DVDs makes this the largest factory ever uncovered in Western Europe in terms of capacity'. The fakes included 'mainstream' Western products, but again the majority consisted of Indian bootlegs. The difficulty for future enforcement efforts was made clear – since, unlike the considerable size of plant required for a comparable VHS replication facility, this operation was spatially compact, required only three operatives and 'From the outside this factory looked like any other suburban semi' (BPI 2005). Access to large-scale DVD replication is thus becoming easier for pirates and more difficult for agencies to detect.

In this respect, it will not be reproductive capacity but access to the masters themselves that will become the most critical aspect of both piracy and anti-piracy operations in the digital era. Both plant investment and media cost are likely to become as widely diffuse for DVD as the exhibition infrastructure was for the VCR – with the networks of association that give reliable access to the film masters and to the consumers becoming the real area of investment, wealth and competition. As is proving to be the case elsewhere, enforcement regimes alone will not change the global dynamics of media piracy. Crucially, there are also cultural factors that must be considered. Indian film viewers are typically 'first-run junkies', where seeing a new film on its Friday release is a desirable form of one-upmanship. This is a mode of habitual consumption long fostered by the industry itself. However, while cultivating a demand for the latest film at the earliest opportunity made sense in the days when 85 per cent of industry profits came from domestic theatrical returns, it has notable drawbacks in the era of playback and cable piracy, where: 'Most look upon viewing pirated DVDs as simply a matter of convenience. And nobody wants to wait till the film comes out (legally) on DVD – the buzz would have died down and they would have already come across as un-cool social misfits at parties' (Lakhanpal 2006). If such attitudes are not easily changed, the majority of future releases will have a relatively short shelf life.

The increasing impatience of overseas consumers expecting an India-on-demand made possible by globally integrated media technologies is an indication that Indian producers will have to move towards instantaneous, or at least swift, worldwide release on playback media. This will require coordinated offshore replication in a number of markets in the manner already being followed by the pirates, with the drawback for producers that it must inevitably reduce the more profitable theatrical window. The continuous deployment of new media applications will also serve to ensure that there will be no permanent solution. In the short term, more local operators will be replicating, packaging and distributing pirate disks onshore at the point of destination rather than trading in smuggled products. Over the medium term, the shift towards download piracy, where replication is undertaken by the consumers themselves, will increase in scale, raising further problems for copyright enforcers, producers and pirates. This constantly evolving situation provides a useful indication of the contradictions of globalization: as the film industry itself adjusts to the changing economic environment by seeking to become more integrated, so the changing nature of technology is making the activities of pirates more diffuse. Nonetheless, the recent intimidation of producers in Mumbai would appear to suggest that greater cooperation with international copyright regimes is now putting pressure upon the pirates to acquire 'legitimate' overseas rights. Intimidation, however, is costly in the long term, since it will provoke police investigations that will ultimately interfere with the efficacy of the 'profit-sharing' that is its primary purpose. As such, a return to the use of lures, such as ready financing, will probably be a more significant method for pirates to retain access to export profits. In the long term, what will most likely be decisive is the extent to which the pirates continue to be the innovators in both technological application and market organization.

Legitimacy, Intellectual Property and Global Ambition

The complex relationships between the Indian film industry and the underworld, between the formal and informal economy, and between media technologies and global trade, all serve to illustrate the dynamics of cultural production in a developing country. This, in turn, highlights the proprietary nature, and limited worldview, of intellectual property rhetoric. The regimes that are currently being implemented to further commodify and control cultural production, and to ensure that digital technologies remain under centralized control, were certainly not developed with the operating conditions of Indian cinema in mind. By contrast, the history of the Indian cinema provides an illustration of how a cultural industry can benefit from the presence of the shadow economy in the face of colonial disinterest, an antipathetic postcolonial socialist economy and, more recently, an era of corporate globalization in which (on paper at least) it enjoys a relatively weak position in the face of external competition. In this context, it is worth recalling that measures such as region coding, digital rights management and the legal frameworks that back them up are being instituted to protect the hegemony of multinational media concerns and to extract the maximum returns from 'low-context' consumers, while retaining maximum control over 'software'. Such initiatives do not consider the complexities of the cultural economy in India. Nonetheless, cultural producers working in a rapidly changing socioeconomic environment in the global South must increasingly conform to a trading regime that has been determined elsewhere (Rajan 2006).

The rhetoric on piracy, legitimacy and sovereignty provided by Hollywood, despite its ready availability and its evangelical black-and-white worldview thus proves to be less than satisfactory in articulating the challenges facing

Indian media in the new global economy. Certainly, the historical relationships between the Indian film industries and the informal economy do not provide a strong position from which producers can cast themselves simply as victims of piracy – since without the success of playback piracy the outside world would probably be no more interested in Indian cinema than it was twenty years ago. More fundamentally, what is at stake here is not simply a contest between legitimate and illegitimate finance or modes of distribution, but rather the newly fashionable agenda to reform the Indian film industry into something more akin to Hollywood. It is about the longstanding desire to make the industry itself legitimate in commercial terms and it also indicates an acceptance, by some at least, of the need to make the transition from an overgrown cottage industry into a streamlined global franchise. Of course, it is the flagship brands of the export-led 'Bollywood' model that are driving this agenda and who seem most likely to benefit from a cultural economy regulated in this way. The vast majority of Indian film producers, particularly in the regional-language industries, lack the means to access lucrative export markets, hard currencies and legitimate international distribution in order to reinvent themselves in this manner (Rajadhyaksha 2003). Even for the bigger production houses, the irony of stronger copyright legislation is that foreign players are now increasingly keen to invoke it for protecting their own intellectual property in India by targeting, for example, the longstanding practice of 'borrowing' stories and themes by Indian film-makers (see Basi 2010; Desai 2005; Narula 2003).

In the decades when Indians had little access to Hollywood films, and vice versa, it was standard practice to produce Indian variants of popular US titles. Presently, however, the practice of retelling or recasting cultural works is as much a target of intellectual property legislation as is the illegal reproduction of originals. Because all commercial cinema is comprised of minor variations within a given narrative formula, this formal limitation of 'inspiration' has very profound implications for the nature of creative labour and cultural performance in the twenty-first century. Indeed, the broader ramifications of the new international framework for intellectual property are undoubtedly one of the most critical aspects of globalization in the present phase. Value judgements aside, the purpose of expanding the legal definition of copyright to its absolute limits is clear cut. With the decline in manufacturing in the developed world, and its relocation to developing economies such as China and India, the United States and its competitors in the developed world have adopted the model of a 'knowledge economy' driven by their advantages in information technologies. By this logic, the material advantages of hosting the means of production will be offset by the intangible commercialized rights exercised over the intellectual content of all economic, social and biological processes held in repository (Thomas and Servaes 2006; Thomas 2010: 117–77). Thus, the balance of trade between the developed and developing worlds will be maintained to the enduring advantage of the West through the payments of royalties on all intellectual products from films to genetic sequences. This is why corporations and individuals from the United States file more patents in India than Indians do.

The visible prosecution of the violators of media copyright is seen as proof-positive of India's new commitment to comply with the broader domain of this radical new regime in knowledge. Beyond that, the direct implications within the media field itself are significant enough. As the world's largest exporter of cultural goods, the United States has used successive international trade agreements as a mechanism for negotiating more favourable access to global media markets (Fleischman 1993; Moore 2005; Wang 2003). In this, the promotion of new intellectual property programmes is not simply intended to reduce the existing piracy of American media content by the cable, computer and DVD vendors of urban India, but also to facilitate a greater market share for US media products in India in the future. There is a long way to go in the cinema, with Hollywood still only achieving a 5 per cent market share against Indian-made films. A strategy of 'glocalization' is therefore being pursued, as the newly constituted Indian subsidiaries of transnational media corporations make their presence felt in film production. All in all, there are considerable international pressures now being exerted on both the regulatory environment and the nature of competition in the Indian film industries. At the same time, a partnership with Hollywood and its logistical and legal resources provides the only practicable means for the Indian film industry to enforce its own intellectual property rights across the ninety-five countries where Indian films have a commercial presence. Due to the entrenchment of piracy and low levels of disposable income in most of these countries, it is hard to estimate the actual cash value of legitimating those markets. It is frequently claimed, however, that in sheer numbers Indian films have a larger audience than Hollywood films, which implies that the overseas market is likely to outstrip the value of the domestic market. There is more than simply profit at stake, however, since the recent agreements with US industry bodies also serve to validate the present ambition within certain sections of the film industries to stake their claim as the world's 'second' global cinema (Punathambekar and Kavoori 2008).

In this sense, Indian film-makers stand to both gain and lose from their incorporation into the global knowledge economy. Needless to say, there is no place in this new paradigm for the traditional creative license of the Indian film, or for the untidy relationship between the disorganized industry and the informal economy. While certain leading film businesses have much to gain from 'internationalization' and 'professionalization', in many ways it remains difficult to see what the bulk of the Indian film industry stands to gain from compliance with Hollywood strictures. Given their disparity in means, it is far from certain that intellectual property agreements will ultimately provide a better means for redressing the global imbalance in the distribution of popular culture than the informal methods used by the Indian cinema in the past. To adjust successfully to the changing conditions of trade, it may prove more fitting to re-examine the historically close relationships between mainstream and informal modes of distribution in the Indian cinema's own history. Such an analysis may well provide the ammunition for stealing the innovations in delivery (as opposed to content) that have constituted the pirates' own intellectual property wealth over the years. In order to tackle the issue of piracy where it really counts, at the level of demand, it remains the case that until there is a sincere attempt to address the needs of consumers as well as (or even better than) piracy networks have been able to do – rather than periodically announcing a naked self-interest for (often illusory) 'lost profits' – only limited progress will be possible at any scale. In this respect, the Indian scenario is comparable to the wider picture being determined by the West.

Further Reading

Boyd, Douglas, Straubhaar, Joseph and Lent, John (1989) *Videocassette Recorders in the Third World*, New York and London: Longman.

Correa, Carlos (2007) *Trade Related Aspects of Intellectual Property Rights: A Commentary on the TRIPS Agreement*, Oxford: Oxford University Press.

Seagrave, Kerry (2003) *Piracy in the Motion Picture Industry*, Jefferson, NC, and London: McFarland and Company.

Sundaram, Ravi (2010) *Pirate Modernity: Delhi's Media Urbanism*, Abingdon and New York: Routledge.

Thomas, Pradip Ninan and Servaes, Jan (eds) (2006) *Intellectual Property Rights and Communications in Asia: Conflicting Traditions*, New Delhi: Sage.

Thussu, Daya Kishan (ed.) (2007a) *Media on the Move: Global Flow and Contra-Flow*, London and New York: Routledge.

5   Digital India: Software, Services and Cybercultures

In the previous two chapters, our analysis of Indian media in the liberalization era has demonstrated the convergence of new media technologies and a new economic paradigm largely through the action of remediation. This is a term that describes the process by which the application of new forms of media technology inevitably reprocesses and reworks existing media forms (McLuhan 1964; Bolter and Grusin 2000). Thus, we have encountered the remediation of television through satellite broadcasting, along with the remediation of feature films into a more highly mobile commodity through playback technologies, first analogue and then digital. At this point, we will now turn our attention to the presence of digital technologies in their own right, that is, beyond their 'updating' of older media systems. In this respect, we need to consider the presence of digital technologies as a distinctive suite of applications that produce new configurations of media usage. In being attentive to the claims made upon those technologies as constituents of the globalization process, we must account for both the structural and symbolic dimensions of the digital domain. First of all, we will outline the mediating function of information technologies in the wider economic processes of globalization. Second, we will survey the new forms of media content and usage that have appeared on the scene with the advent of personal computers. Accordingly, the initial focus of this chapter is on largely structural developments, including the rise of an indigenous software industry and the impetus behind the steady 'outsourcing' of information technology work to India from other parts of the world. In the latter part of the chapter we direct our attention towards the assimilation of new media within the Indian public sphere, from new forms of interactive content to new patterns of connectivity enabled by transnational web dialogues, social networking and mobile media. In drawing together these two aspects of mediated social change, we begin to get a sense of the present reality of a digital India and its place in the emerging global mediascape.

Globalization and Information Technology

Manuel Castells made his mark as one of the leading theorists of globalization during the late 1990s, with the publication of a trilogy of works heralding the advent of the 'information age' (1996, 1997, 1998a). For Castells, it was the interaction between economic liberalization and computer technologies that defines the present epoch, both socially and politically. The present form of globalization was therefore described by Castells as being symptomatic of a new social order driven by the internationalization of capital and rise of 'informational' economic and political processes. Central to this account of the present epoch is Castells's use of terminologies drawn from the operating metaphors of mass computing. This language is reflective, at one level, of the central role played by information technologies in his particular theoretical model. At another level, these words and phrases are also an indicator of the ubiquitous presence of information technology in the developed world. As such, for those seeking to understand the dominant language of mediation within the field of globalization, Castells's work is highly suitable for interfacing communications technologies and social theory as a ready means of expressing social change. For Castells, the phenomenon of globalization is shaped by:

> The emergence of a new technological paradigm organized around new, more powerful, and more flexible information technologies, making it possible for information itself to become the product of the production process ... A networked, deeply interdependent economy emerges that becomes increasingly able to apply its process in technology, knowledge, and management to technology, knowledge, and management themselves. (1996: 67)

The new model of social organization that emerges from the operation of 'informational' capitalism takes a form that mirrors the distinctive architecture of the Internet after the advent of the World Wide Web – that is, the diffuse, global trajectories of data that flow around the world by means of telecommunication cables connecting a vast web of file servers which in turn disperse/collect processed information from millions of personal workstations. This radically decentred information architecture provides the technical means for entirely new forms of institutional organization at a global scale. This is reflected in the emergence of what Castells calls the 'network society', 'a society that is structured in its dominant functions and processes around networks' (Castells 2000: 133). The global network society constitutes: 'a comprehensive social form, able to link up, or de-link, the entire realm of human activity', a form which 'resulted from the historical convergence of three independent processes' (ibid.). Castells identifies these as: the information technology revolution, the restructuring of capitalism/statism and cultural social movements.

Fundamentally, Castells's network society is structured by the exchanges of knowledge, people and wealth that take place between the 'nodes' where information, and thus economic power, is increasingly concentrated. The global network society takes the spatial form of increasingly interconnected global cities joined together by dense 'flows' of information. It is guided in its operations by those who inhabit the global network and its particular archi-tectures (airports, financial markets, file servers, transnational media broad-casts, luxury hotels). For Castells, these are the 'networkers' who live within the 'space of flows'. In its global effects, the space of flows is highly selective, in that it remakes older geographies by turning off hinterlands, connecting some city districts into global flows while bypassing others (1997: 386). As such, the space of flows is not a 'global village' but is instead a new network of power that operates above previous modes of living, 'concentrating the direc-tional, productive, and managerial functions of all power over the planet; the control of the media; the real politics of power; and the symbolic capacity to create and diffuse messages' (2009a: 434). The space of flows is unremittingly urban in its origins and in its destinations and, as such, 'Megacities articulate the global economy, link up the informational networks, and concentrate the world's power' (1998b: 8). In this sense, the media are primarily an enabling technology for the network society but their symbolic content, like digitized capital itself, flows within its matrix of power. Favoured cities see concentrations of information flows, and thus take on an extra-physical form in their articulation of this power, making 'informational cities' themselves a mediatized urban form, a symbolic rather than geographical expression of power. The reason for this concentration of power in select urban centres is the necessity of a critical mass of technological expertise, reflecting a situation where:

> the highest tier of science and technology, the one that shapes and commands overall technological development, is concentrated in a few dozen research centres and milieus of innovation around the globe, overwhelmingly in the United States, Western Europe and Japan. Russian, Indian and Chinese engi-neers, usually of very high quality, when they reach a certain level of scientific development, can only pursue their research by linking up with these centres. Thus highly skilled labour is also increasingly globalized, with talent being hired around the globe when firms and governments really need the talent, and are ready to pay for it… A case in point is Silicon Valley, the most advanced information technology-producing region in the world, which can only main-tain the pace of innovation by recruiting every year thousands of engineers and scientists from India, China, Taiwan, Singapore, Korea, Israel, Russia and Western Europe, to jobs that cannot be filled by Americans because they do not have proper skills. (Castells 1999: 3–5)

Silicon Valley, then, is a (if not the) primary hub of the global network society, working in connective exchange with the global entertainment hub in nearby Hollywood, the financial hubs of New York and London, and the concentrations of electronics manufacturing in Tokyo, Taipei and Seoul. India, as Castells himself notes, has emerged as a vital contributor of human capacity to the operation of the global network society. Since the 1980s, the technological expertise of Indians, previously directed towards heavy engineering for national development programmes, has been significantly diverted into the new field of information technologies and the international opportunities that it offers to its key personnel. At the same time, India has also engineered a similar concentration of information technology expertise within the country, reflecting a global phenomenon where 'in Bangalore, Mumbai, Seoul or Campinas, engineers and scientists concentrate in high-technology hubs, connected to the "Silicon Valleys" of the world, while a large share of the population in all countries remains in low-end, low-skill jobs, when they are lucky enough to be employed at all' (Castells 1999: 3). For Castells, this strategy of 'clustering' the infrastructure and institutions that support information processing, along with the highly skilled workforce required to perform those operations, becomes a prerequisite to participation in the new global economy, where 'there is little chance for a country, or region, to develop . . . without its incorporation into the technological system of the information age' (ibid.).

IT in India

Given the technological and scientific ambitions of India's postcolonial elite, there was an early recognition of the importance of electronics and the necessity of acquiring computer technologies. As with other 'high-technology' fields monopolized by the developed world, the goal of India's state planners was to acquire the latest electronics technologies and subsequently replicate them within India for the purposes of serving a self-sufficient domestic market (Dedrick and Kraemer 1993: 466–7). This was entirely consistent with the import substitution objectives of the Nehruvian era, but the knowledge complexity of these new fields was considerable, with much of the expertise being held by foreign corporations with little incentive to release their intellectual property. It was in recognition of India's lack of independent capacity in new technology research and development that the Nehru-led Congress governments made considerable investments in tertiary institutions for technical training in the 1960s (such as the Indian Institutes of Technology (IIT) and the Indian Institute of Science (IISc)). Before the benefits of an expanded human capacity came on-stream in the 1970s and 1980s, India was also disadvantaged by its lack of industrial capacity for supporting the design and manufacture of electronics. As such, in order to gain access to computer technology on a commercial basis, India had to enter agreements with two leading foreign companies, International Business Machines (IBM) from the United States and International Computers Ltd (ICL) from the United Kingdom. It was the former that quickly proved to be the more significant player. According to Dedrick and Kraemer, IBM subsequently dictated terms that the Indian government saw as unfavourable to its own interests in information technology, since:

> [IBM] dominated the computer market in India (from 1960–72, IBM accounted for over 70% of all computers installed in India). From 1966 to 1968, the Indian government tried to get IBM to share equity with local capital in its Indian operations, but IBM said it would leave the country before agreeing to equity sharing and the government let the matter drop. (1993: 475)

Rather than leave the field of digital technology in the hands of foreign companies, Indira Gandhi oversaw a series of state interventions in electronics in her early years in power. The public-sector Electronics Corporation of India was established in 1967 in order to support India's efforts in nuclear, space and defence technologies. In 1971, an Electronics Commission was founded to formulate policy for developing an Indian electronics industry. A Department of Electronics (DOE) was established with a regulatory remit to enforce those policies. At the beginning of the emergency period (1975–7), the DOE was given licensing powers over computer imports. The DOE also announced in 1975 that all imported computer systems in India would be maintained by the state-owned Computer Maintenance Corporation (CMC). All of these initiatives were designed to reduce the stranglehold of multinational companies over electronics and to create a favourable environment for an indigenous manufacturing sector to get off the ground (Grieco 1984; Sridharan 1996). The National Informatics Centre (NIC) was also established in 1975 to serve the IT needs of the state bureaucracies. The new regulatory regime also brought the high-technology sector within the broader policy of industrial self-sufficiency. As such, the Foreign Exchange Regulation Act 1973 (FERA), which limited foreign ownership to 40 per cent in Indian subsidiaries, was extended to the computer industry. IBM refused to comply with these requirements and, after two years of negotiations, made good on its threats by finally ending its Indian operations in 1978. Indira Gandhi's Congress government thus made a major impact upon the private-sector computer and electronics industries in India by ousting IBM, reducing ICL's holdings in its Indian subsidiary and thereby encouraging joint-equity partnerships (such as the venture between

US manufacturer Burroughs and Tata, India's extensive private-sector conglomerate) (Subramanian 1992).

However, as with other media sectors, the initiatives undertaken in the IT field were deeply contradictory. On the one hand, the longstanding domination of foreign companies was brought to a close, but Indira Gandhi was also deeply antipathetic to the big Indian business houses that dominated the Indian private sector in almost every field. Thus, in order to prevent players such as Tata taking up the space left by IBM, restrictions were put into place on the size of electronics manufacturing concerns. This led to the proliferation of many small companies alongside the state-giant ECIL, as it was intended to do, but this inevitably meant that India's electronics manufacturing sector was highly fragmented. This prevented economies of scale being achieved in the production process and also restricted growth in the capacity of research and development. Indian-made components were more expensive than imports, and few companies were of sufficient size to justify substantial investments in improving their designs. As a result, Indian efforts in the electronics field were quickly eclipsed by the rise of the 'Asian Tiger' economies in Taiwan, South Korea and Singapore that came to dominate the global trade in cheap high-quality electronic components. Before long, this led to a situation where India's computer companies were primarily assembly operations, building comparatively expensive machines from imported components. Thus, while the government wanted to encourage an export-led industry in consumer electronics, it ended up institutionalizing a heavily protected and relatively inefficient hardware industry that made computers three times more expensive than they were in the developed world. In turn, this slowed down the introduction of information technology into the wider economy and held back the intended benefits of computerization.

Balaji Parthasarathy nonetheless observes that the departure of IBM was a watershed for computing in India, not least because many of the former employees of its Indian operations went into the software business (2010: 251; Heeks 1996: 69). At the time, India had no software industry, and internationally the software domain had lagged behind the development of hardware for computing. As Parthasarathy explains:

> With the availability of increasingly more powerful and inexpensive hardware, there was a proliferation of computer usage in various economic sectors, creating a huge demand for software. However, while automated, capital-intensive operations permit the mass production of high quality hardware, software production, in comparison, has remained a craft-like, labour-intensive affair, plagued by uneven productivity and quality, relying more on trial and error to achieve its goals . . . The result is that software development is notoriously prone to 'bugs', delays and cost overruns. In other words, software productivity

and quality have lagged behind those of hardware, creating a 'software bottleneck'. (2004: 667)

In seeking to overcome this bottleneck, IBM made the momentous decision in 1969 to separate the commercialization of hardware and software, allowing customers to buy IBM hardware and commission their own software elsewhere (ibid.). Over the next decade, this customization option would drive the popularity of IBM hardware designs but it would also fatally undermine IBM's global dominance over information technology. Similarly, the government of India, with its characteristic emphasis on manufacturing, sought to artificially create a situation where the state-owned ECIL would dominate industrial-process computer manufacturing with microcomputers left to the myriad small private companies. The intangible, problematic, development of software was also left to the private sector. In this respect, both IBM and the Indian government failed to see that the future of computing lay not in mainframes but in small microcomputers. They also failed to see that it was in software, not hardware, that the fortunes of the 1980s would be made. At the global scale, Bill Gates's Microsoft was the big winner from IBM's error, but in India a vital new industry was to emerge outside of the state's technological planning regime.

Since tariffs on electronics imports were also applicable to software products, imported software packages continued to be relatively expensive in India in the early 1980s. By contrast with the situation in the hardware sector, however, India had a ready resource from which to produce an indigenous software industry. With 150,000 engineering and technology graduates now emerging each year from its tertiary system, there was a highly skilled workforce that could be deployed into computer programming and software design (Arora et al. 2001: 1270). The adoption of the open-source UNIX language as a global standard also made the raw material for a software industry available without cost (Parthasarathy 2004: 671). Nonetheless, given the problems in the hardware sector, computer take-up within India remained low and large-scale computerization projects were inevitably sited in the public-sector industries, with all their inherent complexities and a timescale that reflected this. For smaller companies seeking to establish themselves quickly in software production, it therefore made much more sense to target an international market. As the Indian software industry worked to establish itself, two major factors provided a strategic endorsement to this export-led approach – most critically, the rapid expansion of computer applications beyond industrial processes and into the vast administrative domain of the developed world that came about with personal computers and networking in the 1980s. With such rapid computerization in so many organizations, the subsequent demand for basic programming, technical support and software servicing could not be fulfilled by the existing IT workforces. Hence, India's software companies, with their growing army of well-educated, English-speaking graduates, were extremely well placed to offer their services on a consultancy basis.

> By this time a number of Indians were working in US firms. Some of them played an important, although as yet undocumented role, in bridging the gap and matching the buyers in the US with the suppliers in India. Responding quickly to the growing demand, a number of Indian firms arose in quick time. Contrary to its normal practice, the State encouraged this growth by considerably simplifying the process for obtaining the numerous clearances and permits that any firm in the organised sector in India typically needs. (Arora et al. 2001: 1271)

The second factor that supported this paradigm, therefore, was quick support from the Indian government. Rajiv Gandhi, who succeeded his mother as Prime Minister in 1984, was keen to be seen as a modernizer, and he favoured liberalization of the high-technology sector. As such, the computer industry was the focus of two new acts of government policy, the Computer Policy in 1984 and the Computer Software Export, Development and Training Policy in 1986 (Heeks 1996; Subramanian 1992). As Parthasarathy notes: 'The 1984 policy, besides easing the local manufacture and availability of computers, recognized software as an "industry", making it eligible for various allowances and incentives. It also lowered duties on software imports and made software exports a priority. The 1986 policy aimed at increasing India's share of world software production' (2010: 252). Thus, the new approach to information technology constituted a switch in emphasis from hardware to software, as well as a rejection of self-sufficiency in favour of export-led integration into the booming global IT economy. Accordingly, quite unlike India's other media industries, which remained focused upon the domestic market, the software services industry has always had a primarily external orientation, consistently doing two thirds of its business in foreign markets, with the majority of this in the United States (Aoyama 2003; Arora et al. 2001; Arora and Gambardella 2004). This new industry grew rapidly from its inception with overall revenues for the software and services sector growing from US$80 million in 1985 to US$50 billion in 2009 (Parthasarathy 2010: 249).

The Space of Flows

Because the core skills in software are intuition, logic and language, the wealth of India's software industry has always been embedded in its personnel. Thus, in the early years, alongside local operations to conduct basic programming tasks for clients in India and overseas, there was a much larger trade in supplying programmers and other IT professionals to overseas clients on a contract basis. Since an Indian programmer could be hired for around one fifth of the cost of an American programmer, there was a rush to hire Indian programmers to work on site for technology firms in Silicon Valley on this basis, referred to as 'bodyshopping'. Through this route, hundreds of thousands of Indians were drawn into Castells's 'space of flows' over the course of the 1990s (Saxenian 2001). Travelling back and forth between California and India, they forged a multiplicity of informational exchanges and personal contacts between India and the world's high-technology hub. As demand for their services surged, the consultancies in India prospered and the software industry grew by as much as 30 per cent year on year. Attrition, however, was seen as a problem, since after completing their contracts in the United States, the best software engineers were often offered positions directly and consequently left their Indian employers to start a new life in the United States. They were increasingly able to do so as the United States revised its immigration policy in the 1990s to encourage the settlement of information technology specialists under the H1-B visa category, with Indians representing the largest cohort in this category (Alarcon 2000). However, the continuing supply of graduates in India meant that these personnel could be easily replaced, even if attrition robbed the Indian companies of the longer-term experience held by their former staff (Arora 2005: 405). From their new base in North America, these non-resident Indian software engineers nonetheless maintained their personal and professional connections in India, and this further strengthened the mutual labour arrangements and communicative pathways between India and Silicon Valley (Saxenian 2005; Tauebe and Sonderegger 2009).

One of the biggest problems for Indian companies in moving beyond the 'bodyshopping' models was that of acquiring sufficient and affordable operating premises with reliable basic infrastructure and high-bandwidth telecommunications. Characteristically, telecom in India was another long-standing government monopoly. Under the British, India had seen early investments in a telephone infrastructure overwhelmingly intended for the benefit of India's numerically small and dispersed foreign rulers. After independence telecoms remained a state preserve, and investments were limited in scope as the technology was seen, like other forms of mass communication, as a luxury that could wait until India had built up its primary industries (Chakravartty 2004). Subsequently, as the telephone network was gradually developed over the course of the 1970s and 1980s, the sheer size of India, geographically and demographically, meant that any significant expansion of reach was always going to be prohibitively costly. India was unable to develop cheap reliable domestic telephone technology and therefore had to rely on expensive, often obsolete, foreign exchanges that were overloaded almost as soon as they were installed (ibid.: 235). The waiting lists for connection were years long and telephone access was extremely limited and famously unreliable. Since telephones were a scarce commodity, priority was given to the most important public-sector institutions and their key staff. For the general public, the situation was somewhat improved in the 1980s by innovations in phone-metering and the franchising of connections to thousands of private operators providing phone booths across urban India (Kulkarni 2001; Ray and Ray 2010). The field of telecoms was extensively liberalized after the government monopoly over supply finally ended in the 1990s. Subsequently, the advent of mobile phone technology circumvented the capacity shortage in fixed lines, giving rise to another sunrise communications industry in the private sector. The mobile phone has since provided personal telecoms access to 130 million Indians, and was itself worth US$18 billion by the mid-2000s (Kohli-Khandekar 2006: 187).

In the earlier years of the software industry, however, there was a pressing need to be in a location where the available communications infrastructure was concentrated and maintained. Although many ventures started out in Mumbai, as commercial ambitions in India generally do, by the 1990s they had relocated to a range of other locations in the South and West of India. By far the most prominent concentration of IT firms was in the city of Bangalore, capital of Karnataka state in South India. It was here that Nehru had decided to concentrate much of India's scientific community, with major space, defence and communications institutions all located in the city (Stremlau 1996: 22). To serve the needs of the scientific community, there was also an array of high-quality higher education institutes. Without the land limitations of peninsular Mumbai, Bangalore had plenty of space available on the fringes of the city for the development of new software technology parks (STPs), supported by superior infrastructure. Bangalore also had a municipal and state-level administration that was conducive to the development of a concentration in the software sector as its over-riding priority. Since attracting a substantial investment by Texas instruments in 1985, Bangalore has worked hard to attract scores of foreign technology companies with cheap land deals, streamlined development approvals, tax incentives and other investment-friendly policies (Parthasarathy 2004). Bangalore is now known internationally as the heart of the Indian IT industry, and home to internationally recognized companies such as Wipro and Infosys. Another Indian heavyweight, Satyam, set up a software development centre in the city during the 1990s. By the 2000s, a majority of the leading multinational

IT companies had established a major presence in Bangalore (Dossani and Kenney 2007, 2009; Parthasarathy and Aoyama 2006).

As investment streams slowed with the end of the first dot.com boom in the United States, cutting costs became a much more important feature of the information technology economy. Many of the leading players in the sector subsequently moved to take advantage of cheaper labour and lower operating costs by setting up their own 'offshore' subsidiaries in India (Dossani and Kenney 2003). Simultaneously, a number of expatriate Indians who had established themselves in Silicon Valley spearheaded numerous US-based joint ventures, carrying out the bulk of their labour-intensive IT work in India (Saxenian 2005: 52). As the 'offshoring' phenomenon has gathered pace, the relocation of programming and software work has been massively augmented by the newfound desire of large foreign companies across a wide range of fields from banking, insurance, utilities and retail to cut their own labour costs dramatically by 'outsourcing' the bulk of their quotidian data-processing and customer-service work to 'call centres' in India (Dossani and Kenney 2007; Kobayashi-Hillary 2005; Nadeem 2011). Given the concentration of communications infrastructure made available for the software technology parks, Bangalore has also been a major beneficiary of this trend. Thus, as Douglas Hill notes:

> The new era of the out-sourcing economy that would transform the city landscape was heralded by the establishment of Software Technology Parks of India (STPI) in 1991, including the country's first satellite earth station (undeniably an important factor in enabling its transition to an offshore and call-centre powerhouse). The announcement of a new IT-focused economic policy in 1997 by the Karnataka Government was aimed at further accelerating the growth of the industry . . . In recent years, the arrival of biotechnology industries has further augmented the suite of hi-tech operations that now largely determine the economic life of the city. (Athique and Hill 2010: 114)

India is now the world leader in the provision of offshore services in business processing operations (BPO). The biggest players in this field are typically either subsidiaries of big Indian companies in the IT and software sectors like Wipro BPO and TCS BPO or former subsidiaries of multinational firms (as with Genpact and WNS). The output of the BPO industry, together with the traditional IT industries, is now measured under the category of Information Technology Enabled Services (ITES) and constitutes over 5 per cent of India's gross domestic product. In 2007, these two sectors, along with IT research and development, created 1,251,000 new jobs (Dossani and Kenney 2009: 79). Employment growth in ITES is now running at 23 per cent per annum, outstripping the supply of engineering graduates, and thus widening domestic recruitment strategies to include management, business and arts graduates. The National Association of Software and Service Companies estimates that industry revenues exceeded NASSCOM 2011 $76 billion in 2011 (NASSCOM 2011). Taking up these wider revenue streams and diversifying into high-end research and development, the major Indian software firms are now of a size and sophistication where they have become competitors to their former clients in global markets. In addition, a range of big multinational companies from outside of the information technology sector have moved into Bangalore in order to set up their own offshore BPOs. With a presence in India's undisputed high-technology capital, these companies are now able to access India's IT expertise for a range of applications without relying on the US companies that formerly provided, or intermediated, those services. In turn, Indian ITES providers are now seeking to develop their own independent global presence by establishing offshore operations of their own. As such, the 'multiplicity of service activities now undertaken in India has ignited a cycle of cumulative causation encouraging exploration of yet further opportunities' (Dossani and Kenney 2009: 78).

The scale of growth in India's ITES industries has been astounding, and competition from Indian companies, along with the snowballing deployment of the 'outsourcing' model by Western companies, has made Bangalore's success synonymous with the loss of white-collar jobs in the US and the UK. Rafiq Dossani and Martin Kenney have recently made the case that, aside from cost, the success of their Indian rivals in moving from 'routine' operations into 'high-value' IT processes has made it imperative for US firms to be on the scene in Bangalore (2009). IBM, for example, has returned to India with an eye to the rising competition, employing 70,000 people locally by the end of 2007 (ibid.: 86). The past decade has seen not only the massive further expansion of basic ITES service provision in Bangalore, but also a significant expansion in commercial research infrastructure and local start-ups (Parthasarathy and Aoyama 2006). As such, Bangalore has confounded predictions that India would remain in a subservient position in the global information economy. Some now estimate that tens of millions of jobs will eventually be moved from the West to India in the broad field of ITES (Bhagwati and Blinder 2009). To keep things in perspective, however, it is worth noting that the US software industry still enjoys a massive lead in the field, possessing a larger global market share than all its major competitors combined. Nonetheless, after the near collapse of the Western financial sectors in 2007–8, the new geopolitical economic reality seems set to further accelerate the outsourcing process in India's favour. One factor is that India's continued growth in the face of worldwide recession is attracting investment inflows that are finding few profitable markets elsewhere. Another factor is the reduced liquidity of major international companies, which is encouraging them to cut costs further.

Nonetheless, detractors of the ITES euphoria in India have pointed out that this field of employment is actually very small in terms of the overall workforce and remains heavily exposed to the vagaries of Western markets (Benjamin 2005: 9). ITES activity is confined to a small number of well-resourced enclaves with few of the benefits reaching the majority of India's population. Even in Bangalore, despite receiving a majority of resource allocation, ITES only constitutes 4–8 per cent of local employment (Athique and Hill 2010: 114). Given the high levels of education demanded by the industry, much of this work also goes to migrants from other parts of India, a factor that is steadily exacerbating communal and class conflicts in the city (Chakravartty 2008; Rao 2007). The STP model has also driven the independent provision of key infrastructure such as power, water, communications and housing to numerous campus developments around the fringes of the city (Aranya 2003; Stallmeyer 2011). In other, older, areas of Bangalore the dated infrastructure is collapsing under the population growth that has accompanied the IT boom, doubling the number of inhabitants from three to six million in twenty years (Census of India 2001). As such, the story of Bangalore's rise as an informational city has been driven by relentless urban growth and the interplay between multinational corporations, state policy and local entrepreneurs (Basant and Chandra 2004). In this respect, there is a clear equivalence with two of the major inputs of Castells's network society (economic liberalization and information technology). To assess the third input, networked cultural and social movements, we need to turn our attention to the 'symbolic capacity' of the digital media

Indian Cybercultures

The success story of India's information technology sector has been an important factor in recasting India's international image as a 'place to do business'. Similarly, India's technological achievements in the field operate as a symbol of progress for the national elite. The futuristic architectures of the STPs and New Economy hubs also make a very public statement of prosperity to the general population. The wealth generated in this area of activity facilitates new practices of consumption that replace or remediate older cultural forms such as cinema and television (Athique and Hill 2010; Mehta 2007). The content industry for new media, however, is very small compared to the surging television sector. The overarching reason for this is that Internet 'penetration' remains very low in India. It is low for mainly three reasons. First, because

PC ownership is growing slowly compared to television and mobile phones. Second, because of the continuing capacity shortage in fixed-line telecommunications. Third, because the content of this 'international' resource has been overwhelmingly delivered in English. As such, a commercial orientation in content design was always going to face serious infrastructure constraints in connections, computers, IP addresses and purchasing power. In keeping with the overall thrust of IT policy, the bulk of Internet resources have been concentrated in locations housing the ITES economy and major research institutions. Beholden to the government monopoly over telecoms, Internet Service Providers (ISPs) charged exorbitant rates, which dissuaded widespread leisure usage (Kohli-Khandekar 2006: 211). After all, a new world of satellite television was simultaneously becoming available at a far lower cost. The Internet has, however, been well suited to the growing population of ITES workers and computing graduates who have the prerequisites of computing literacy and ready access. As such, according to Gopinath:

> Internet usage has . . . evolved more in 'depth' than in 'spread' in its decade long presence in India. This is to be expected in a highly stratified society as exists in India. According to a study conducted in 2005, there are about 17 million regular users, with casual users being 5 million, with the penetration of Internet amongst urban Indians being around nine per cent and amongst all Indians about 2 per cent. However, almost a third of urban Internet users are heavy users ('depth'), logging more than three hours per day. For Internet to grow rapidly in urban India, Internet would need to break two major barriers. The first barrier is that of low speed and connectivity which makes online experience a poor one. The second barrier is the 'perceptual' one of creating a more 'persuasive' relevance of Internet in people's overall lives rather than it being restricted to the work domain. (2009: 299)

In the West, Microsoft's bundling of Internet Explorer with its Windows 95 operating system was critical in spreading Internet usage from the work environment to the home. In India, however, time-shared access to the Internet by means of cybercafés was a more significant factor in developing a leisure audience. The content being accessed in the late 1990s was necessarily English-language content, much of it hosted elsewhere in the world. Although web content in the vernaculars has increased markedly in recent years, there were, and still are, a number of technological, linguistic and conventional restraints upon building up a major presence for Indian languages online. Indian web content was hampered in a similar fashion to the rest of Asia, with a lack of well-supported non-Roman scripts and the dominance of an exclusively English search and retrieval infrastructure. Indeed, India's internal linguistic diversity has made achieving a critical mass of local content much harder than it was for China, Korea and Japan. India's comparative advantage, or some would say disadvantage, is the advanced English-language skills of its upper middle classes and elites. Given, however, that this cohort represents the wealthier segments of the population, Indian companies were relatively quick to examine the potentials of the Internet in light of the rapid growth in advertising revenues that came with liberalization (Mazarella 2003).

Vanita Kohli-Khandekar identifies three major Indian web portals that commenced operation in the late 1990s, India World, Rediff and Indiatimes (2006: 210–15). India World was launched by Rajesh Jain in 1995, providing an information and news service that included electronic editions of a major English-language paper, the *Indian Express*, and the English-language business weekly, *India Today*. India World subsequently expanded its web portal with search, sports, finance, food and history domains. Rediff was started up by Ajit Balakrishnan, founder of a successful advertising agency as well as a former computer manufacturer. The Rediff portal started out in 1995 with a similar service. Indiatimes, by contrast was a cross-media venture by the Indian publishing giant Bennett, Coleman and Company Ltd (BCCL). Putting out free online editions of its major publications, Indiatimes launched in 1998 with the women's magazine *Femina* and the movie-oriented *Filmfare*. During the 1990s, one thing that these three ventures had in common was that their content was in English and their primary users were the millions of Indians living offshore, along with the longer-term émigré South Asian population in the Western world. Internet take-up in both groups was high. In the former case, the large-scale migration of Indian IT professionals helped to shape one of the most computer-literate migrant communities in the world. In the latter, the swifter penetration of Internet into the domestic habitat in the developed world brought certain overseas Indian communities online much quicker than the population of India. The keenness of advertisers to reach these particular audiences also provided critical funding to support these new media services. Internet media production skills are well supported within India by the technical colleges and the outsourcing industry.

Carrying banners from venture capitalists through to marriage brokers, the Indian portals slowly but steadily expanded in the early 2000s beyond their initial user base to include the more affluent urban youth in India. In search of content and visual styles, India's Internet portals have all made extensive use of film-related material, promoting themselves with movie gossip and downloads of star images. Accordingly, film producers, distributors and film fans in India were well placed to make use of the new medium for promotional purposes. Following *Filmfare*, the market leader, other film magazines have also put out extensive electronic editions. Major film projects, production houses and film stars have produced lavish websites as part of their promotional strategy for some years now. Arguably, this Internet presence has been instrumental in developing a new global infrastructure for promoting Indian films and film stars around the world. This official material has been substantially augmented by the large numbers of homemade fan sites dedicated to film-based discussion and image-swapping. Add to this the co-location of film stars and consumerism in the images produced by the Internet advertising industry, and you begin to get a sense of the sheer scale of what Ananda Mitra has called 'bollyweb' (2008: 268–81). The culture of the popular film therefore constitutes the largest contingent of an Indian presence on the World Wide Web. At the same time, there is strength in Gopinath's argument that the predominance of the English language in all this 'Indian' content, including much of the Bollywood-themed material, has also had the effect of privileging a vision of India that speaks primarily to Indians overseas and globally oriented elites at home (2009: 303).

By the mid-2000s, the Internet content industry in India had revenues of some 20 billion rupees, making its annual turnover a good deal smaller than the mobile phone sector. Nonetheless, the economics of the industry had stabilized, with portals such as Rediff expanding their user base beyond 40 million users and individual Internet subscriptions reaching 7.5 million. In making a financial assessment of the sector, Kohli-Khandekar identified several major strands of commercial content: Internet retail, employment services, marriage services, travel bookings, consumer advertising, brokerage and buyer-to-buyer selling (2006: 205). Of these, travel and trade revenues were expanding at 100 per cent per year with other services growing at 25–35 per cent. A web presence has also become requisite for Indian companies of any size, particularly those with a corporate and/or international agenda. Beyond its focus on trade, a culturally distinctive feature of Indian Internet services is the growing importance of online matrimonial services in facilitating the complex social system of arranged marriage in India, as constituted by numerous local traditions of kinship as well as broader pan-Indian customs of acceptable heterosexual pairings. For many centuries, marriage specialists have operated as intermediaries for locating and selecting suitable matches by virtue of faith, caste, colour, language, race, class, wealth, profession or favourable cosmology. With the advent of print media and growing urbanization, it became customary for many families to seek marriage partners by means of classified advertisements in the press. As such, there was an established practice of mass-mediated marriage, which made online matrimonial searches an obvious service provision for India. Accordingly, marriage portals such as Shaadi and Bharatmatrimony have attracted significant investments (including foreign investment), promoting themselves heavily through banner advertisements on Indian-themed websites, and more recently through targeted advertisements for Internet users with Indian (or potentially Indian) surnames.

Submerged at first glance beneath the marriage ads, investment opportunities and consumer goods, the Internet has also provided a new infrastructure for India's tenacious civil society. Increasing demands for more accountable government have prompted many of the major state institutions to establish some form of online information service. India's relatively small but vocal academic sector has also made full use of the medium during the past decade. Similarly, India's many non-governmental organizations (NGOs) and charity projects have used the Internet extensively to publicize their work and to attract donations and volunteers from India and overseas. Thus, for these established actors in civil society, the advent of the Internet has provided for a far greater scale of information exchange with the outside world than was previously possible. For academia, the new accessibility of international publications along with email connection to their colleagues around the world has contributed to a far more globalized research environment. Similarly, the capacity of the Internet to mediate linkages with the growing number of Indians working in the Western universities over the past two decades has done much to enmesh the Indian academic community into the global knowledge economy. It has also made Indian expertise much more readily available to international institutions and foreign researchers. Another important development was the use of the Internet by non-state cultural and political movements to mobilize their global constituencies. TamilNet, for example, became the major organ of communications for the Tamil-separatist LTTE in Sri Lanka which, prior to its crushing military defeat in 2009, used this platform to promote its cause amongst Tamils in India as well as Sri Lankan Tamil refugees in the West (Jeganathan 1998; Whitaker 2004). The use of the Internet to reach out to migrant communities around the world was also in concord with the global agenda in Hindu majority politics during the 1990s, and this was reflected in the web strategies adopted by the World Hindu Council (Vishva Hindu Parishad) and other similar groups (VHP 2011).

The Internet has also been significant for civil society in the domestic realm, being put to innovative use by a small, technologically savvy intelligentsia who have employed electronic publishing formats to record and debate the critical social issues of recent years (see, for example, SARAI, CRIT). At a regional level, the Internet has also provided a unique space for transnational commentary on cultural and political issues in the online *Himal South Asian* magazine, based in Kathmandu. A more contentious example of Internet activism was the online news portal, Tehelka, that conducted a series of sting investigations in 2001 that allegedly exposed corruption in defence procurements. As the story spread to the mainstream news outlets, senior government officials were forced to resign. In response, the government launched a series of extensive investigations into the affairs of Tehelka, followed by a legal process that soon bankrupted the company (Trehan 2010). The Indian government also expressed its public concern over the uses of cybercafés for accessing the global pornography industry that has been fuelled by the Internet. In 2000, an Internet law was passed which instituted strict penalties for disseminating or viewing pornography in India. This legislation also covered a wider range of cyber-crimes including website defacement, hacking and hate campaigns. To extend the enforcement of the Internet Law, cybercafés were required to log the identities of all their users from 2004 onwards.

These measures have not dissuaded the rapid growth of cybercafés in urban centres, extending the Internet user base well beyond those able to afford their own subscriptions. A vibrant culture has subsequently emerged in bulletin board discussions, chatrooms and social networking in recent years. Indians have also taken to blogging as a platform for both self-expression and social commentary. User-generated content on bulletin boards has tended to focus on topics permissible for discussion in the public realm, such as communal politics, film culture and occidental/oriental comparisons. By contrast, as Pramod Nayar has noted, the blogging format has opened up more transgressive spaces for intimate self-expression and more radical political commentary (2009). For this reason, certain blogs in India have caused controversy despite reaching a very small audience. Once again, the Indian government was moved to take action to restrict access to some blogs. The question of Internet censorship also became intertwined with a national security agenda after the series of terrorist attacks in Mumbai in 2006–8. In its subsequent attempt to crack down on clandestine electronic communications, the government of India has claimed the right of complete access to data held by Skype and Google, as well as demanding that BlackBerry hands over the encryption key for its handheld devices so that all personal communications can be effectively monitored by the state (BBC News Online 31 August 2010). Clearly, the advent of cyberspace has raised similar questions of governance in India as it has around the world. It is fair to say that the stance taken by the Indian government towards Internet regulation has been simultaneously reactive and proactive, in that the government has moved with uncharacteristic speed to suppress undesirable practices as they emerge on the World Wide Web.

The infrastructure bottlenecks that have held back growth to date are now being addressed by innovations in wireless systems (Raman 2007). Similarly, over the past decade, Internet content and service providers have taken note of the significance of the very rapid penetration of mobile phones in India and diversified into SMS and other services. The trend towards a mobile Internet environment has greatly increased access for the rural population and the lower middle classes. This means that close attention is being paid to the new opportunities offered by 3G mobile technologies for expanding handset-based Internet services to 250 million mobile phone users. Addressing the language barrier therefore becomes the most pressing concern for interfacing the textual form of the Web with the vernacular compatibility of speech technology. If this can be achieved, we may well see yet another example of 'leapfrogging' in information technology as India makes use of the latest global innovations in order to bypass the infrastructure constraints of 'traditional' computer-based services. Although the Internet audience in India remains small in terms of the overall population, a tenth of the users reached by television or mobile phones, the global nature of its development has given rise to a vibrant cyberculture within its user base that justifies Gopinath's categorization of 'depth' in both its complexity of content and in the degree of engagement by users. A small user base in proportionate terms still constitutes almost twenty million people, which is sufficient critical mass for a many-to-many system to be maintained in terms of diversity of local content. In that sense, the public authorship of Internet content negates effective comparison with older mediums like television. Equally, the simultaneously live and global nature of the Internet makes it a unique medium, and it is important to recognize the significant extent to which access to international content and communications remains intrinsic to its appeal.

India and the Network Society

As has been the case elsewhere in the world, India's emerging cyberculture is increasingly dominated by commercial services, advertising and entertainment in the form of an interactive fanbase for popular culture. Although players such as Rediff have made significant investments in vernacular content, the Indian Internet still addresses a primarily English-speaking audience, albeit with a greater proportion of those users now coming from within India. Thus, in many respects, Indian cyberculture shares a constituency with the domestic English-language press. Given the use of English as an educational medium in the tertiary sector, this audience has shaped the present form of the Internet through an emerging field of popular commentary and web-based activism that goes well beyond the technical fraternity. In the Indian context, the politics of the cultural and social movements now being formally expressed online appear to be more traditionally left and right in their orientation than the pink and green traces of radical politics that Castells saw as representing the 'progressive' elements of network society in the West. Nonetheless, the inherent gendering of India's discussions around modernity and the prevalence of female authors in this new arena seems likely to make the Internet a significant platform for India's enduring feminist movement. Taken as a whole, this rich expression of civil society nonetheless remains limited in its social base as well as in its geographic reach, and to date the benefits of the Internet have naturally accrued to the better educated and socially advantaged. In that sense, both the cultural form and user base of the 'network society' in India supports Castells's propositions of informational advantage and selective connectivity.

Parthasarathy and Aoyama have noted that, in the original edition of *The Rise of the Network Society*, Bangalore was assigned a marginal position within the global information technology industry (2006). The rationale was that Bangalore would remain oriented towards labour-supply and low-end services, since India was lacking in venture capital networks and an efficient, diverse research base for innovation. From our present standpoint, however, we can see that informational capitalism is more than prepared to redirect investment flows, not only amongst peripheral territories and the older manufacturing economy, but also away from its own established infrastructure in the West. Like many theorists of globalization, Castells arguably failed to take sufficient note of the wider significance of Indian manpower in the IT economy, and subsequently underplayed the West's diminishing technological advantage in human capacity. To be fair, most commentators at that time underestimated the full extent to which the new mobility of 'bread-and-butter' activity inevitably transfers technology and wealth (Brewer and Nollen 1998). The heyday of Silicon Valley in the 1990s, the end of the Cold War and frenzy of profit-taking in the West all resulted in a lacuna towards redistribution effects in globalization theory.

In terms of Bangalore's place within the hierarchy of the global network society, the rhetoric of 'cyber-coolies' in Asia also seriously misjudged the likely outcome of bringing together large volumes of over-qualified and ambitious people within a state-supported and competition-driven development cluster (Taeube 2003). Florian Taeube has also recently taken note of the 'cultural support' provided for technical-linguistic skills by India's Brahmanic traditions (2009). Given India's consistent ambitions in high-technology acquisition, the recent move into more sophisticated areas of the information economy could be seen as being more or less inevitable once India's human capacity was co-located with adequate, even barely adequate, communications infrastructure. In many other respects, however, India's ITES sector stands as an exemplar of Castells's 'global network society' theory. The entire industry is more or less concentrated in half-a-dozen 'hubs' around the country, with the vast majority of its dealings oriented towards actors and markets located in other parts of the globe. Indeed, the case of Bangalore powerfully illustrates how one part of a city can be intricately wired to the global information economy, while other neighbourhoods are left in 'information darkness'. Within the ITES enclaves, career prospects are dictated by an international labour market that is entirely oblivious to the rural economy of Karnataka State (D'Costa 2004). Since the domestic market will not require even the present level of IT capacity for some years, Bangalore relies absolutely on the density of its transnational communication networks, and the consistent capacity of its personnel to traverse the space of flows.

Further Reading

Castells, Manuel (1996) *The Information Age: Economy, Society and Culture, Vol. I: The Rise of the Network Society,* Cambridge, MA, and Oxford: Blackwell.

D'Costa, Anthony and Sridharan, E. (eds) (2004) *India in the Global Software Industry,* New Delhi: MacMillan India.

Greenspan, Anna (2004) *India and the IT Revolution: Networks of Global Culture,* Basingstoke: Palgrave Macmillan.

Heeks, Richard (1996) *India's Software Industry: State Policy, Liberalisation And Industrial Development,* New Delhi: Sage Publications.

Nadeem, Shehzad (2011) *Dead Ringers: How Outsourcing is Changing the Way that Indians Understand Themselves,* Princeton, NJ: Princeton University Press.

Stallmeyer, John C. (2011) *Building Bangalore: Architecture and Urban Transformation in India's Silicon Valley,* London and New York: Routledge.

Subramanian, C. R. (1992) *India and the Computer: A Study of Planned Development,* New Delhi: Oxford University Press.

6   Bollywood, Brand India and Soft Power

Previously, we looked at the global presence of Indian films in terms of a nexus between technological advances, economic geography and intellectual property. Going beyond this, we must also take account of the cultural impact of this dispersal of media content. As such, in order to understand the significance of the Indian film as a global artefact, we also need to assay the combination of human and textual geographies that constitute what Kaur and Sinha have dubbed 'Bollyworld' (2005). The topography of this particular cultural terrain can be seen as being shaped by a varied set of forces that include: the shifting sands of geopolitics, the cultural knowledge of audiences, the movements of people over time, and the iconic placement of paradise as a textual device in both Indian and occidental signifying structures. Because these are complex and, often, competing and contradictory influences, the map of Bollyworld is geometrically lumpy. For example, the lakes of Switzerland, where Bollywood films are barely seen, are a commonplace location for romantic Indian films. By contrast, the great rivers of Nigeria and Pakistan, where Indian films are a prominent form of popular culture, do not flow on to the silver screen. In the Swiss case, the association of cool mountain holidays with romantic encounters is textually reminiscent of the colonial era. The astute substitution of Switzerland for the favoured Himalayan valley of Kashmir in the 1990s, as insurgency made the 'original' an impracticable location for filming, is a useful illustration of how contemporary political realities impinge upon the geography of Bollyworld. Similarly, the oblique absence of Pakistan in the verbal and textual forms of Hindi cinema is an indication of the continuing contradictions between cultural familiarity and political divorce (Athique 2008b). Bollyworld, then, is inevitably a product of what Nitin Govil (2007) has called the 'frictions of global mobility' and this is as true of the symbolic universe represented by the films themselves as it is of the nature and extent of the transnational audiences formed around their consumption.

Brand Bollywood and Soft Power

Ashish Rajadhyaksha has described recent export flows towards Western markets, and the wider international rebranding of Indian commercial cinema, as a process of 'Bollywoodization' (2003). Indeed, the majority of popular discourse in circulation now seems to present Indian cinema and 'Bollywood' as effectively synonymous. Rajadhyaksha, however, is at pains to maintain a distinction between the two: 'the cinema has been in existence as a national industry of sorts for the past fifty years . . . *Bollywood* has been around for only about a decade now' (2003: 28). Rajadhyaksha insists on making this distinction between Indian cinema and Bollywood for two major reasons, first, because the cultural industry surrounding the 'Bollywood' brand extends far beyond the production and consumption of feature films, and second, because the high-budget gloss and transnational themes of the major Bollywood films are far from representative of the majority of Indian film production.

> Bollywood is *not* the Indian film industry, or at least not the film industry alone. Bollywood admittedly occupies a space analogous to the film industry, but might best be seen as a more diffuse cultural conglomeration involving a range of distribution and consumption activities from websites to music cassettes, from cable to radio. If so, the film industry itself – determined here solely in terms of its box office turnover and sales of print and music rights, all that actually comes back to the producer – can by definition constitute only a part, and perhaps an *alarmingly small* part of the overall culture industry that is currently being created and marketed . . . While Bollywood exists for, and prominently caters to, a diasporic audience of Indians . . . the Indian cinema – much as it would wish to tap this 'non-resident' audience – is only occasionally successful in doing so, and is in almost every instance able to do so only when it, so to say, *Bollywoodizes* itself, a transition that very few films in Hindi, and hardly any in other languages, are actually able to do. (2003: 27–9)

By Rajadhyaksha's definition, the Bollywood brand denotes something like a broader culture industry in terms of the media mix that it employs, but at the same time Bollywood also denotes a restricted field in industrial and aesthetic terms. Bollywood does not encompass India's small art, or 'parallel', cinema which, in days gone by, were the only products of Indian film-making recognized on the global stage through the film festival circuit (Bannerjee 1982). Furthermore, Bollywood does not incorporate the regional-language cinemas that constitute the bulk of film production and consumption in the subcontinent in purely numerical terms. Even as a sector of Hindi cinema that produces some 200 features a year, the Bollywood brand effectively excludes the large stable of low-budget comedies and action exploitation films. Instead, the Bollywood archetype is defined by the high-budget saccharine upper middle-class melodrama, which represents a tongue-in-cheek blockbuster repackaging of the *masala* movie of old within an affluent, nostalgic and highly exclusive view of Indian culture and society. It is also notable that the sixty or so productions per year that fall into this category have become increasingly saturated with product placements for global consumer fashions and multinational sponsors. So, if Bollywood is not the Indian cinema per se, as Rajadhyaksha points out, it might be described instead as the 'export lager' of the Indian cinema, since Bollywood productions are the ones that dominate India's film exports. The high-budget Bollywood Hindi-language film generates the vast majority of export returns and has become centrally positioned in the international imagination as the 'trademark' Indian film.

The rise of Bollywood can be understood as an indication of generational change in the film industry, as the major stars and directors of the 1970s and 1980s hand over the reins to their children. Many of the current stars come from established film families (such as Abhishek Bachchan, Karisma and Kareena Kapoor, Hrithik Roshan, Saif and Soha Ali Khan) as do many of the new directors working in the Bollywood vein (such as Aditya Chopra and Farhan Akhtar). The explosion of transnational television, international brands and global aspirations has produced a very different outlook on the cinema amongst these younger players. This is very much a post-satellite generation that is acutely aware of international trends in the cinema. Thus, Bollywood films are more outward-looking in their film style than the films made by the previous generation, whose attention was much more focused on long-term trends in a closed domestic market. At the same time, the latest crop of film-makers clearly remain conscious of the legacy that they are inheriting, and the prevalence of 'retro' references to the formula films of the past is a notable feature of Bollywood films. Much of this attention to the old Indian cinema is expressed in terms of ironic affection, a trope that sometimes mobilizes a surprisingly effective nostalgia for classic Indian cinema, but at other times has the effect of making contemporary Bollywood appear to be something of a slick parody of itself.

Bollywood gloss has not been restricted to sentiment alone. We have also witnessed the rise of the impossibly beautiful body as the central focus of contemporary films. This trend was led by the entry of former Miss World, Aishwarya Rai, into the film industry with Subhash Ghai's *Taal* (1998) and has subsequently been augmented by the fetishistic representation of the male body in the forms of Hrithik Roshan and John Abraham. Impossibly beautiful bodies set in impossibly beautiful lives have been further augmented by the saturation of the Bollywood frame with impossibly beautiful products, like Coca Cola (*Taal*) or Mercedes (*Dil Chahta Hai*). Thus, we begin to see Bollywood articulating the collapse of distinctions between advertising and narrative entertainment common to the media-saturated cultures of late capitalism found in Europe and North America. It does seem that the bigger stars like Shah Rukh Khan and Amitabh Bachchan have advertised everything from axle oil to light aircraft during the last ten years. Aishwarya Rai also delivers considerable cultural capital for companies targeting affluent Indian consumers, as well as representing the preferred 'fair and lovely' face of the new India for international advertisers. There is no doubt, therefore, that the Bollywood brand articulates a universe that is light years away from the Manmohan Desai potboiler and the more visceral Indian cinema of the immediate past.

In an attempt to capitalize on a new configuration of international trade and respond to favourable press interest from abroad, leading industry figures, including 1970s superstar Amitabh Bachchan and veteran director Yash Chopra, launched the International Indian Film Awards (IIFA) in 2000 (IIFA 2011). The IIFA is an Oscars-style glamour event designed to connect with key overseas constituencies and to promote Indian cinema on the international stage. As the IIFA web portal claims: 'As global cinema rapidly emerges, a prominent place for Indian cinema is reserved. IIFA constantly endeavours to showcase to the world the wealth of talent that Indian cinema has to offer' (IIFA 2011). The list of sites chosen for these events can be read as a useful list of Bollyworld hubs, where the symbolic placement of international glamour is balanced by proximity to significant offshore audiences. The first event was held at London's Millennium Dome in 2000, and since then events have been held in Sun City, South Africa (2001), Genting Highlands, Malaysia (2002), Johannesburg, South Africa (2003), Singapore (2004), Amsterdam (2005), Dubai (2006), Yorkshire, UK (2007), Bangkok (2008), Macao (2009), Colombo (2010) and Toronto (2011). Organizers of the IIFA claim that each of these events has driven significant growth in the consumption of Indian films in the local territory as well as generating invaluable publicity in the mainstream media of the host nation, catching the attention of the wider community outside of the established fan base (2011).

While operating with great effectiveness as a set of marketing strategies by which the Indian cinema has launched itself into a new era, Bollywood simultaneously operates as a symbolic performance of India in the liberalization era (Deshpande 2005). Bollywood productions have increasingly been seen as iconic of India's global ambitions, and described as a major source of cultural capital in the mediation of the global (Tharoor 2008). Joseph Nye, perhaps the best-known exponent of the political benefits of cultural prestige, has frequently identified Bollywood films as a clear example of what he calls 'soft power' in the global field (Nye 2005; Diwakar 2006; Hannifa 2011). Nye's notion of soft power is intended as a counterpoint to the 'hard' economic and military power wielded by nation-states in the pursuit of their global interests. Hard power, however implicit in its usage, is essentially a coercive tool in international relations. By contrast, soft power is persuasive in nature, relying on the external perception of a country as a benign influence in the world (Nye 2004). In this sense, the democratic credentials of a nation as well as the quality and popularity of its cultural exports are both useful contributors to soft power. In exactly the same way that Hollywood cinema was perceived as an ambassador for the American way of life during the twentieth century, Bollywood films have been increasingly seen as transmitters of India's cultural prestige.

The value of projecting an attractive brand in international affairs has been taken up with enthusiasm in recent years by the India Brand Equity Foundation, which is administered jointly by the Indian Ministry of Commerce and the Confederation of Indian Industry (IBEF 2011). The idea of soft power has been endorsed explicitly by successive governments, with India's current Prime Minister, Manmohan Singh, observing in 2011 that 'India's soft power is an increasingly important element of our expanding global footprint . . . The richness of India's classical traditions and the colour and vibrancy of contemporary Indian culture are making waves around the world' (Singh 2011). Long-serving diplomat, writer and now Minister of State, Shashi Tharoor also describes the popularity of Bollywood films around the world as a concrete indication of India's capacity to project a 'good story' that the world wants to hear (2008). Soft power is also an intrinsically comparative measure, with the rising hard power of China appearing to make foreign commentators particularly receptive to a new image for India, as Per Stahlberg notes: 'An American opinion institute recently ranked India as number 18 on an index of successful "Nation Brands" – a measurement of how consumers around the world perceive different countries. And, as the Indian media enthusiastically reported, "Brand India" was stronger than Asian competitors like "Brand China" and "Brand South Korea"' (Stahlberg 2006).

As we have seen, the new image of India as a global economic player in the popular imagination has also been shaped by India's considerable success in the global IT industry. The potential spending power of India's middle classes as an 'emerging market' for restless global capital, an established operational nuclear capability and India's continued growth in the face of recession in the West have also backed up soft power with some hard power, the effective combination of which Joseph Nye is fond of calling 'smart power' (2008). India's rebranding on the international stage is also strategic on the part of other nations, being indicative of the desire of some countries to find a balance to China's growing economic clout. As such, a new picture of India has been established in the pages of anglophone news and business publications, replacing its previous role as a speaker for the 'traditional' societies of the Third World with a new role as a democratic, modernizing, capitalist society amenable to incorporation into a new world order. For good or for ill, the widespread adoption of the logic of marketing nations and cultures like movie franchises has seen the two parallel projects of rebranding the Indian cinema and rebranding India itself become intertwined.

Transnational Audiences for Indian Films

The notion of cultural imperialism was a product of the Cold War era, when the mass media were seen as capable of readily reprogramming the minds of their audiences, and where international relations were understood in terms of clear ideological boundaries. In the twenty-first century, we have come to recognize the influence of the media as being contingent, negotiated and, in practical terms, much more diffuse. Similarly, our general understanding of the present international order reveals quite different ideological contests, the boundaries of which are not as readily apparent. For this reason, the obvious problem in equating a global media presence with the diffuse projection of cultural influence would be an intellectually lazy tendency to equate hard and soft power, that is, to see public perception as synonymous with substance. In practice, it would be somewhat ridiculous to assume that India's global rise would be hampered by a bad year in the Bombay film industry. It is vitally important, nonetheless, that the very notion of soft power directs us to think of the conversation that takes place between media narratives and their audiences in contexts where that exchange is variously international and transcultural. For some viewers, it might be a perceived cultural proximity that makes Indian films appealing, enacting discourses of affinity, cultural affirmation or 'imagined community' (Anderson 1991; Straubhaar 1991). To others, perhaps it is the degree of cultural distance that makes Indian movies attractive, mobilizing aesthetics of exoticism (Athique 2008c; Choudhuri 2009). In order to avoid the pitfalls of simplistic causal explanations between hard and soft power, we must be attentive to the very human contradictions of media audiences, and to the subjective distinctions that continue to exist between national cultures and nation-states. With this in mind, we need to approach transcultural media reception in ways that are sensitive to the social conventions, cultural geography and individual subjectivities that are brought into play in those encounters.

Diasporic audiences

In his influential exposition of the cultural dimensions of globalization, Arjun Appadurai claimed that the consumption by migrants of media artefacts addressing their own ethnic specificity provides the catalyst for the imagining of 'diasporic public spheres'. These are defined by Appadurai as mobile post-national communities, constituted by globally dispersed ethnic networks linked through electronic media (1996: 22). In India, the 'non-resident Indian', much like the Indian film industry, has made a marked transition in recent years from being configured as an errant native seduced by the wealth and glamour of the West, at the expense of Indian values, to being an icon of the desirable cosmopolitan Indian citizen straddling the globe. For their adopted nations, naturalized Indian migrants are increasingly seen as valuable for fostering business connections with a liberalizing Indian economy. However, the same migrants are also seen as potentially damaging to the cohesion of the national public sphere in the country of settlement, given their 'cultural differences' from the majority population. The project of 'multiculturalism' in Western nations has explicitly sought to harness the positive potential of a more culturally diverse society in an era of global economic connectivity. Simultaneously, multicultural policy frameworks are intended to manage the potentials for what is seen as a dilution of the existing 'national' culture. In the process of this elaborate dance, a large body of literature has emerged from the Western academies on 'migrant communities', describing their economic structures, cultural practices and social behaviours. Thus, although there are sizeable populations of Indian origin in Africa, the Caribbean and elsewhere in Asia, research on the media use of Indian diasporic communities has tended to focus on Indians located in Western countries (Gillespie 1995; Ray 2000; Dudrah 2002a/b; Thompson 2002).

In part, this is a reflection of the relative dominance of Western academia, and its concerns, over the production of 'global' knowledge. A Western-centred notion of the Indian diaspora, however, is not simply a Western or an academic predisposition. It is also a marked feature of official discourses emanating from the Government of India, as well as in the popular discourse of the Indian media, in the print and electronic press, on television, in literature and in movies. From 1998 to 2004, the BJP-led coalition government made considerable efforts to capitalize on the growing wealth of India's expatriate communities through the promotion of the concept of cultural citizenship. The desire of non-resident Indians (NRIs) and persons of Indian origin (PIOs) for a cultural connection with the 'homeland' was given emphasis in official discourse, as was their potential as ideal foreign investors (Singhvi 2000). In September 2000, the Government of India commissioned a high-level committee on diaspora, which produced the L. M. Singhvi Report in 2000. Amongst its recommendations were a dual-citizenship scheme for NRIs and PIOs in 'selected [read Western] countries', a central body for fostering the national-diaspora relationship, and a diaspora day (Pravasi

Bharatiya Divas) to promote cultural links with the diaspora, including an awards ceremony (Pravasi Bharatiya Samman) for high achievers from Indian communities overseas. Claiming that a 'deep commitment to their cultural identity has manifested itself in every component of the Indian Diaspora', the Singhvi Report emphasizes the role of the media in fostering the close cultural connections between India and the diaspora (2000). This was a position echoed by Sushma Swaraj, then Union Information and Broadcasting Minister in the NDA government:

> The exports of the entertainment industry from India which in 1998 stood at 40 million US dollars have in 2001 crossed more than 180 million US dollars. This entertainment and media explosion has brought India closer to our diaspora. More important is the fact that the diaspora has also majorly contributed in fuelling this growth. Perhaps geographical division between Indians in India and the Indian diaspora is blurring if not disappearing altogether. And with the announcement made by the Hon'ble Prime Minister at the yesterday's inaugural session, the dual citizenship will bring the diaspora closer to us not merely due to our cultural bonds but also by a legal system. Each entertainment and media icon of the Indian diaspora remains our unofficial ambassador abroad. We salute these leaders and assure them of our conducive policies to facilitate their endeavours. (Swaraj 2003)

Given the longstanding antagonism between the Government of India and the film industry, these officially sanctioned attempts to capitalize upon the reach of Indian films in strategically important countries represent something of a *volte face*. The rationales on offer from two quite different administrations in the past two decades have thus sought to reverse-engineer explanations for the appeal of Indian films in ways that reflect their own ideological positions. For the BJP-led government of 1998–2004, Bollywood was figured as a transmitter of timeless Hindu values, while for the presently governing Congress party (2004–), the contemporary Indian film is a modern avatar of India's rich syncretic culture. In both cases, however, the diasporic audiences for Bollywood are positioned explicitly as instruments of soft power in their own right, capable of influencing both Indian and Western societies.

Ronald Inden (1999) and Rajinder Dudrah (2002a) have both observed that, prior to the mid-1990s, 'foreign' Indians were typically villains in film texts, financially enriched and morally corrupted by the West and lacking in the 'Indian values' of humility and integrity. Such characterizations of overseas Indians were an extrapolation of the conflicts between tradition and modernity, often implicitly (or even explicitly) played out in Indian cinema as a contest between Indian and Western values. The turning point commonly identified by commentators was the spectacular success of a Yash

Raj film directed by Aditya Chopra (Dwyer 2000; Rajadhyaksha 2003: 26). *Dilwale Dulhania Le Jayanege* (1995) marked the transition of the persona of the NRI, from villain to hero. In this film, the British-Indian hero and heroine fall in love on a 'grand European tour' before returning to the Punjab to play out a love triangle against the patriarch's preferred choice of son-in-law. Ultimately, the non-resident Indian suitor proves himself to display greater integrity than his spoiled and macho Indian counterpart, thus winning the dutiful British-born bride (as the title of the film suggests). This film was one of the most successful Indian films of the decade. Furthermore, it was one of the first features to make full use of its potential in the overseas markets, where it was incredibly popular with migrant audiences – positioning male lead Shah Rukh Khan as the biggest export draw in Indian cinema for the next decade. From that moment onwards, the cinematic NRI was rapidly reconfigured as a returning hero and as an 'Indian at heart' – with every other film appearing as 'Dil this' or 'Dil that' in the late 1990s. According to Rajinder Dudrah:

> Bollywood of the nineties took note of the NRIs as cosmopolitan in mind, speaking in English or American accents, but with their heart and soul in the right place respecting all things Indian. Nineties film plots spanned several cities across several continents with diasporic characters taking centre stage . . . characters could be in middle-class India or the urban diaspora of the West thereby opening up affinities with audiences across the globe. (Dudrah 2002a: 29)

In reference to high levels of 'diasporic' consumption of Indian films, as well as the increasing characterization of transnationally located subjects in film narratives, Vijay Mishra states that 'A study of Bombay cinema will no longer be complete without a theory of diasporic desire because this cinema is now global in a specifically diasporic sense' (2002: 269). Manas Ray has described the participation of ethnic Indians overseas in Bollywood spectatorship as an expression of 'cultural affirmation' by these groups (2000, 2003). Immediately prior to the boom in Western export markets in the mid-nineties, Marie Gillespie also saw the domestic consumption of Indian films by British Asians as an act of cultural affirmation and communal identification, in this case acting as a response to the inherent racism of the national media in Britain (1995). Rajinder Dudrah reminds us that the limited representation of South Asians in the British media also has to be considered alongside their marginalization in the wider social sphere, and 'in the context of a racist Britain in which Black settlers had made their home' (2002a: 27). Here diasporic cultural practices are seen as structured by a form of 'cultural resistance' compensating for social exclusion. On the other hand, this engagement with Western spaces can also be figured triumphantly, for example, by Gargi Bhattacharyya who claims that: 'We occupy by force the place that Asian modernity must learn to become, the place between over here and back home, another form of double consciousness for a global age' (2003: 10). This is a good example of the heroic description of diasporas where migrants are both victims (of Western racism) and colonizers (of Western knowledge and capital).

As a projection of soft power premised on ethno-cultural loyalty, it has to be said that Indian popular films are not especially convincing as transmitters of an Indian-ness deployed as a timeless ethnic text. The Bollywood refashioning of Indian film culture enacts a relatively 'Westernized' model of cultural consumption, building upon the strong Euro-American influences already at play in the Indian cinema. Contemporary Bollywood films provide audiences in India with a diet of free romance and consumer affluence, which continue to be associated with Western culture. Simultaneously, the same films also provide a source of cultural consumption often associated with ideas of 'Eastern' and 'Asian' cultures by South Asians who reside in the West, and for whom its Western influences become less apparent. Therefore, the dual address of Bollywood's 'NRI' films is ridden with powerful contradictions structured around the orientalist binary. In any case, the extent to which non-resident Indians are willing to accept those narratives as indicative of an Indian 'real' also appears to vary considerably (Athique 2005; Banaji 2006; Bhattacharya 2004; Kaur 2005). Therefore, as Raminder Kaur observes, 'It is too glib and cursory to say that Bollywood enables a religion-like nostalgia for people of the Indian diaspora; or that it serves some kind of identity orientation in the midst of a West-induced anomie' (Kaur 2005: 313). It is, however, fair to say that the now ubiquitous presence of Indian media products around the world has transformed the cultural experience of migration for many, and, in so doing, the global dispersal of Indian films has radically transformed the distance perception of migrant communities.

We should also note that the globalizing effect of media exchanges is not restricted to the migrant-homeland axis emphasized exclusively by the Indian government. The cultural connections within and between South Asian migrant communities around the world have also multiplied. For example, Hindi film songs are remixed by DJs in Birmingham, England, and blasted out at India-themed dance events in Toronto, Suva and Sydney. Increasingly they are also, depending on your point of view, either exported or 'returned' to India. The Indian cinema has provided much of the *materiel* for this global subculture, although it is equally clear that these diasporic practices intersect with other media flows in these far-flung locations to produce a set of hybridized cultural products which draw upon influences such as Jamaican Dub, Afro-American rap and mainstream urban club cultures. This hybridity does not preclude, or necessarily diminish, the significance of the ideologically coded offshore subjects envisioned by the Indian state. However, it does suggest that if we are to understand the function of soft power in signifying cultural identity at a global scale we need to understand the diasporic audience beyond the confines of any instrumental *ideal type* shaped by foreign policy.

The crossover audience

The notion of a 'Western viewer' is as old as the study of Indian cinema. Since the days of Satyajit Ray and the Indian Film Society movements in the 1950s there has been a comparison between an Indian audience, typified by illiteracy and an enthusiasm for escapist fare, and an occidental viewer acculturated to a diet of realism rather than fantasy, drama rather than melodrama and psychological motivation over musical excess (see Vasudevan 2000). Of course, aside from the music, this realist model of Western audiences rather contradicts the popular fare consumed in European, North American and Australasian cinemas. It did, perhaps, suit the kind of audiences addressed by art-house cinemas and film festivals, which in anglophone countries have traditionally been the most common environment for the screening of foreign-language films. Prior to the 1990s, the only Indian films to reach any significant Western audiences were art films operating in this niche market, described by Jigna Desai as:

> based on positioning 'foreign' films as ethnographic documents of 'other' (national) cultures and therefore as representatives of national cinemas. In particular, foreign Third World films that can be read as portraying the other through cultural difference (i.e., gender and sexual experiences or nativist renderings of rural village life). (Desai 2004: 39)

The art-house audience in the West represents a collection of consumers with various degrees of investment in an ethno-cultural scheme of 'World Cinema'. This coalition of interests might include those with an academic or professional interest either in cinema or in the 'producing culture'. It also encompasses viewers whose consumption of foreign films represents a mixture of auto-didacticism and aesthetic pleasure-seeking, gaining them a measure of cosmopolitan cultural capital. Art-house outlets often co-locate a Third World 'exotic' with European *auteur* cinema and with the alternative or independent sector of the host nation's local film culture. During the last decade, however, Indian films have escaped this aesthetic ghetto and begun to appear in the popular domain. Part of the reason for this is that diasporic audiences resident in the West, and inhabiting the same metropoles as the old art-house audiences, have given *popular* Indian cinema a commercially viable presence in the new context of multiplex exhibition (Kerrigan and Ozbilgin 2002: 200).

A further factor at play in the 'buzz' surrounding Bollywood in the West has been the success of a number of directors of Indian origin, working within various Western film industries, who have produced Indian-themed films which have successfully targeted Western audiences (see Desai 2004). Despite the obvious differences between these films and mainstream Indian cinema, the films of US-based Mira Nair, Canada-based Deepa Mehta and UK-based Gurinder Chadha have frequently been conflated with Bollywood in the Western media. Both Indian and expatriate directors have benefited from this fallacy: mainstream Indian films have been associated, for example, with the success of Nair's *Monsoon Wedding* (2001), while the 'colour as culture' connotations of Bollywood branding have been used to market the films of non-resident Indian (or NRI) directors, such as Chadha's *Bride and Prejudice* (2004). The success of crossover films with niche audiences has encouraged the staging of events designed to promote Indian films amongst a more 'mainstream' audience. In 2002, the British Film Institute (BFI) organized an extensive showcase of Indian cinema, *ImagineAsia*, as part of a nationwide *Indian Summer* festival which also included the use of Bollywood themes in department store merchandize, visual art exhibitions and theatrical productions. This celebration of Indian popular culture under the rubric of 'multiculturalism' was designed to promote Indo-British trade exchanges, emphasize official recognition of Britain's large South Asian population and to draw profits from providing a context for the consumption of Indian cultural products by the UK's majority white population. The BFI's *ImagineAsia* festival of Indian cinema was considered a success, *primarily* since it drew almost a third of its audience from outside of Britain's South Asian population (White and Rughani 2003).

The term 'crossover' deserves some attention because, as Desai has also observed, its use is synonymous with the quest for white audiences for 'ethnic' media artefacts (2004: 66). The crossing described by the term is unidirectional, from a niche audience to a larger 'mainstream' audience that promises greater exposure and profits. The term is generally not used, for example, to describe the consumption of mainstream media by niche audiences or minority-to-minority media exchanges. The 'crossover audience' for both Indian-produced and NRI-directed films is imagined as a desired market based upon a collective notion of culturally literate cosmopolitan members of the majority population willing to extend their consumption of media cultures (and media *as* culture). Within the context of multicultural-ism, this crossover can be defined as the success of a media artefact located in one ethnic culture with a majority audience located in the dominant culture. This is because, while the logic of multiculturalism challenges the idea of a culturally homogeneous national audience, it continues to assume 'that there are certain audiences that are commensurate with communities and demo-graphic populations' (Desai, 2004: 66). As such, 'the emphasis on crossover success shifts discussion away from the issues associated with the burden of representation and the relations between cultural producers and black British communities to appealing to white demographic markets' with Indian films becoming 'integrated into capitalist expansion through the logic and rhetoric of multiculturalism' (Desai 2004: 66).

Of course, multiculturalism is not only a rhetorical project, but also con-structs and naturalizes an industry with both internal and external aspects. Within the host nation, the acquisition, possession and display of products of foreign cultural provenance are facilitated by a range of leisure industries providing music, textiles, movies, literature, furniture and food. The external interests of the multicultural industry facilitate this trade in commodities between the importing and exporting nation, but are also incorporated with other aspects of interstate trade and the movements, in both direc-tions, of financial, military and ideological capital. In the case of cinema, the celebration of the media projects of other 'cultures' is also related to furthering desires to extend economic opportunities for the national media industry in those markets. Western media companies now view India as a potentially lucrative media market and, with Indian production budgets also increasing dramatically, a number of national film industries have been keen to court Indian producers and their appetite for offshore production and post-production facilities (Hassam and Paranjape 2010). At the same time, Western film-makers have been keen to draw upon the Bollywood aesthetic for their own ends, from Baz Luhrmann's stylistic borrowings in *Moulin Rouge* (2001) to Danny Boyle's Oscar-winning *Slum Dog Millionaire* (2008), which applied a Bollywood-inspired makeover to the previously successful formula of Mira Nair's *Salaam Bombay* (1988). It is significant then, perhaps, that the big crossover successes have originated in the West, despite the considerable efforts made by India's most talented producers to capitalize on the fashionable status of their own productions (Schaefer and Karan 2010).

The rebranding of commercial Indian films in the West as postmodern pop art, as exemplified by the trope of Bollywood, is very much part of the continuing cycle of orientalism. From the Western perspective, it is possible to discern a certain cultural ennui couched in this latest commercialization of liberal multiculturalism as cosmopolitan 'ethnic chic', while in India the imagination on screen of a transnationally orientated middle class, and its occupation and consumption of the West, represents the symbolic coun-terweight of the orientalist binary. It is imperative, therefore, to recognize that any discussion of cultural consumption that juxtaposes East and West remains powerfully inflected by the historical exercise of power in the Indo-European encounter. Beyond the present geopolitical context, the Bollywood fad can also be seen as the latest manifestation of India's status as one of the most successful nations in the erstwhile Third World at having its cultural produce 'appropriated' in Western markets. India has always been one of the heavyweights for multicultural products: from rustic tribal jewellery, orien-tal fabrics, sixties-style spiritualism, ethnocultural and adventure tourism, New Age music, exotic foodstuffs, ethnographic texts and 'new literatures'. Popular Indian films have now joined this considerable bankroll as another source of foreign-exchange earnings and another form of cultural currency in the ongoing encounter between India and its highly significant 'Western Other'. As such, the machinery of Western appropriation clearly functions with the support of equally significant machinery in the Indian economy, which works to sell 'India' abroad.

It is also worth pointing out that the promise of an off-the-peg experience of exotic authenticity is one of the primary strategies employed in the market-ing of multiculturalism (and specifically media-culturalism). This is, in each and almost every case, a fallacy convenient to all of those involved. As such, the dusting-off of Indian popular cinema and its new life as the camp, glam-orous and low-context 'Bollywood' is typical, rather than atypical, of market-ing Asian cultures in the West. Nonetheless, the wider circulation of Indian films, and the spin-off of Bollywood club cultures and Bollywood dance schools emerging around the world, are helping to make the Bollywood dance routine the acceptable, Western-friendly, face of multiculturalism at a time when other markers of difference, such as the *hijab*, have become symbols of conflict and irrational fear. In that sense, it is possible to make a strong argument that Bollywood films represent an effective projection of soft power within the global imagination of the West. It remains to be seen, however, whether this recent flirtation with Bollywood will be a passing fash-ion or whether it will become an ongoing addition to the cultural repertoire of Western multiculturalism. Further, it remains a point of likely contention whether this crossover effect emerges from the particular aesthetics of the films themselves, or whether Bollywood has merely been signified as a con-venient intangible brand whose 'colourful' meanings can be easily appropri-ated by a cultural economy firmly anchored in the developed world (Schaefer and Karan 2010).

The parallel audience

In the naming of this category, I take the term 'parallel' from Brian Larkin's work on the interpretation of Indian films in Nigeria (1997, 2003). Among the Hausa people, Larkin records the emergence of new cultural forms modelled on the themes of familial loyalty and romantic desire as played out in locally popular Indian films. Larkin notes that the renunciation, negotiation and appropriation of modernity found in Indian films, emanating as it does from another 'non-Western' perspective, has proved highly resonant with the experiences of Nigerian audiences. In seeking to provide an explanation for this instance of transnational consumption, Larkin proposes that the Hausa people understand Indian films as representing a 'parallel modernity, a way of imaginatively engaging with the changing social basis of contemporary life that is an alternative to the pervasive influence of a secular West' (1997: 16). Larkin's notion of parallel modernities thus provides a useful model for recognizing transnational relationships that exist between different parts of the 'developing world'. This is not a utopian proposition, however, since there is no reason to assume that the 'parallel' nature of mediated exchange, and of modernity itself, existing amongst so many different locations should be understood as constituting any equitable exchange system between non-Western states. Similarly, the popularity of Indian films amongst parallel audiences does not predispose any coherent Third World public. Not all parallel audiences for Indian films are equally foreign, perhaps, and such audiences are in any case unlikely to be foreign in the same way.

The first example that I will employ here is the Indonesian case where Indian films first appeared in the last years of Dutch rule. Indeed, as the Indonesian film industry was attempting to establish itself in the 1950s, a strike was staged against Indian film imports, due to their popularity with the mass audience and the fact that they were cheap for local distributors to import. This made them a direct form of competition for Indonesian producers, whereas American films mostly patronized by the upper classes were not (Said 1991: 44). These brief protests proved unsuccessful and the importation of Indian films into Indonesia has continued to the present day. Pam Nilan has observed that in contemporary Indonesia, wider geopolitical events have 'been reflected in the ratings decline for American programs and films while other exogenous content – South American soap operas, Bollywood films, and Hong Kong martial arts epics – remain hugely popular' (2003: 188). Nilan believes that: 'A major reason "Bollywood" has millions of non-Indian fans in the Middle East, Africa and Southeast Asia is because of the non-American quality of Indian films' (2003: 296). In the years following the Asian currency crisis of 1997–8, Indian films certainly became far more commercially viable for Indonesian distributors than the more expensive American product. The production of Indonesian films was also virtually halted by the increased cost of film stock and processing and it was Indian and Hong Kong films which filled the vacuum (See Sumarno and Achnas 2002: 160). However, the consumption in postcolonial Indonesia of films imported from other Asian nations has been too consistent to be only a phenomenon of current affairs. As an alternative explanation, a contributor to the Indonesian website Taman Bollywood points out the historical influence of Indian narrative forms upon Indonesian culture:

> Most Indonesian people, especially who live in the island of Java (about 60% of Indonesian population lived here), have a Hindu background. Their culture, dances, language (based on Sanskrit), philosophy, and their traditional ceremonies, all reflect this Hindu influence in their lives, which has come to be a mix between Hinduism and Islam (Sufism). We don't say that Hindi films are only loved by the Javanese, but also loved by so many Indonesians who live in other islands and also watched by many people who live in Islamic countries. (Khan 2003)

It may be unwise to overemphasize such a direct link for two periods of cultural exchange between South and South East Asia, which are separated by some 500 years, but there is doubtless some sense of a more contemporary inter-Asian dialogue in Indonesian discourse on Bollywood. India has historically been a major centre of culture, as well as an exporter of culture, within Asia, and it is relatively unsurprising that it remains so today. Having said that, the same website also offers other reasons for the popularity of Indian films in the archipelago, such as the physical and symbolic attraction of film stars, the cross-cultural appeal of pop music and the desire for entertainment 'when many people are "crazy and bored" with political issues and bad economic conditions' (ibid.). The longstanding popularity of Hindi cinema in Indonesia is paralleled by its continuing popularity in other Asian nations, such as nearby Malaysia and Burma, the more distant Uzbekistan and Tajikstan, and the newest Asian nation of East Timor. Generally speaking, the trans-Asian spread of Indian cinema is found in Southern rather than Northern Asia, although Indian films have enjoyed occassional success in both China and Japan. It is worth recognizing, however, that the reception of Indian films in distant parts of Asia is qualitatively different from their reception by audiences in countries that are India's near neighbours.

In the first instance, the fact that the national divisions within South Asia do not have a linguistic basis means that Indian films remain intelligible for large audiences located across India's borders. The second point to note is that the South Asian region was a single multi-lingual market for a number of Indian film industries prior to the advent of the modern political map of Pakistan, India, Sri Lanka and, later, Bangladesh. One legacy of this period is a commonly shared and inter-referential cinematic tradition, in terms of visual and narrative style as well as industrial practices. However, since independence, the relative presence of Indian films in other parts of South Asia has been affected by the political relationship between the governments of the postcolonial nation-states, which have attempted to serve as both arbiters and guardians of their national publics. For this reason, it is far from insignificant that Hindi cinema retains a large following in Pakistan. For Indian film-makers, and for the Hindi cinema in particular, the population of Pakistan represents a large and loyal audience that it would clearly like to access commercially. In an interview in 2003, actress Urmila Matondkar said: 'Human suffering has no religion. We should work together for the betterment of our next generation. Let me tell you, Pakistanis love Indian films. Why not make them legal in Pakistan? This will help bridge the cultural gap between our two countries' (Ashraf 2003). Matondkar has not been alone in this sentiment, with many other members of the Hindi industry lobbying for normalized trade links with Pakistan (ibid.). Nor is it only the film industry that sees Indian films as a resource for bridge-building between the two states, with academics also making similar claims during the intermittent attempts at rapprochement between the two states (see Bharat and Kumar 2007).

However, it is worth remembering that these invocations of cultural fraternity are interspersed with periods of intense nationalist hostility. Throughout the 1990s, working against the backdrop of the festering situation in Kashmir, Muslim terrorists and their reputed sponsors in Pakistan became explicit targets for big-screen accounts of Indian nationalist fervour. As such, for the film wallahs, the economic potential of audiences on the other side of the border has to be balanced by what constitutes a permissible articulation of India–Pakistan relations within the regional political environment at any given time. Strangely enough, this does not appear to have diminished the popularity of Indian films, as Rahimullah Yusufzai records: 'films, which depict the Indian view of the Kashmir Issue, are being secretly rented after a ban by the government, which of course clubs them all as Indian propaganda. Video stores in Islamabad report brisk demand for Bollywood films, including the "anti-Pakistan" ones' (Yusufzai 2001). Indeed, Cable TV operators in Pakistan went as far as striking in 2003 when the government of Pakistan attempted to restrict their broadcasting of Indian entertainment channels, an event recorded with some triumphalism by India's *The Hindu*: 'every new attempt by Islamabad to deny its people access to Indian entertainment has had the opposite effect. Bollywood films, soap operas, filmi and non-filmi songs and Indian pop groups (mostly Hindi) have become the staple diet of the majority of the Pakistani society' (Reddy 2003).

Thus, for their part, Pakistani audiences for Hindi films seem prepared to take the occasional jingoistic outburst with a pinch of salt. These acts of transnational consumption on the part of Pakistani film fans are paralleled to a lesser extent by the market for Pakistani-produced Urdu dramas in India. Thus, in the South Asian context, the illicit trade in media products across the border can be seen as a major component in maintaining the cultural connections that have now been discouraged politically over a lengthy period. It may be unwise, however, to overstate the extent to which Indian films are able to exert soft power over their audiences in neighbouring Pakistan. Their long-standing presence there does not yet appear to have reduced the overall levels of mistrust and hositility between the two nations, and the cultural familiarities which they invoke could be seen as being as much part of the nationalist problem in South Asia as they are part of any solution. It is entirely possible for Pakistanis to enjoy Indian films while maintaining a deepseated mistrust of their neighbours. However, we should also be wary of cementing the nationalist clichés of mutual loathing that entrench senseless confrontation in South Asia. Working against the official strictures of reflexive otherness, and in marked contrast to the state-owned media of either nation, the role played by Hindi cinema in perpetuating cultural exchange between India and Pakistan is a highly significant one.

In the east of the subcontinent, the exchange of Bengali media products and personnel between India and Bangladesh also serves to sustain cultural contact in the aftermath of political division (Raju 2008). Indian films and film stars have proved both popular and controversial in Nepal over the years (see BBC Online: 27 December 2000; Burch 2002). The resumption of screenings for Indian films in Afghanistan was one of the first media developments following the invasion of 2001, and their ongoing popularity in that country has recently prompted US diplomats to suggest the deployment of Bollywood stars there as an Indian 'soft power' asset (Srivastava 2000; *Guardian* 2010). It can be argued, therefore, that Indian media exports are currently playing an important role in the development of a South Asian media sphere that might, over time, contribute to better understanding between the South Asian nations. At the very least, the role of the Indian film undermines the ideological (mis)alignment of cultural and political geographies in the subcontinent. Nonetheless, the continuing popularity of Indian cinema in the rest of the subcontinent has also been seen as damaging competition for local film production in neighbouring states. Thus, while Indian films might be seen as a non-threatening alternative to US cultural production in Southeast Asia and Africa, they have frequently been regarded as a source of cultural imperialism acting upon other South Asian states (see Sonwalkar 2001). In any case, the available evidence suggests that sustained demand for Indian films by culturally proximate audiences throughout South Asia will continue into the future.

Further afield in Asia, it seems equally clear that the degree of cultural literacy required to enjoy the pleasures of Indian cinema is relatively low in practical terms. For this reason, Indian films have been able to cement their popularity amongst audiences with only a scant knowledge of Indian culture and society. More broadly, the longstanding dispersal of Indian films across the developing world does appear to provide support for Larkin's notion that Bollywood operates as the bearer of a 'parallel modernity' (1997) – that is, if we understand the popularity of Indian films in terms of their distinctive narrative engagement with the competing forces of tradition and modernity, and their particular focus upon the tensions between familial duty and romantic desire in a feudal society. It is also reasonable to some extent to back Pam Nilan's assertion that Indian films are understood comparatively to Western media products that articulate a more individualistic, technologically determined and sexualized social environment. Neither of these cultural narratives is an accurate rendition of social conditions: Western society is by no means as liberated and Indian society is by no means as romantic as the movies they respectively produce. In that sense, the general appeal of Indian films can be attributed to the conscious mismatch between the Bollywood diegesis and the burden of faithfully representing an Indian social milieu. To demand anthropological veracity of cultural representation, or to assume that this is expected by audiences, is to somewhat miss the point of popular culture. At the same time, Indian films are still seen by their overseas audiences as being ethnically marked media products that signify at some level the sensibility of the society from which they come. Thus, in many ways, their soft power relies precisely on the simultaneous substitution and transferability of 'Bollyworld' for India itself.

Indian Films as Global Currency

The global circulation of Indian movies provides fertile ground for discussions that indicate a number of disparate imaginings, such as Indian and South Asian identities, inter-Asian dialogues, Third World fraternity and anglocentric cosmopolitanism. The now ubiquitous presence of Indian media products around the world has transformed the cultural experience of migration for many. Brand Bollywood has helped to project the 'new' reality of an Asian modernity to the developed world. The distribution channels of both

Mumbai and Dubai have successfully dispersed a distinctive blend of pop styling and feudal melodrama that enjoys widespread appeal in developing societies. As a field of practices, therefore, we can say with confidence that 'Bollyworld' cannot be overwhelmingly characterized by similarity of experience, and within its broad ambit the cultural capital of the Indian movie is spent quite differently. It is difficult, however, to find hard evidence that the soft power exerted by Indian films inculcates long-distance nationalist sentiments amongst migrants, reduces racist ignorance in the West or overwrites the political antagonisms fostered by state actors in Asia.

Demanding such evidence, perhaps, indicates a somewhat wilful ignorance of the difference between soft power and the older discredited notions of mass media effects and propaganda. Despite the obvious investment of the academy in linking social anthropology to clear political objectives, we must at least consider the possibility that the linkages between media consumption and overt personal and political loyalties may not be as strong as the theoretical paradigm of the past twenty years has suggested. We should remember that watching an Indian movie is not *only* a personal or social statement of identity. It is also a choice of entertainment and therefore a source of gratification. Further, it is also not likely to be the only choice being made. This does not negate the importance of Indian films as a source of soft power in the field of globalization. If anything, such a configuration would imply that their influence is both 'softer' and more powerful than the bare logic of nationalist politics is capable of recognizing. For that very reason, the 'globalized' social imagination is manifested within a pluralized mediasphere, where it appears to be more than capable of transcending ethno-cultural barriers as well as state authority.

Further Reading

Appadurai, Arjun (1996) *Modernity At Large: Cultural Dimensions of Globalization*, Minneapolis, MN, and London: University of Minnesota Press.

Banaji, Shakuntala (2006) *'Reading Bollywood': The Young Audience and Hindi Films*, Basingstoke: Palgrave Macmillan.

Basu, Anustap (2010) *Bollywood in the Age of New Media: The Geo-Televisual Aesthetic*, Edinburgh: Edinburgh University Press.

Kaur, Raminder and Sinha, Ajay (eds) (2005) *Bollyworld: Popular Indian Cinema Through a Transnational Lens*, New Delhi: Sage.

Mishra, Vijay (2002) *Bollywood Cinema: Temples of Desire*, London: Routledge.

Punathambekar, Aswin and Kavoori, Anandam P. (eds) (2008) *Global Bollywood*, New York and London: New York University Press.

Rai, Amit (2009) *Untimely Bollywood: Globalization and India's New Media Assemblage*, Durham, NC: Duke University Press.

7   Media Provision and the New Leisure Economy

One of the central tenets of economic and political thinking in the anglo-phone countries, in the present phase of globalization, has been the inevitability of a permanent shift away from manufacturing as the central plank of the economy in favour of a new scenario where technical innovation, creative performance and information management are the main sources of activity. A modernist worldview typical of the 1950s would likely characterize this as a process of 'undevelopment'. In a changing world, however, we could see a measure of this process as a necessary rebalancing of the uneven industrialization of the colonial era. More commonly, under the varied influences of international finance, ecological pressures and scientific futurism, the notion of a 'post-industrial' society has been postulated not as a lapse into a pre-industrial epoch or a lasting redistribution of productive wealth, but rather as marking a paradigm shift into a new stage of postmodern social and economic development (Bell 1973; Masuda 1980; Kumar 2005). By this reading, the most developed countries are deemed as having passed through certain stages in economic and social organization due to technological progress (namely, agricultural society and industrial society) prior to the pursuit of a post-industrial society. This teleology naturally causes us to question the implications of this new paradigm for a country like India, which has invested so much in industrialization as the goal of the development process. In the wider context of contemporary globalization, we must also be attentive to correlations between the Indian media industries and the influence of international business models that favour 'post-industrial' activities such as entertainment and services.

The Post-Industrial Paradigm

One of the most influential early exponents of a post-industrial ideal was Harvard sociologist Daniel Bell, who noted during the 1960s the steady decrease in labour-intensive manufacturing as a proportion of the American economy. Bell concluded that:

> A post-industrial society is based on services. Hence, it is a game between persons. What counts is not raw muscle power, or energy, but information.

131

> The central person is the professional, for he is equipped, by his education and training to provide the kinds of skill which are increasingly demanded in the post-industrial society. If an industrial society is defined by the quantity of goods as marking a standard of living, the post-industrial society is defined by the quality of life as measured by the services and amenities – health, education, recreation, and the arts – which are now deemed desirable and possible for everyone. (Bell 1999: 127)

In a post-industrial society, the consumption of material goods is surpassed by the consumption of services. In daily life, 'white-collar' work predominates over 'blue-collar' work, and political consensus is enforced by the educated middle classes, rather than by unionized working classes. As a developmental model, the post-industrial society has been developed in conjunction with the idea of a knowledge economy, which has also been around since the 1960s (Drucker 1969). At that time, the notion of a 'knowledge worker' sought to differentiate between the manual labour of the working classes and the intellectual work of white-collar workers and managers. By redirecting the definition of value away from material production and towards the acquisition, application and production of knowledge, the purpose of the knowledge economy paradigm was to emphasize the economic importance of work deemed 'unproductive' under the materialist paradigm. As such, both the 'post-industrial society' and the 'knowledge economy' sought to recast the divisive politics of the industrial era. In doing so, they took note of the new body of knowledge produced by the expansion of mass marketing techniques, and gave primacy to consumption over production. In the developed world, these ideas were taken up as an intellectual framework in support of a new economic model, driven by consumer services, organizational innovation and the diffusion of information technologies, following the oil shocks of the 1970s.

During the high tide of the first dot.com boom in the late 1990s, thinkers like Danny Quah and Diane Coyle characterized this new world of work as a 'weightless economy' where wealth was generated by activities in which innovation and creativity were more important than industrial skills, and where the products that people valued and consumed were becoming largely intangible (Coyle 1999; Quah 2001). That is, people's lives were increasingly organized around producing and consuming audiovisual information, rather than physical products. In Britain, Charles Leadbeater proclaimed a new era where software programmers, web designers, pop performers and advertising executives had become the new labour elite. In this world, consumers spend their disposable income on data services and multimedia entertainment. Individuals invest in virtual paperless banks and compete with each other primarily on the basis of creative resources and thinking skills. For Leadbeater, this constituted an economy by which the inhabitants of the developed world would live 'on thin air' (2000). Many of these ideas, of course, are broadly resonant with Manual Castells's contemporaneous model of 'informational capitalism' (1996). They subsequently proved to be enormously influential in business and political circles and have probably constituted the nearest equivalent to a governing ideology for the global IT industries. As such, their influence has spread widely throughout the world, reaching countries such as India which have generally been seen as being located in the earlier stages of the development process.

In this respect, it is important to give some broad consideration to the relationship between this field of discourse and the development of the 'new economy' in India since 1991. At the outset, it is obvious that the very foundation of these ideas is almost entirely antithetical to the strategic ambitions and ideology of Nehruvian industrialization pursued by India in the first four decades of independence. Given the enormous commitment made by millions of Indians in the lengthy pursuit of an industrial economy, the advent of a post-industrial ideal represents a significant shift of the goalposts within the developmental process. Further, given the motivation to 'catch-up' that is inherent to developmentalism as a doctrine, the viability of a leap-forward beyond the industrial age inevitably comes into play. In that respect, however, we must question whether a fully industrial society is a prerequisite for the post-industrial transition, or whether the industrialization stage could be partial or even bypassed entirely. Beyond the abstract, and on the ground, these socio-economic models encounter the stark realities of material lack in any society where development is uneven in its progression and distribution. Further, some very fundamental questions remain about the implicit assumptions of the post-industrial paradigm in its recent application by the developed world. Seemingly, no one assumes that material production is no longer necessary to sustain a post-industrial society. Rather, the notion has been that in the context of globalization, the developing countries would be happy doing the polluting, labour-intensive industrial work for the benefit of thinkers and shoppers in post-industrial countries. We might well ask, then, how could this powerline be maintained in a world increasingly defined by the interchange of information?

Looking at India in the broadest sense, the ideal of promoting intangible creative labour and directing purchasing power towards recreation and popular culture seems somewhat anachronous. After all, this is a developing economy where disposable incomes are typically marginal at best, and where the majority of the population lack the most basic provisions of clean drinking water, sanitation and a sufficient diet. Under these conditions, consumption readily appears a luxury and, as such, has been intrinsically understood as a leisure activity rather than as a functional necessity. It was by this very logic, of course, that the state prescribed austerity for India's middle classes over many decades. Correspondingly, consumption remains powerfully associated with higher social status. In the post-industrial West, by contrast, proletarian consumption is now understood as an economic necessity, and even as a civic responsibility. Nonetheless, whether formally sanctioned or not, modern India has always had a large consuming economy by merit of its sheer size. Equally, that consumption has extended well beyond material goods to accommodate the intrinsic cultural needs of complex social organization. Here, the enthusiasm for a range of pursuits (from sports to movies, from pilgrimages to shopping trips and from texting to eating out) has formed an ever increasing constituent of the nation's social and economic life. Accordingly, one of the most striking features of India's engagement with liberalization and globalization has been the runaway success of a sector that was seen as a secondary concern by India's planners during the socialist era.

Until recently, this was also a domain little understood by Western exporters and investors. For this reason, early international expositions of liberalization in India focused on blue-sky projections for the consumption of consumer durables by India's middle classes. However, this overarching notion of India as an emerging market for imported goods was soon supplanted by a widespread recognition of the new prominence of India as a source of global media 'flows' and as a service provider to the global economy. This shift in emphasis from tangible consumption to a 'knowledge economy' provider has been paralleled by two decades of rapid growth in India's media industries. On the back of rising investment, the entertainment and services category has consistently enjoyed a greater rate of growth than the rest of the economy during the liberalization era (PriceWaterhouseCoopers 2008). These rising trends have been exemplified by the expanding global ambitions of the film industry, the domestic television boom, critical mass in ITES, the rapid diffusion of mobile telecoms and the explosion of cross-media advertising. As such, the vaunted 'new economy' of India as it stands today is largely imagined in terms of the cumulative aspirations enshrined in the software park, the shopping mall and the multiplex (Athique and Hill 2010; Voyce 2007; Stallmeyer 2011). Thus, it is reasonable to argue that, in its present phase at least, India's experiments in post-industrial economy signify a nascent leisure economy, one that is manifested within a highly particular physical and human geography.

Media Structures

The media industries are doubtless the most critical component in the present form of the leisure economy, and their prominence has been shaped by significant structural changes in mass communications. Prior to the liberalization era, there was a longstanding tripartite division in the Indian media. The primary division within the formal economy was between the state-owned industries and the privately owned business houses. In India, these are collectively referred to as the 'organized' sector. The counterpart to both is the 'unorganized' sector, made up of small businesses and traders reaching deep into the unregulated informal economy. Prior to the 1990s, broadcasting, telecoms and documentary film were all state preserves. Publishing and the press, along with the manufacturing of consumer electronics, were located in the 'organized' sector of the economy. Commercial films operated in the 'unorganized' sector, and therefore at the margins of the informal economy. To be entirely accurate, most media forms crossed these boundaries in some form, but they nonetheless remained stratified by them. Information technology, for example, was developed by both state and private actors in the formal economy, with the 'big stuff' going to the government (Subramanian 1992). Elsewhere, the demarcation was an aesthetic one. Classical Indian music, for example, was produced for state-owned All India Radio. Vinyl records were manufactured and marketed to a small upmarket customer base by privately owned HMV in the 'organized' sector. For much of the 1980s, popular music and film music reached the masses via the cassette medium, a business that operated in the 'unorganized sector' (Kohli-Khandekar 2006: 148–50).

The term 'unorganized' may itself be somewhat misleading given the great complexity of small-business activity in India, which continues to dwarf the state-owned and corporate concerns which constitute the 'organized' sector (Dutt and Rao 2000: 26). Given the considerable coordination requisite for any industrial mass media system to operate, I prefer to use the term 'disorganized', which implies a dispersal of organization rather a lack of it. In that sense, the Indian film industry appeared to be 'disorganized' when compared with the model of formally integrated operations set by the film industry of the United States, where a handful of corporations control the entire product chain from production through to exhibition. By contrast, the 'disorganized' film industry in India was characterized by the dispersal of working capital and assets amongst large numbers of small, independent operators with a common interest in the successful exploitation of cinematic culture. Typically, these ventures were dispersed across the delivery chain and often had competing interests. The 'disorganized' structure made sense against the backdrop of tight regulations applied to larger businesses and the incentives introduced by Indira Gandhi for private businesses to remain relatively small. In that sense, the state protected government industries through formal monopolies, and protected India's larger private businesses from foreign competition and smaller private businesses from the bigger ones. The 'disorganized' sector, when it was considered, was sporadically targeted for enforcement of regulations and for taxation.

The adoption of the liberalization doctrine has rewritten those rules. Private enterprise was given the lead first in information technology (1984) and subsequently in television (1997), telecoms (1999) and radio (2000). Large state-owned entities such as broadcaster Doordarshan and the Electronics Corporation of India continue to play a major role, but deregulation has directed the majority of growth towards the private sector. Similarly, regulatory changes have also removed many of the disincentives for media companies to grow larger, as well as incrementally loosening the restrictions on international trade and investment that had kept the Indian media within what was, effectively, a closed market. The shift from a state-dominated media economy to one that is overwhelmingly private-sector led has also been symptomatic of a 'post-industrial' approach to the media. Previously, the importance of media was seen to lie in three areas: dissemination of information to the public, facilitation of public communications and the promotion of indigenous cultural forms. None of these functions was overtly commercial in orientation. Today, the primary importance given to the media lies in quite different areas: the generation of intangible commodities of trade, facilitation of new forms of consumption, dissemination of technical literacy and the provision of entertainment services (Kohli-Khandekar 2006). Within this context, previous distinctions between cultural and commercial value, and between public and private interest, have been significantly eroded. Thus, arguably, the logics that for decades guided state regulation of the media have been overwhelmed by the commercial potentials of an expanding media environment.

Nonetheless, we also need to consider the 'pull' factors that may have influenced policy changes. In that respect, the fostering of profitable creative and communications industries has clearly underpinned a wider strategic engagement with the globalization experiment. Media deregulation has transformed costly public services into lucrative commercial services attracting investment, which is also reclaiming 'entertainment' areas such as film and music from the tax-averse informal economy. It has also facilitated new revenue streams that could transcend basic infrastructure shortages in ways that the old manufacturing economy could not. Attention to areas such as advertising and ITES has allowed India to leverage the commercial benefits of its large population and its investments in education. In many respects, the change of heart towards the media industries in recent years is symptomatic of a shift from a formal economic logic centred on production capacity to one driven by consumption growth. For all these reasons, it is worth paying attention to the degree to which the media revolution has not been so much grudgingly conceded to the market by a weakening state, but actively facilitated by government policy at the federal and state levels. The phrase 'deregulation' which has commonly been associated with the transformation of India's media industries can be misleading, since it is not simply the repeal of legislative obstacles that has benefited the sector but also the introduction of new legislation that has consciously favoured the development of a 'post-industrial' economic base in urban India (Ahmed, Kundu and Peet 2010). This intervention by government has functioned at a number of levels, from tax exemptions to the re-zoning of residential, agricultural and industrial land for ITES, media and retail developments (Aranya 2003; Athique 2009; Athique and Hill 2007).

Global Integration

While many of the idiosyncrasies of India's liberalization programme do need to be understood within a national frame, it is also important that we consider the impetus for these changes within the wider global context. In the first place, liberalization is an intellectual position with a long pedigree and a global constituency. It has always had its adherents within India, but they were in a minority for much of the independence period due to the relative weakness of Indian industry in comparable terms and, equally, due to the historical exploitation of India by the British in the name of free trade. By the 1980s, however, the business community that had grown considerably during three decades of state-protection became more frustrated with government bureaucracy and more confident about its competitiveness. Accordingly, a significant cohort within Indian business became vocally supportive of a less regulated operating environment. Enthusiasm for a turn away from manufacturing and towards media and services has been a more recent development, and this has been undertaken largely in emulation of (or in concert with) the profits generated by 'post-industrial' strategies in the developed countries. The media industries, therefore, can be seen as a test case for the ongoing experiments in both privatization and globalization. In the first scenario, they have seen the withdrawal of state monopoly from key areas of activity, and, in the latter, they have made a transition over two decades from an almost wholly indigenous pattern of ownership to an operating environment where international business models and foreign direct investment (FDI) now play a major role.

Prior to liberalization, the role of foreign companies in India was generally limited to the marketing, importation or assembly of their products in a minority partnership with an Indian concern or through a part-stake in an Indian subsidiary. Two decades on, 100 per cent foreign investment is now permitted across the film industry, in television programming and in most forms of publishing aside from news. As such, the size and scope of foreign holdings in the Indian media sector has increased dramatically. Japan's Sony, for example, after entering the Indian television market in 1995 with Sony Entertainment Television (SET), has developed further subsidiaries in film production, radio and recorded music, along with its core activity in consumer electronics. News Corporation has expanded its interests across the delivery chain of television, from satellite broadcasting to programming, cable operation and direct-to-home (DTH) systems. Britain's Vodafone Group has become the second largest provider of mobile telecoms with 135 million subscribers through its majority-owned Indian subsidiary. The expanding interests of these international media companies, along with increased foreign investment portfolios in Indian media companies, provides some evidence for India's incorporation into a broader global media apparatus. The close integration of the Indian ITES sector with the global IT industry is an even stronger example of this, evidenced by the operational presence of all the major multinational IT companies in India today. It is also significant to note that the remaining restrictions on FDI in media, where they do not pertain to news services, are centred on ownership of delivery infrastructure, rather than on content. In that sense, the doors have been opened wide to foreign media content, which is really now only restricted by general censorship laws, linguistic barriers and the cultural filters constituted by Indian audiences.

Accordingly, we can see the newfound interest of international media outlets in Indian popular culture as a reflection of the extent to which those companies now see themselves as players in the Indian market. In turn, this recognition overseas has stoked the ambitions of Indian media companies and leveraged a higher degree of domestic investment from the banks and business houses that previously showed little interest in media sectors (such as film) that were open to the private sector. Initially, it was the massive growth in Indian television from the mid-1990s onwards that provided much of the impetus for re-evaluating the commercial potentials of media. This operated in tandem with the rapid expansion of the advertising industry, which has promoted a new agenda for establishing Western-style retail businesses to serve an expanding middle class. The success of the ITES experiment within 'Special Economic Zones' (SEZs) delivered a marked increase in disposable income to its employees, as well as a greater engagement with 'international' lifestyles that made them an obvious constituency for this new culture of consumption. Presently, both domestic and international businesses remain highly attentive to the potentials of India's new middle classes, albeit for slightly different reasons. For domestic investors, the change in overall policy direction is opening up new commercial opportunities in media, circumventing the tight hold of state companies and established business houses in many other sectors. For foreign investors, it is the obvious saturation of markets for leisure and services in so many developed countries that is driving their search for new markets in the developing world.

It is also critical to note that the influence of foreign companies exceeds their formal business holdings by a considerable margin. It is not only capital and new technologies that they have brought into the Indian market in recent years, but also a new set of operational procedures, structures and terminologies. These are business models established under quite different socio-economic conditions, and for the most part, they have been necessarily adapted to the Indian context through various strategies of what Robertson called 'glocalization' (1994). At the same time, however, the inculcation of 'international' business models amongst their Indian staff has been influential in transforming the overall business culture throughout their respective areas of activity. It is significant to note, therefore, that many of India's successful new media companies have been guided by former employees or business partners of the multinationals. This broader influence upon the business culture has been strengthened by the longstanding convention for the Indian elites to seek an overseas tertiary education for their children. While the UK is a favoured provider for historical reasons, it has been the United States that has become the most significant destination over the past two decades. As India's middle classes have expanded, their upper echelons have sent their children to join this temporary diaspora, and in the process a growing cohort of students has come into contact with the new managerial disciplines that have formalized the worldview of contemporary American business culture within the university system. Upon returning to India, these overseas graduates have often been instrumental in reorienting their family businesses towards this new international standard in commercial motive, innovation and operation. Thus, just as international companies have sought to 'glocalize', their Indian competitors have acquired, emulated and 'indigenized' international business models with considerable success.

The Corporate Agenda

Traditionally, Indian commercial culture has been dominated by a family business model, from the lower reaches of the informal economy right up to the small number of big business houses that dominate commercial activity in the organized sector. Capitalization through share markets has been far less commonplace than it is in developed economies. Organizational structures were often strictly hierarchical and feudal, with a small number of centralized decision-makers and a public image that was significantly personalized in the social status of the business owners. The counterpart to this mode of operations was formed by the public-sector enterprises, where the stratified hierarchies of the civil service were reproduced within a more secular, but similarly top-down, mode of operations. In that sense, India's newspaper families were 'press barons' in the older sense of the term, and the directors of the state media were bureaucratic managers rather than business leaders. As investors from India and abroad have begun to invest heavily in media platforms, however, these old operating logics have been infused with a new commercial epistemology modelled on the competitive corporatism of North American capitalism. In this context, there is a significant divestment of operational control to an expanded management strata, a fostering of internal competition and a greater focus on the projection of 'brand value' within the market. The media companies that are seen to exemplify this new ethos are generally referred to as 'corporates' in contemporary business literature. As a signifier, this term denotes a larger, publicly financed company, a transparent business model and an impersonal, meritocratic operational structure. This self-conscious public image is a direct result of the inflow of external investments and share capital into the media business, and the subsequent need to cultivate market confidence.

In the past decade, concerted efforts have been made to reorient the film industry away from the margins of India's informal economy and into the ambit of the big business houses. This is a goal that requires a large-scale aggregation of interests within what has traditionally been a highly fragmented industry with largely informal organization. The agenda of 'corporatization' has proffered a substantial degree of operational change within the film industry, as it redefines its primary markets in terms of higher-value customers, both overseas and in the domestic market. Corporatization in this arena is directed by a business model that is strongly influenced by the post-Reagan Hollywood milieu. However, given the uniquely fragmented nature of the Indian film industries as a starting point, the corporate agenda remains very much a work-in-progress at the present time. After a decade of official recognition as an industry suitable for legitimate investment, the bulk of the film industry, and the regional language industries in particular, continue to operate within the informal economy. Nonetheless, the transformation of the film industry is much more advanced now than it was even just a few years ago. The leading Bollywood producers are targeting international revenues, undertaking their own marketing and distribution, and getting access to new sources of legitimate finance. Overseas distributors such as Eros, Indian Films and UTV have also raised significant sums on international exchanges. These activities are steadily transforming the relationships between exhibitors, distributors and producers, and unsurprisingly all of this has upset the balance of power in the film world. At the same time, however, even the largest production houses still fall well short of anything comparable to a Hollywood studio, typically operating as a family business with an output of less than a dozen films a year.

Where the corporate model has been more expansive is in the exhibition sector. Here, significant share capital has been raised by a raft of newly constituted companies, in support of a new exhibition infrastructure targeting the more affluent segments of the population (Athique 2009). In this context, the international format of the multiplex cinema has operated as a demarcation between the corporate media paradigm and the loose network of single-screen one-size-fits-all family-owned cinemas that previously constituted the delivery infrastructure for the film industry (Athique and Hill 2010). By targeting a high-end audience, a handful of multiplex companies now dominate the domestic box office, attracting investment from India's big league. As a result, they have diversified into the production and distribution of films, as well as pursuing interests in food courts, gaming and other areas of entertainment. Initially, the multiplex experiment began in 1997 when Ajay Bijli entered into a partnership with Australian exhibition chain Village Roadshow, in order to reinvigorate his family cinema business in New Delhi. Subsequently, Mumbai-based distributors Shringar Films (1999) and film-processing company Adlabs (2000) launched their own multiplex projects. All three companies subsequently raised share capital on the markets to fund rapid expansion programmes. Benefiting from targeted tax exemptions and readily available commercial premises via the shopping mall boom, the multiplex chains spread rapidly in the major urban centres. As a result of this success, both Shringar Cinemas and Adlabs were subsequently acquired by larger businesses from outside of the film industry. Adlabs was acquired in 2005 by the land investment arm of the Reliance ADA Group, one of India's biggest corporate business houses. Shringar Cinemas was absorbed in 2010, by INOX Leisure Ltd, a wholly owned corporate subsidiary of Gujarat Flourochemicals.

Another player in the multiplex boom has been Subhash Chandra's Essel Group. The Essel Group, which started out in 1982 as a packaging company, famously diversified into the media in 1992 when chairman Subhash Chandra launched ZEE television, India's first satellite channel. During periods of both partnership and competition with Rupert Murdoch's STAR, ZEE has been a giant of India's television boom. ZEE TV presently operates a suite of regional, national and international television channels. The parent company, Essel, had made earlier forays into the leisure economy with a number of theme parks, starting with Essel World in Mumbai in 1988. Subsequently, new ventures have been undertaken in the media sector under the auspices of E City Ventures, launched in 1999, which is composed of five divisions: E-City Entertainment (developing and running shopping malls since 2001), E-City Films (film distribution since 2001), E-City Digital Cinemas (rolling out digital distribution and exhibition technology since 2004), E-City Property Management Services (offering management expertise to private shopping mall owners) and, finally, FUN Multiplex. This broad range of interests is also characteristic of ZEE's regional competitor in South India, SUN TV, which was India's first privately owned television broadcaster in 1992. A public company since 2005, SUN now operates around twenty television channels, six newspapers, two large radio broadcasters, and a film production and distribution company. In 2010, SUN founder Kalnidhi Maran took a major stake in low-cost airline SpiceJet.

The Reliance ADA interest in the multiplex business has been extended by the acquisition of cinema assets in Malaysia and the United States, along with major holdings in radio, television, computer gaming, websites and event management. Reliance ADA is also the third biggest provider of mobile telephone services in India, with 120 million customers. The telecoms holdings of the group are massively extended by the ownership of the world's largest private undersea cable network, providing information capacity around the world. Both Reliance ADA Group and Reliance Industries (textiles, petrochemicals) have emerged from the business empire of Anil Dhirubhai Ambani, an entrepreneur who turned a polyester business into one of the largest conglomerates in the world by tapping into middle-class investors through the stock market. Probably, the inverse of the exuberant new money of Reliance in the media sector would be Bennett, Coleman and Co. Ltd, founded in the colonial era and owned since 1946 by the Jain family. Nonetheless, the BCCL's Times Group has also diversified from its flagship English-language newspaper and magazine assets into web content, television, radio, film production and event management. BCCL has also acquired regional newspapers in India as well as extending the publication of the *Times of India* into regional editions. This expansion of the 'old media' has been largely funded by the rapid growth in advertising revenues throughout the media boom, with BCCL well placed at the outset to command a large slice of this market. There are still some major players who pursue a more singular focus. *The Hindu*, for example, continues to operate as a traditional, family-owned newspaper, albeit with a hugely successful online edition. Bharti Airtel, as the largest mobile phone provider in India, and fifth largest in the world, remains focused upon that business, recently expanding into the provision of international services across Africa and Asia. Diversification, however, appears to have become the norm amongst the corporate media.

The biggest brands in information technology, Wipro, Infosys and Satyam, have seen sufficient expansion in that sector to sustain their ambitions for growth. Given the expanding domain of ITES, however, they have diversified substantially from software programming and consultancy into a broad array of BPO and service transactions across the financial, healthcare and travel sectors. Given their close engagement with global business, the ITES companies are often seen as the most genuine corporates in India. Infosys began as a business partnership amongst technically minded entrepreneurs in much the same way the US giant Microsoft operated in its early years. Wipro, despite having emerged out of a parent concern in vegetable oils, has been listed as a public company since the 1940s. As a consequence of serving its shareholders, and being aware of the importance of a comparable business culture to its overseas customer base, Wipro chairman Azim Premji has fostered the corporate model over many decades. Hyderabad-based Satyam, however, has become a much more problematic representative of corporate India. Despite the outward similarity of Satyam to its competitors, in terms of its business model and organization this company continued to be guided behind the scenes by the feudal loyalties of its founders. In 2009, this led to the biggest corporate scandal in India, when it was discovered that Ramalingu Raju, chairman of Satyam, had been funnelling billions of company revenues into the businesses and bank accounts of his close family members. The Satyam scandal, which has been referred to as 'India's Enron', has clearly tarnished the image of the corporate sector, but, inversely, it has also revealed the extent to which a new business culture has taken root. While the cross-subsidization of feudal conglomerates has been a marked feature of Indian capitalism over a long period of time, it was against the new corporate paradigm that the affairs at Satyam were judged and found wanting.

Convergence and the Leisure Economy

Prior to the liberalization era there was a very clear distinction between the major media industries in India, and it was entirely defensible to analyse the Indian media as distinct entities with their own specialized markets. This is clearly no longer the case because, as the commercial media industries have expanded their fortunes, they have become increasingly interlinked. One highly visible outcome of this influx of capital is the collapsing distinction between the various media industries, as the film industries find new profits in television schedules, TV companies begin to invest in film production and multiplexes, and advertisers use film culture to market fashion and telecoms. Across the world, liberalization of the media has tended to strengthen processes of 'vertical integration' where dominant players acquire interests across all stages of production and delivery at the expense of small or more specialized companies. Similarly, the repeal of restrictions on cross-media ownership opens the gates to 'horizontal integration', where established media corporations diversify their interests across a range of other media formats. In the present phase of globalization, these related processes of integration and expansion have also been determined by the impact of digital technologies upon the production and delivery of previously distinct media forms. In that respect, the growth of multimedia capacity in software and consumer electronics has significantly eroded the technical, commercial and aesthetic distinctions between media products. As a result, the experience of media consumption has become characterized by a multimedia environment in which cultural goods and communication services are co-located.

In conceptualizing the technical and commercial developments of the present era, Henry Jenkins has predicted that the future media environment will be determined by a matrix of technological integration, capital accumulation, institutional diversification and cultural synthesis that can be best understood as a multifaceted process of convergence (2006). The rise of large-scale media conglomerates under the auspices of business houses like Reliance ADA is an indication of the incorporation of the 'convergence' paradigm in the present remaking of the Indian media. It is in this new operating context that the difficulty of analysing the media in isolation from the interests of the wider economy has become increasingly apparent. Thus, not only do we need to recognize the expansion of various media and their growing importance within the wider economy overall, but we also need to be aware of the ways in which their activities are being integrated into India's formal economy. In that respect, the contours of media convergence in India are being dictated not simply by technological remediation, but to a similar extent by the dynamics of India's metropolitan real estate, the ambitions of the retail sector and the diversification projects of companies originating in previously favoured heavy industries such as textiles, chemicals, sugar and plastics. Over the past decade, liberalization has unleashed processes of cross-media integration, which seem likely to be furthered by the ambitions of these big companies to combine media interests with other sites of leisure such as food courts, shopping malls and theme parks. This is a powerful indication of the growing interface between traditional media and a larger and more tightly orchestrated leisure economy. By consciously identifying the epicentres of the 'new economy' as its target market, the new leisure infrastructure emerging from the corporate agenda further cements the link between post-industrial production and recreational consumption.

Jenkins model of convergence also directs us towards the cultural trends within a new world of technologically integrated consumption (2004). As such, the very proposition of an Indian leisure economy indicates three major pairings of culture and economy: the political economy of the cultural industries, the anthropology of commercial activity and the cultural specificity of India which attaches particular symbolic meanings to leisure. Most likely, the interchanges between these three pairings will determine the future direction of the leisure economy. Having addressed the first two pairings to some extent, it is fitting that we now turn our attention towards the culture of contemporary media content, and the broader culture of consumption to which it relates. It is in this context that the ascendance of the Bollywood brand, and its dominant position within an expanded field of popular culture, plays a central role in the exposition of a recreational consuming economy. As the pre-eminent resource within a restricted field of popular culture under the earlier paradigm of development, it was inevitable that the new outlets of commercial television and Internet content would turn to the popular film for their central aesthetic. As much as the emulation of an international standard in the audiovisual field predisposed the adoption of Western media formats, it was the semi-illicit cultural capital of the Indian cinema, and its ritualized iconicity, that presented itself as the most suitable vehicle for the 'glocalization' of those formats. Accordingly, the runaway success of the British quiz format, *Who Wants to be a Millionaire?*, for STAR TV was largely guaranteed by the presence of veteran movie star Amitabh Bachchan as its host. As Amit Rai has noted, 'For some years after the advent of liberalization in India, one dominant trend of potentializing and capturing screen space was product placement . . . now whole segments are shot as if they were in fact commercials for a product . . . as veritable vehicles for Amitabh Bachchan's career as a product endorser' (2009: 114).

On the big screen, the new hero, as he moves between business in New York, shopping in London and endless marriage celebrations in Punjab, articulates an 'ideal' globalization for the Indian middle classes. Explicitly, these discursive attempts to stabilize Indian-ness via the paradigm of the global Indian are intended to assert cultural particularity against the tide of cultural convergence associated with a global media apparatus dominated by the West. Implicitly, however, the 'global Indian' as a privileged subject of popular culture marks the diegetic appropriation of the hybrid subject as a metaphor for occidental pleasures (Kaur 2002). As such, the current refashioning of Indian popular culture is infused with referents to indigeneity at many levels, while being simultaneously encoded with an overtly 'Westernized' model of cultural consumption. This dual address, which is intended to mitigate the contradictions of globalization within a consciously nationalistic frame, has also been identified as the most suitable vehicle for commercial persuasion in a developing society where the tradition/modernity binary still holds sway (Mazarella 2003: 149–211). Outside of the screen space itself, the limited availability of recognized celebrities has seen a small stable of Bollywood stars dominating the brave new world of commercial advertising. The huge painted images of movie stars that previously dominated the facades of Indian cinemas are now surrounded by countless billboards across the urban landscape, where those same faces promote mobile phones, cars and cosmetics. Although it is not readily apparent whether Shah Rukh Khan advertising scores of different products really constitutes star value for the advertisers, as opposed to simply extending the brand value of Shah Rukh Khan, it is clear that the iconic status of the star image formally expresses the wedding of culture and commerce that guides the new leisure economy. As Sudhanva Deshpande notes, 'this new, consumable hero wears Gap shirts and Nike sneakers, and when he dances, it is in front of McDonalds outlets in white man's land, or Hollywood studios, or swanky trains, and has white girls – not Indian peasants – dancing with him' (Deshpande 2005: 197).

As with most areas of India's new economy, the cultural field of the leisure economy is demarcated by a very particular social imagination. This worldview is overwhelmingly determined by the perceived aspirations of an expanding middle class 'unfettered' by liberalization. Although longstanding speculation on the economic potential of India's middle classes as a consumer market has given us a textbook case of optimistic, and self-interested, marketing literature, there is no doubt that the extent of the median ranges in India's population has grown steadily in recent decades. In the process, the old, bourgeois culture of the neo-colonial class, and its autocratic socialism, has been supplanted by a more emotive, populist and middlebrow culture that is assertive in its material aspirations and highly conscious of its newfound status. It is this group that now bears the burden of the development process, being given an instrumental definition as the 'consumer classes' by the National Council of Applied Economic Research (NCAER 1994). Under this scheme, India's middle classes, situated between the tiny elite and the utterly destitute have been classified under three bands, 'consumers', 'climbers' and 'aspirants' (Varma 1998: 171). According to Leela Fernandes, this 'culturally constructed' imagined community is intended to embody 'a cultural standard associated with the globalizing Indian nation' which 'proponents of liberalization have sought to deploy . . . as an idealized standard that other groups can aspire to' (2004: 2418). One of the best known of those proponents is Gurcharan Das, whose book *India Unbound* makes a powerful case for rebuilding Indian economy and society around the industriousness and aspirations of these new middle classes (2002). According to Das, 'When half the population is middle class, its politics will change, its worldview will be different . . . Thus to focus on the middle class is to focus on prosperity' (2002: 351).

In this context, it is perhaps unsurprising that the cultural form of media content in the present epoch has been particularly indicative of a consistent, if not always coherent, push to create a hegemonic cultural address that articulates the ideal of a 'globalized' consuming middle class. After all, it is the capacity and propensity of these groups to consume that underpins the business models for commercial media expansion, and that provides the 'eyeballs' that attract investment flows into the media. As such, the symbolic dominance of the consuming class in the social imagination is inevitably played out in both textual and material realms. It is the prevailing trope across the intertextual range of what Anustap Basu has called the 'geo-televisual aesthetic' of contemporary Bollywood style (Basu 2010). It is materialized in the new infrastructure of shopping malls and multiplexes that allows the corporate leisure economy to physically distance itself from the 'Third World' media economy of the recent past (Athique and Hill 2007). At the same time, the explicit alignment of the emerging corporate leisure economy with the urban consuming classes undermines its substitution for the universal, pan-Indian domain claimed by the old 'national' media systems. At present, we could assert anything from 100 to 250 million people as a broad estimate of the full extent of the consuming classes across the county (Fernandes 2006; Scrase and Ganguly-Scrase 2010), that is, between one tenth and one fifth of the population overall. The remainder, while they may wish to avail themselves of an expanded range of media services and new leisure environments, lack the financial capacity to do so, in some cases by a large margin. Furthermore, the new hybrid dialect of 'Hinglish' fostered by commercial television (and its intrinsic mentality) does not speak to, and is not spoken by, the majority of the population. For this reason, even on the streets of New Delhi, the roving television reporter appears to approach the common man as a foreign subject in much the same way as Western reporters encounter Third World citizens within the already-tired conventions of rotating global news.

In this respect, the enlargement of the leisure economy under the present paradigm necessarily encounters the inherent dichotomy of the mass media. That is, in laying claim to a universal address they make an implicit commitment to the entire population, even when their commercial rationale and the interests of their sponsors do not extend beyond a fraction of that audience. To date, the liberalization era has seen a rapid profusion of new media content and services become available for the high- to middle-income groups of urban India, but the same cannot be said for larger groups that are poor, rural or both. For the urban poor, the continued existence of the old leisure infrastructure, in the form of dilapidated family-owned cinemas, open grounds and street vendors, alleviates to some extent their exclusion from the ambitions of the new leisure economy. At the same time, the differences in ownership, operation and, increasingly, content between the two infrastructures is glaringly apparent. In the former, imported models of retail operation, American jeans and the multimedia Bollywood aesthetic rub shoulders with branded advertising, cell phones and Hinglish conversation. In the latter, the regional-language films that have been largely eschewed by the corporates are played for an audience that marks the intermission by chewing paan, smoking beedies and buying snacks from itinerant vendors on the pavement outside. This is by far the larger part of the film audience in India, although it is already considered to be of lesser importance than the 'creamy layer' that can spend at the multiplexes and the nearby shopping malls. The pressing question of whether the corporate leisure economy will eventually seek to service the bulk of the Indian population remains debatable, since it would be dependent upon the capacity (and the desire) of organized leisure to cater to audiences whose purchasing power is small. For example, a television environment driven by advertising revenues has little incentive to consider the villages of India that lie beyond the spillover of its existing footprint.

Media Provision and Economic Development

At the present time, there are two distinctly different tiers of operation for the Indian media industries that are serviced respectively by organized and disorganized entertainment infrastructures. The distinction has emerged largely on the basis of their physical location and the wealth of their customers. Since it is unlikely that the half-a-billion Indians living a hand-to-mouth existence are likely to join the ranks of cosmopolitan consumers any time soon, we can expect to see the continuation of both tiers of leisure infrastructure for many years to come. Needless to say, the widening distinction between these two tiers, and the differential in their market value, has many implications for the professionals who work in the cultural domain. Already, the pursuit of a one-size-fits all approach to media content is becoming a thing of the past. At one level, we could see this positively as evidence of a more mature market where consumers can be targeted effectively on the basis of their personal interests and assets. More negatively, we could see this as the narrowcasting of divergent taste cultures separating the haves and have-nots in the new India. Looking forward, it certainly seems entirely plausible that the middle and lower classes will become formally separated in terms of their cultural environment and their leisure entitlements. Already, during a period of unprecedented media expansion, we have seen fault lines appearing between metropolitan and district audiences, between richer and poorer regions of the country, and between the older and younger generations. Inevitably, this raises serious questions about the viability of a common media culture capable of operating across the different strata of Indian society, and this is likely to have significant implications for the operation of the public sphere in the years to come.

The limitations of the constituency for the new leisure economy, large as it may be in numerical terms, is an indication of the inherent difficulty of media provision in a developing country. In that sense, the sheer scale of Indian society provides a useful illustration of the applicability of a post-industrial model of development. With its enormous human resources, India has demonstrated within a short space of time that it possesses the intellect, organization and acumen to develop a sophisticated range of post-industrial activities. It is also clear that within the confines of the consuming classes there is sufficient wealth and demand to justify the formalization of the leisure economy in India. This domain has already proved large enough to accommodate significant competition from major international media companies, thereby connecting India to the global media apparatus without being reduced to a franchise operation. The successful translation of the overlapping logics of liberalization, corporatization and convergence would appear to indicate that the post-industrial model has real economic potential for the developing world. It would also appear that this model is readily available to countries that have not yet achieved a fully industrialized economy or a fully developed national infrastructure. Along with take-up of investment opportunities in media and services, new technological innovations have allowed India to quickly overcome the infrastructure bottlenecks that previously restricted the spread of communications. The willingness to pursue this particular path has also been reflective of a desire to develop the leisure economy in a form comparable to the 'global standard', and the means chosen for doing so are in themselves an indication of the much closer cultural relationship with the United States that has been intrinsic to the liberalization era. This becomes particularly apparent in the media sectors, where the influence of American business and management culture is symbolically reinforced by the broader influence of American popular culture.

On a more cautious note, the fact that the majority of India's post-industrial activity either serves overseas clients or competes for the attention of an overall minority of the domestic population is also an indication that the post-industrial model can only be applied selectively. Indebted farmers

149

committing suicide on a large scale and the hardships now being caused for the urban poor by the rising cost of basic foods provide obvious indicators that the post-industrial stage of development remains very much dependent upon the prior, and continuing, operation of agricultural and industrial systems (Dev and Chandrasekhara 2009). In that respect, the fact that the recent expansion of the leisure economy in urban India has been accompanied by deepening distress in the agrarian sector points us towards inherent flaws in the 'staged' approach to development. The whole of India is no better placed to make a transition into a fully post-industrial society than the world is as a whole. Of themselves, media technologies cannot alleviate the poverty that removes the larger section of the Indian population from the radar of commercial investors. Better communications and the expansion of knowledge can lead to improvements in health, productive efficiency and the perceived quality of life, but they cannot overwrite the material constraints of environmental degradation, population growth and the scarcity of resources. In that sense, taking the Indian case, it would appear that the leisurely ideal of a post-industrial society can only be realized as a subset of activities within a larger and more diverse society.

Further Reading

Ahmed, Waquar, Kundu, Amitabh and Peet, Richard (2010) *India's New Economic Policy: A Critical Analysis*, London and New York: Routledge.

Athique, Adrian and Hill, Douglas (2010) *The Multiplex in India: A Cultural Economy of Urban Leisure*, London and New York: Routledge.

Das, Gurcharan (2002) *India Unbound: From Independence to the Global Information Age*, New Delhi: Penguin.

Fernandes, Leela (2006) *India's New Middle Class: Democratic Politics in an Era of Democratic Reform*, Minneapolis, MN, and London: University of Minnesota Press.

Kohli-Khandekar, Vanita (2010) *The Indian Media Business*, 3rd edn, New Delhi: Response Books.

Kumar, Krishan (2005) *From Post-Industrial to Post-Modern Society: New Theories of the Contemporary World*, Oxford: Blackwell.

Mazarella, William (2003) *Shovelling Smoke: Advertising and Globalization in Contemporary India*, Durham, NC, and London: Duke University Press.

Thomas, Pradip Ninan (2010) *Political Economy of Communications in India: The Good, The Bad and the Ugly*, New Delhi: Sage.

Afterword: Indian Media and the Asian Century

Over the past decade, India has come to occupy a prominent place in the discussion of globalization. Within this context, it has typically been India's economic potentials that have been given greater emphasis over its political or cultural influence. In many respects, this constitutes a broad reversal of the general perception of India's position on the world stage. As of today, India is widely predicted to become one of the world's major commercial powers over the first part of this century. At the same time, however, India's rise is most commonly considered in comparison with the recent emergence of China as the second largest global economy and one of the most powerful trading nations. In that context, we now hear of India as the world's fastest-growing major economy (after China), the fastest-growing audience for television (after China), the largest emerging market for goods and services (after China), and so on. Inevitably, then, given their geographical proximity in the Asian region and their parallel size and importance in the contemporary world, the two countries have become objects of mutual comparison over the past decade. It is equally inevitable that such comparisons bring to light the many differences between the two nations. India is a complex and vibrant democracy, while China is ruled by an unelected autarchic elite. China's ethnic diversity remains subject to the longstanding dominance of the Han culture, while India has no similarly hegemonic culture. Religion is firmly off the agenda in Chinese politics, while taking centre stage in contemporary Indian politics. As such, there are very marked differences in the cultural and political domains operating in the two Asian giants.

During the golden era of the liberalization-led global economy after 1991, the two countries have also received disparate assessments from global markets. It could be said that international investors have appeared to favour the autocratic operation of Chinese state-capitalism to the democratic realities and bureaucratic complexities of doing business in India. However, within the specific domains where India has been able to make use of its earlier investments in technical education, India has developed quite different niches within the globalization paradigm. Media and information technologies are a case in point, and in this domain India holds many advantages (Curtin 2010). Presently, China's greatest strength and weakness is its newfound status as a manufacturer for a post-industrial United States. India, by comparison, is much less exposed to the changing fortunes of North America. Chinese manufactures, however, do represent significant competition for their Indian counterparts. Thus, in so far as the focus of comparison is centred on their shifting status as developing societies pursuing economic growth, we could identify key differences in economic outcomes stemming from their respective approaches to export-led and import-substitution manufacturing (Das 2006). Of course, one broad similarity is that both countries spent several decades attempting to achieve economic take-off in relative isolation from the global capitalist economy. For much of the twentieth century, China's communist ideology implied a far more radical rejection of the Western model than did the Fabian socialism of postcolonial India. However, what they shared in their previous inclination for nationalist economics was a keen awareness of the subordinate positions imposed upon them during the long reign of European imperialism.

In the making of the present epoch, the conversion of China from a communist to command capitalist economy has marked a much greater ideological reorientation than has India's incremental liberalization of its mixed economy. As a simplification, we could see the zeal of outright conversion as outperforming India's longstanding inclinations towards caution and compromise. However, when we begin to look in greater depth at the trajectory of the two countries, it becomes apparent that a competitive comparison may not be the most suitable approach, partly because there are significant differences in their respective strengths, and partly because in most areas of direct comparison China enjoys a clear lead (at least for the short term). Jairam Ramesh has suggested that instead of focusing on the competing interests of the two countries, we should pay more attention to the potentials for a mutually beneficial relationship between what he calls 'Chindia' (2007). By this reading, a commitment to significant areas of cooperation could form the basis for a closer bilateral relationship by which each nation benefits from the success of the other, as opposed to both countries wasting their energies competing for Western markets, for hegemony in South East Asia or for resources in Africa. The most commonly cited example for cooperation has been a putative linkage between India's expertise in software and China's capacity for hardware production in information technologies (Athwal 2008: 94). However, as a primarily Indian initiative, it has also been noted that India has more to gain from the 'Chindia' paradigm than does China, which has been relatively lukewarm to the idea (Raj Isar 2010). Further afield, the term 'Chindia' has taken on a different significance as commentators have tended to read the combination of the two rising economic powers as heralding the demise of Euro-American dominance over the global economy, and the beginning of an 'Asian century' (e.g., Jacques 2009; Mabhubani 2008).

Thus, while the critical relationship between the two countries has seen little development on the ground, the growing status of the two nations is seen to signify a broader phenomenon where the development process in Asia has finally progressed beyond the tutelage of the West. By this reading of the term, it is the emerging relationship between 'Chindia' and the rest of the world that counts rather than their bilateral relations (Straubhaar 2010).

The Case for Connectivity

In its own right, the Indian case provides some powerful examples of how advances in technological mediation work to circumscribe distance, enhance transnational linkages and multiply the breadth and scope of social communication. As such, the increased outward connectivity of India today is paralleled by the increasing density of internal communication within the country. These are the two public faces of the globalization process in India, a process which has been in operation for more than a century and which is now characterized by the forging of a new social imagination amongst significant sections of the population. The Indian media, via screen, print or voice, now reach more people in more languages than ever before, and the extent of access to information in India today outstrips any period in its long history. Correspondingly, the newfound confidence with which Indians now locate themselves in the world marks a quantum shift in the national self-image. Massive advances in literacy thus prove to be every bit as significant as the new geopolitical reality through which the options for the future have finally transcended the old alternatives of dependency versus isolation. At the same time, the potency of this emerging worldview continues to be undermined by the uneven distribution of development outcomes. While some parts of India, and its many social groups, have leapt forward in their development trajectory, others have seen few of the benefits from this process, with hi-tech investments going elsewhere and the global economy showing little interest in many regions beyond controversial extraction projects. As a result, dissatisfaction with the pace and conduct of national development, and the role of international capital, are hotly debated topics in the various fora of the Indian media. Thus, although the media by its very nature operates as the vanguard of globalization, it inevitably forms the most significant arena for articulating resistance to those processes. This is as true today as it was in the days of the colonial press.

The form and function of media within the development process has been subject to a series of technological advances that have favoured different potentials and affordances within the various strata of Indian society.

The printing press introduced an expanded and impersonal public sphere that nonetheless brought the emotive forces of cultural nationalism to the forefront of political life. The obstacles of linguistic plurality gave rise to a distinctly regionalized media structure that has subsequently been reproduced in other mediums such as cinema and television. For print, the pushing back of the literacy barrier has proved to be a long and slow process, and it has not been pushed far enough back yet for the full potentials of the medium to be realized. For the broadcast media and for telecommunications, it was the requirement for 'heavy' infrastructure that slowed the pace of media development over several decades. Since the state was the only actor capable of providing such investments, the economic priorities and political whims of various administrations were what shaped a media environment characterized by the top-down imposition of an official culture. The shift from analogue formats and their large-scale national circuits to the independent, cellular structures of digital technologies circumvented the infrastructure barrier by providing selective connectivity and favouring a grassroots model of self-expanding capacity. Clear examples of this shift can be found in playback media, computers, mobile and satellite communications. At the same time, the consistent pursuit of the latest technological advances before the completion of earlier media deployments has been characteristic of a long-term commitment to accelerated technological development, a commitment that seemingly outweighs the imperatives for universal provision.

To a significant degree, the impetus for this approach comes from the symbolic status of technology within the development paradigm. As much as technology has been proffered as the primary means of achieving the modernization of a society, the existence of technological infrastructure is generally taken as proof positive of development, and thus a goal in itself. This is why the media development programmes of both the state-led and liberalization periods have shown a marked continuity of purpose in their commitment to high-technology programmes over the completion of more basic infrastructure. In all likelihood, this is an approach that we can expect to continue into the future. Nonetheless, we must also consider whether the realization of technical ambitions has actually facilitated a diffusion of knowledge exchange or democratic access across the society as a whole. Further, the development of communicative infrastructure can only act as a guarantor for cultural diversity in circumstances where its operation becomes embedded in the mores and rituals of everyday life. These goals have typically been subsumed within the development ideologies of the state media and largely ignored by the commercial interests of the liberalization era. Nonetheless, it is possible to argue that the Indian media have still managed to perform a critical role in furnishing an expanded public sphere as well as providing a situated cultural idiom that has evolved over time. In the former case, we could point to the synthesis of the press with India's vernacular traditions, and in the latter we can take note of the particular styles of performance that have emerged in the Indian cinema.

A Field of Diversity

The aesthetics of the Indian media are as critically important as their technological form. There can be no doubt that the popular film has exerted a profound influence over the sensibilities of modern India. As the predominant form of mass visual culture, the style and form of the Indian movie is either reproduced or closely referenced in other media forms such as television, magazines, pop music, graphic art and advertising. The film world has also intruded into a wide range of other cultural rituals and practices, such as fashion, portrait photography and contemporary dance. It has exerted its influence upon numerous aspects of the modern Indian wedding (Sengupta 1999; McMillin 2003) and upon the rhetoric of Indian politics (Appadurai 1996: 36). In the fashioning of its aesthetic, the cinema has synthesized many of the diverse classical and folk traditions of India, while simultaneously importing themes and styles from Europe, America and the Middle East. In its uniquely regional organization, the cinema has also become closely aligned with the major regional cultures of India, juxtaposing those identities with the steady solidification of a pan-Indian polity. In the cinema hall itself, the social ritual of the cinema has become infused with a wide variety of Indian mannerisms, both sacred and profane. If the range of social practices which have been subject to its influence are taken into account, as well as the many strands within its syncretic tradition, then the cultural footprint of the commercial cinema is undeniably large. Given that the popular Indian film has represented the major source of modern visual culture for almost a century, it has become commonplace to correlate its discursive agency with the modern forms of Indian social life (Basu 2010; Mishra 2002). This aesthetic seems set to outlive the technological form through which it originally emerged.

In a broader sense, however, the triumphant hybridity of the popular aesthetic also sits alongside major ruptures in the public sphere. The longstanding opposition between officially sanctioned culture and the domain of the popular may have become less pronounced than it was, but there is still an elite–popular divide with clear social and aesthetic dimensions. The markedly different tone and content of the news media across different linguistic and demographic markets is a formal representation of this divide, amongst others. As a result, despite numerous national media projects, there is still no single address or unified constituency available for the Indian media. Instead, the broad field of media culture interweaves a large number of disparate publics within the diverse fabric of Indian society. This is, in itself, a significant achievement, and the extent of interchange between these social formations could be read positively as being indicative of a healthy democratic polity. In its European formulation, the health of the public sphere is often correlated to its capacity for consensus-building within a homogeneous public culture, a context in which cultural diversity is habitually identified as a crisis of fragmentation (Habermas 1996). By comparison, however, India's intrinsically multicultural public sphere, constituted through the interaction of its strong regional and communal cultures, mobilizes an entirely different field of discourse, presenting a context in which globalization is not so much a challenge to cultural singularity, but rather an extension of the existing scale of diversity. This is no utopia, however, since there are clearly many groups whose voices are yet to be heard in the public domain, mainly due to poverty, illiteracy, marginal location or social exclusion. The fate of these people is a common topic of discussion in civil society, and a contested one in political society, but they have yet to wield media power in their own right.

Partha Chatterjee has emphasized a simultaneous division between private and public life in Indian society, stemming from the colonial presence (1993). Accordingly, the media industries are frequently called to account for transgressing the blurred demarcations between a celebratory public modern and a firmly entrenched conservative outlook in the personal domain. In recent years, television, via its domestic situation, has done much to quietly destabilize this status quo. In this medium, there is a complex interchange between the global and local, but also a new configuration of the personal and the social. The impact of this on the cultural politics of the public sphere is yet to be determined. For the adherents of the cultural imperialism thesis, there is plenty to be concerned about in the increased inflows of American programming and the aping of television formats from various parts of the West. For the adherents of the indigenization thesis, the primacy of local-language content and the far greater popularity of domestically produced content would appear to provide a reasonable degree of support for a 'glocalization' effect. Nonetheless, we have yet to see whether the Indian reversioning of Western television conventions operates as a more effective Trojan horse for cultural homogenization than the presence of the original artefact itself. Alternatively, since the regionalization of Indian television has brought it much closer to the strongholds of Indian culture, we may see instead (following the example of cinema) that very particular idioms of 'Indian' television emerge over time.

The cultural dimensions of globalization can be readily located across the spectrum of local, national and global subjectivities contested within the Indian mediasphere. At another level, we must also contextualize our previous analysis of the outward media flows that have projected an Indian presence within global media markets. India can now muster a significant roster of media exports that constitute contra-flows within global media markets traditionally dominated by American and European exports. Brand Bollywood is the most instantly recognized face of India on the world stage, but we have also taken note of the important role played by software exports and the recent expansion of transnational television and telecoms services across Asia and Africa. As much as the Indian media have historically concentrated upon their domestic markets, the present era has seen a wholesale shift in emphasis towards new possibilities available in international markets. In turn, the growing visibility of these media exports is inextricably tied up with the cultural diplomacy by which India seeks to capitalize on a new market-friendly, technologically savvy and aesthetically alluring image. Nonetheless, the cultural geography of India's media exports proves to be complex in its make-up. Certainly, contradictions remain in place, with the postcolonial fixation with Western markets and acquisitions, for example, seemingly at odds with the obvious advantages of India's established position in Asian and African markets. Even so, the present level of attention being paid to the export arena provides a ready illustration of the global ambitions that now infuse India's newly corporate media industries.

Cultural goods are undoubtedly the most context-dependent commodity of trade, and thus the marked variance in the social context applicable to Indian media exports in Dubai or Jakarta, in London or New York, becomes highly significant in any assessment of their future potentials. From a more quantitative perspective, there continues to be a marked disjuncture between the numerical extent of India's offshore audiences and their 'box-office' value. Indian media find large audiences in poor countries, and very small audiences in rich countries, and this dichotomy has yet to be resolved within the international ambitions of film and television companies. For exporters of ITES and telecoms, the 'cultural fit' exerts a far lesser structuring effect upon their international trajectory. In these industries, the prerequisite for success is literacy in the mores and conventions of the global business culture that infuses the network society. Given the international standards in coding and protocols, the provision of infrastructure services to clients offshore requires relatively little local knowledge of the receiving markets themselves. Culture, nonetheless, does become critical in the provision of offshore customer services from an Indian base. That is why the call-centre industry has invested heavily in 'Western literacy' programmes for its staff, albeit with some relatively bizarre outcomes (Wood 2009). Of course, the colonial legacy of the

English language has also furnished India with a particular set of cultural skills that have given its BPO operators a natural advantage over potential competitors elsewhere in the world. China and Brazil, for example, lack such a ready resource for servicing Western clients, with nascent competition coming instead from South Africa and the Philippines. These providers have yet to present a serious threat to Indian dominance in this area of trade, however, since a comparable linguistic resource does not by itself provide those countries with the advantage of a well-developed, and co-located, IT concentration.

A Moment of Uncertainty

While much of the academic discussion of globalization emphasizes the critical importance of communication technologies and cultural diversity, these tend to become subservient to the economic dimension when globalization is debated in the wider public domain. Concluding upon this terrain, we must remain attentive to the interactions between these phenomena – that is, the functional role of media as an enabler of economic processes, as well as the critical importance of cultural diversity to the operation and assessment of global media markets. There is more, however, that we must consider within the economic dimension itself. The global spread of particular forms of business organization has proved to be highly significant in the current form of the Indian media. The neo-liberal economics promoted by world trade bodies have also played a critical role in the changing relationship between the state and the media since 1991. Similarly, intellectual property regimes, on which the very model of the knowledge economy is now seen to rest, are increasingly being brought to bear upon the media industries in Asia. The fine-tuned commoditization of creative works, and other intangible goods, via these regimes seems likely to play a determining role in the aesthetic form and economic fortunes of the Indian media in the future. For this new operating context to become normative, however, the formalization of the Indian leisure economy must extend much further than it does at present, and the incentives to go beyond the confines of the 'consuming classes' have yet to become great enough to accelerate this process. Indeed, in areas where this market has been saturated, there appears to be a tendency to pursue new markets offshore, rather than cater to the rump of Indian society. Nonetheless, the emergence of a formal leisure economy in the past decade is a landmark development, providing a clear indication of the potency of the post-industrial economic model operating at a global scale.

Writing at the present time, however, it is impossible to ignore signs that the fundamental logics of the liberal phase of globalization have entered a state of flux. For twenty years, a mutually conducive commitment to deregulation, privatization, financialization, corporate convergence and international expansion has characterized the economic orthodoxy that has operated in tandem with the technological and cultural dimensions of the globalization process. Since 2007, the collapse of global financial markets due to insufficient regulation, undue complexity and corporate corruption has left this model holed below the waterline. With regulators and taxpayers in the developed world reluctantly coming to the rescue of the international finance industry at enormous cost to future generations, serious questions have been raised about the fundamental premises of a free market that operates above national jurisdictions, and beyond public accountability. In an era where an expanding global market encouraged corporations to place their own interests above national loyalties, and their investments elsewhere at the expense of local workforces, the continuing requirement for the citizens of their home countries to carry their losses at a time of crisis has come as something of a shock to many people in the Western world. Amongst the hubris of the 'knowledge economy', it could be argued that the West as a whole failed to seriously consider the possibility that the financial tsunamis triggered by the computer-driven expansion of global trading could also 'blowback' on their instigators' home territory (Stiglitz 2010). It is notable, in this regard, that the capacity of India and China to weather the storm of the global financial crisis, this far at least, has much to do with the fact that their economies continue to enjoy significant regulatory protection alongside the natural advantages of internal scale.

'Chindia', then, may have proved more adept in balancing expanding opportunities in the global economy with robust hedges against the vagaries of global markets. At the same time, the acute inflationary pressures now being felt across the world are putting the brakes on the 'miracle' growth in both countries, and inflicting hardships upon the countless millions of Asians who still toil below the poverty line. Thus, for the project of the 'Asian century', the recession presents a new opportunity to play a much larger role in the direction of the world's economic affairs, but it also puts the hard-won gains of the past three decades in jeopardy. The future, therefore, is highly uncertain in the economic dimension. A new paradigm may come to the fore, or the present one may survive in some modified form. It is too early to tell. What we can be sure of is that Asia will be more central to the global imagination in this century than it was in the last, even as the challenges to be faced may well become greater. India, given its prominent role in the region, will undoubtedly play a decisive role in its success or failure. We can be equally certain that, whatever transpires in the economic domain, the exponential increase in the capacity of global communications technologies will continue, as will the incremental extension of the public sphere and the growing volumes of cultural exchange taking place across the globe. For this reason, the Indian media industries will most likely play a substantive role in articulating the coming phase of globalization.

References

Agrawal, Binod C. (1981) *SITE Social Evaluation: Results, Experiences and Implications*, Ahmedabad: Space Application Center.

Agrawal, Binod C. (1984) 'Indianness of the Indian Cinema', in Dissanayake, Wimal and Wang, George (eds), *Continuity and Change in Communication Systems: An Asian Perspective*, New Jersey: Ablex Publishing Group, pp. 181–92.

Ahmed, Ishtiaq (1996) *State, Nation and Ethnicity in Contemporary South Asia*, London and New York: Pinter.

Ahmed, Waquar, Kundu, Amitabh and Peet, Richard (2010) *India's New Economic Policy in India: A Critical Analysis*, London and New York: Routledge.

Aiyar, Shankhar (2005) 'Black Money Boom', *India Today International Edition* (19 December): 22–9.

Alarcón, Rafael (2000) 'Migrants of the Information Age: Indian and Mexican Engineers and Regional Development in Silicon Valley', *Working Paper 16*, The Center for Comparative Immigration Studies (CCIS), San Diego, CA: University of California.

Albarran, Alan (2009) *The Media Economy*, London and New York: Routledge.

Anderson, Benedict (1991) *Imagined Communities: Reflections on the Origins and Spread of Nationalism*, London: Verso.

Anderson, Benedict (1998) *The Spectre of Comparisons: Nationalism, Southeast Asia and the World*, London and New York: Verso.

Ang, Ien (1985) *Watching Dallas: Soap Operas and the Melodramatic Imagination*, London: Methuen.

Aoyama, Yuko (2003) 'Globalization of Knowledge-Intensive Industries: The Case of Software Production in Bangalore, India', *ANREG*, 12: 33–50.

Appadurai, Arjun (1996) *Modernity at Large: Cultural Dimensions Of Globalisation*, Minneapolis, MN, and London: University of Minnesota Press.

Appadurai, Arjun (2000) 'Spectral Housing and Urban Cleansing: Notes on Millenial Mumbai', *Public Culture* 25/3: 627–51.

Aranya, Rolee (2003) 'Globalisation and Urban Restructuring of India: Growth of the IT Industry, its Spatial Dynamics and Local Planning Resources', 39th ISOCORP Congress, at: <http://www.isocarp.net/Data/case_studies/255.pdf>; accessed 10 December 2005.

Armes, Roy (1987) *Third World Filmmaking and the West*, Berkeley and Los Angeles, CA: University of California Press.

Arora, Ashish (2005) 'The Emerging Offshore Software Industries and the U.S. Economy,' *Brookings Trade Forum* (2005 edn): 399–409.

Arora, Ashish, Arunachalam, V. S., Asundi, Jai and Fernandes, Ronald (2001) 'The Indian Software Services Industry', *Research Policy*, 30: 1267–87.

Arora, Ashish and Gambardella, Alfonso (2004) 'The Globalization of the Software Industry: Perspectives and Opportunities for Developed and Developing Countries', *Working Paper 10538*, Cambridge, MA: National Bureau of Economic Research.

Arora, Poonam (1995) 'Imperilling the Prestige of the White Woman: Colonial Anxiety and Film Censorship in British India', *Visual Anthropology Review*, 11/2: 36–50.

Ashraf, Syed Firdaus (2003) 'Why Bollywood Wants Peace', at: <http://specials. rediff.com/movies/2003/dec/20bolly.htm>; accessed 12 September 2004.

Asthana, Sanjay (2003) 'Patriotism and Its Avatars: Tracking the National-Global Dialectic in Indian Music Videos', *Journal of Communication Inquiry*, 27/4: 337–53.

Athique, Adrian (2005) 'Watching Indian Movies in Australia: Media, Community and Consumption', *South Asian Popular Culture*, 3/2: 117–33.

Athique, Adrian (2006) 'Bollywood and "Grocery Store" Video Piracy in Australia', *Media International Australia*, 121: 41–51.

Athique, Adrian (2008a) 'The Global Dynamics of Indian Media Piracy: Export Markets, Playback Formats and the Informal Economy', *Media, Culture and Society*, 30/5: 699–717.

Athique, Adrian (2008b) 'A Line in the Sand: The Border Films of J. P. Dutta', *South Asia: Journal of South Asian Studies*, 31/3: 472–99.

Athique, Adrian (2008c) 'The "Crossover" Audience: Mediated Multiculturalism and the Indian Film', *Continuum: Journal of Media and Cultural Studies*, 22/3 (June 2008): 299–311.

Athique, Adrian (2009) 'Leisure Capital in the New Economy: The Rise of the Multiplex', *Contemporary South Asia*, 17/2: 123–40.

Athique, Adrian M. and Hill, Douglas (2007) 'Multiplex Cinemas and Urban Redevelopment in India', *Media International Australia*, 124: 108–18.

Athique, Adrian and Hill, Douglas (2010) *The Multiplex in India: A Cultural Economy of Urban Leisure*, London and New York: Routledge.

Athwal, Amardeep (2008) *China–India Relations: Contemporary Dynamics*, London and New York: Routledge.

Azad, Maulana Abul Kalam (1959) *India Wins Freedom: An Autobiographical Narrative*, Bombay: Orient Longman.

Badam, Ramola Talwar (2005) 'Bollywood Pirates: Piracy Gnaws At Indian Movie Profits, Leaves Filmmakers Anxious', *Span*, (July/August): 45–7.

BAFTA (2006) 'Roundtable with Yash Chopra, Shah Rukh Khan and Karan Johar', *BAFTA Goes Bollywood* (15 July), at: <http://www.bafta.org>; accessed 9 September 2006.

Bamzai, Kaveree (2006) 'Soft Power, Hard Sell', *India Today International Edition* (6 March): 36–8.

Banaji, Shakuntala (2006) *'Reading Bollywood': The Young Audience and Hindi Films*, Basingstoke: Palgrave MacMillan.

Bannerjee, Indrajit (2002) 'The Locals Strike Back: Media Globalization and Localization in the New Asian Television Landscape', *Gazette: The International Journal for Communication Studies*, 64/6: 517–35.

Bannerjee, Shampa (ed.) (1982) *New Indian Cinema*, New Delhi: National Film Development Council.

Barnouw, Erik and Krishnaswamy, S. (1980) *Indian Film*, New York: Oxford University Press.

Basant, Rakesh and Chandra, Pankaj (2004) 'Capability-Building and Inter-Organization Linkages in the Indian IT Industry: The Role of Multinationals, Domestic Firms and Academic Institutions', in Anthony D'Costa and Eswaran Sridharan (eds), *India in the Global Software Industry*. New Delhi: Macmillan India, pp. 193–219.

Basi, Hariqbal (2010) 'Indianizing Hollywood: The Debate Over Bollywood's Copyright Infringement', at: <http://works.bepress.com/hariqbal_basi/2>; accessed 12 March 2011.

Basu, Anustap (2010) *Bollywood in the Age of New Media: The Geo-Televisual Aesthetic*, Edinburgh, Edinburgh University Press.

Bayly, C. A. (1999) *Empire and Information: Intelligence Gathering and Social Communication in India 1780-1870*, New Delhi: Cambridge University Press.

BBC News Online (17 December 2000) 'Nepal Bans Bollywood Films', at: <http://news.bbc.co.uk/1/hi/world/south_asia/1088100.stm>; accessed 9 December 2004.

BBC News Online (30 July 2002) 'Bollywood Stars Win Protection', at: <http://news.bbc.co.uk/2/hi/south_asia/2161726.stm>; accessed 30 September 2003.

BBC News Online (12 August 2002) 'Devdas "Funded by Gangsters"', at: <http://news.bbc.co.uk/2/hi/entertainment/2188675.stm>; accessed 30 September 2003.

BBC Online (30 September 2003) 'Indian Movie Mogul Convicted', at: http://news.bbc.co.uk/2/low/south_asia/3151036.stm>; accessed 30 September 2003.

BBC News Online (2 December 2003) 'India Seeks Film Piracy Action', at: <http://news.bbc.co.uk/2/hi/entertainment/3255726.stm>; accessed 10 December 2003.

BBC News Online (15 March 2005) 'Police in Bollywood Piracy Raid', at: <http://news.bbc.co.uk/2/hi/entertainment/4350689.stm>; accessed 4 June 2004.

BBC News Online (27 May 2005) 'Major Fake Bollywood Discs Haul', at: <http://news.bbc.co.uk/2/hi/entertainment/4585473.stm>; accessed 4 September 2003.

BBC News Online (14 June 2006) 'Shots Fired in Bollywood Office', at: <http://news.bbc.co.uk/2/hi/entertainment/5080364.stm>; accessed 14 June 2006.

BBC News Online (31 August 2010) 'Google and Skype Could Be Hit by India Data Curbs', at: <http://www.bbc.co.uk/news/technology-11137647>; accessed 31 August 2010.

Beattie, Meriel (2002) 'Cleaning Up Bollywood', BBC Online (7 January 2002), at: <http://news.bbc.co.uk/2/hi/programmes/crossing_continents/asia/1747426.stm>; accessed 30 September 2003.

Bell, Daniel (1973) *The Coming of Post-Industrial Society: A Venture in Social Forecasting*, New York: Basic Books.

Bell, Daniel (1999) *The Coming of Post-Industrial Society: A Venture in Social Forecasting (Anniversary Edition)*, New York: Basic Books.

Benjamin, S. (2005) *The Lifestyle Advertisement and the Marxist Manifesto in a City of Stealth*, New Delhi: Institute of Social Studies Trust.

Bhagwati, Jagdish and Blinder, Alan S. (2009) *Offshoring of American Jobs: What Response From U.S. Economic Policy*, Cambridge, MA: MIT Press.

Bhattacharya, Nandini (2004) 'A "Basement" Cinephilia: Indian Diaspora Women Watch Bollywood', *South Asian Popular Culture*, 2/2: 161–84.

Bhattacharyya, Gargi (2003) 'South Asian Cultural Studies – Lessons from Back Home', *South Asian Popular Culture*, 1/1: 3–12.

Bharat, Meenakshi and Kumar, Nirmal (2007) *Filming the Line of Control: The Indo-Pak Relationship Through the Cinematic Lens*, New Delhi: Routledge.

Bolter, Jay David and Grusin, Richard (2000) *Remediation: Understanding New Media*, Cambridge, MA: MIT Press.

Booth, Gregory D. (1995) 'Traditional Content and Narrative Structure in the Hindi Commercial Cinema', *Asian Folklore Studies*, 54/2: 169–90.

Boyd, Douglas, Straubhaar, Joseph and Lent, John (1989) *Videocassette Recorders in the Third World*, New York and London: Longman.

BPI (2005) 'Piracy Raids Uncover Europe's Largest Fakes Factory', at: <http://www.bpi.co.uk/news/apu/news_content_file_948.shtml>; accessed 4 September 2006.

Brewer, Thomas L. and Nollen, Stanley D. (1998) 'Knowledge Transfer to Developing Countries after WTO: Theory and Practice in Information Technology in India', *Working Paper 98–14*, Pittsburgh: Carnegie Bosch Institute.

Brosius, Christine (2005) 'The Scattered Homeland of the Migrant: Bollyworld through the Diasporic Lens', in R. Kaur and A. Sinha (eds), *Bollyworld: Indian Cinema Through a Transnational Lens*, New Delhi and London: Sage, pp. 207–38.

Brosius, Christine and Butcher, Melissa (eds) (1999) *Image Journeys: Audio-Visual Media and Cultural Change in India*, New Delhi: Sage.

Brown, Judith and Parel, Anthony (2011) *The Cambridge Companion to Gandhi*, Cambridge: Cambridge University Press.

Burch, Elizabeth (2002) 'Media Literacy, Cultural Proximity and TV Aesthetics: Why Indian Soap Operas Work in Nepal and the Hindu Diaspora', *Media, Culture & Society*, 24: 571–9.

Butcher, Melissa (2003) *Transnational Television, Cultural Identioty and Change: When STAR Came To India*, New Delhi: Sage.

Castells, Manuel (1996) *The Information Age: Economy, Society and Culture, Vol. I: The Rise of the Network Society*, Cambridge, MA, and Oxford: Blackwell.

Castells, Manuel (1997) *The Information Age: Economy, Society and Culture, Vol. II: The Power of Identity*, Cambridge, MA, and Oxford: Blackwell.

Castells, Manuel (1998a) *The Information Age: Economy, Society and Culture, Vol. III: End of Millennium*, Cambridge, MA, and Oxford: Blackwell.

Castells, Manuel (1998b) 'Why the Megacities Focus?: Megacities in the New world Disorder', The Megacities Project Publication MCP-018, at: <http://www.megac-itiesproject.org/pdf/publications_pdf_mcp018intro.pdf>; accessed 18 April 2003.

Castells, Manuel (1999) 'Information Technology, Globalization and Social Development', *UNRISD Discussion Paper No. 114*, New York: United Nations Research Institute for Social Development.

Castells, Manuel (2002) 'An Introduction to the Information Age', in Gary Bridge and Sophie Watson (eds), *The Blackwell City Reader*, Oxford: Blackwell, pp. 125–34.

Castells, Manuel (2009a) *The Information Age: Economy, Society and Culture, Vol. I: The Rise of the Network Society*, revsd edn, Cambridge, MA, and Oxford: Blackwell.

Castells, Manuel (2009b) *Communication Power*, Oxford: Oxford University Press.

Census of India (2001) At: <http://censusindia.gov.in/>; accessed 14 October 2009.

Chacko, Priya (2002) 'Culture and Politics in an Age of Global Media: The Impact of Satellite Television and the Internet in India', *Fjhp*, 22: 110–23.

Chadha, Kalyani and Kavoori, Anandam (2000) 'Media Imperialism Revisited: Some Findings from the Asian Case', *Media, Culture & Society*, 22/4: 415–32.

Chakrabarty, Bidyut and Kujur, Rajat Kumar (2009) *Maoism in India*, London and New York: Routledge.

Chakravarty, Sumita S. (1993) *National Identity in Indian Popular Cinema 1947–1987*, Austin, TX: Texas University Press.

Chakravartty, Paula (2004) 'Telecom, National Development and the Indian State: A Postcolonial Critique', *Media, Culture & Society*, 26/2: 227–49.

Chakravartty, Paula (2008) 'Labor In or As Civil Society: Workers and Subaltern Politics in India's Information Society', in P. Chakravartty and Y. Zhao (eds), *Global Communications: Towards a Transcultural Political Economy*, Lanham, MD: Rowan and Littlefield, pp. 285–307.

Chatterjee, Partha (1993) *The Nation & Its Fragments: Colonial & Postcolonial Histories*, New Delhi: Oxford University Press.

Chatterjee, Partha (1998) 'Beyond the Nation? Or Within?', *Social Text*, 56 (fall): 57–69.

Chatterjee, Partha (2004) *The Politics of the Governed*, New Delhi: Permanent Black.

Chatterji, P. C. (1991) *Broadcasting In India*, New Delhi: Sage.

Choudhuri, Shohini (2009) 'Snake Charmers and Child Brides: Deepa Mehta's Water, "Exotic" Representation, and the Cross-cultural Reception of South Asian Migrant Cinema', *South Asian Popular Culture*, 7/1: 7–20.

Congdon, Tim, Graham, Andrew, Green, Damian and Robinson, Bill (1995) *The Cross Media Revolution: Ownership and Control*, London: John Libby.

Contractor, Noshir, Singhal, Arvind and Rogers, Everett (1993) 'Satellite Television Development in India: A Utopian, Dystopian, Neutral and Contingency View', in K. S. Nair and Shirley White (eds), *Perspectives on Development Communication*, Thousand Oaks, CA: Sage, pp. 230–50.

Correa, Carlos (2007) *Trade Related Aspects of Intellectual Property Rights: A Commentary on the TRIPS Agreement*, Oxford: Oxford University Press.

Coyle, Diana (1999) *The Weightless World: Strategies for Managing the Digital Economy*, Cambridge, MA: MIT Press.

CRIT (2007) 'Collective Research Initiatives Trust', at: <http://www.crit.org.in/>; accessed 1 February 2007.

Curtin, Michael (2003) 'Media Capital: Towards the Study of Spatial Flows', *International Journal of Cultural Studies*, 6/2: 202–28.

Curtin, Michael (2010) 'Comparing Media Capitals: Hong Kong and Mumbai', *Global Media and Communication*, 6/3:263–70.

Das, Dilip K. (2004) *Financial Globalization and the Emerging Market Economy*, London and New York: Routledge.

Das, Dilip K. (2006) *China and India: A Tale of Two Economies*, London and New York: Routledge.

Das, Gurcharan (2002) *India Unbound: From Independence to the Global Information Age*, New Delhi: Penguin.

Dasgupta, Ajit (1993) *A History of Indian Economic Thought*, New York: Routledge.

D'Costa, Anthony (2004) 'The Indian Software Industry in the Global Division of Labour', in A. D'Costa and E. Sridharan (eds), *India in the Global Software Industry*, New Delhi: Macmillan India, pp. 1–26.

Dedrick, Jason and Kraemer, Kenneth (1993) 'Information Technology in India: The Quest for Self-Reliance', *Asian Survey*, 33/5: 463–92.

Desai, Jigna (2004) *Beyond Bollywood: The Cultural Politics of South Asian Diasporic Film*, London: Routledge.

Desai, Rachana (2005) 'Copyright Infringement in the Indian Film Industry', *Vanderbilt Journal of Entertainment Law and Practice* (spring): 7/2: 259–78.

Deshpande, Sudhanva (2005) 'The Consumable Hero of Globalised India', in R. Kaur and A. Sinha (eds), *Bollyworld: Indian Cinema Through a Transnational Lens*, New Delhi and London: Sage, pp. 186–203.

Dev, S. Maehndra and Rao, N. Chandrasekhara (eds) (2009) *India: Perspectives on Equitable Development*, New Delhi: Academic Foundation.

Dhar, P. N (2000) *Indira Gandhi, the 'Emergency', and Indian Democracy*, New Delhi: Oxford University Press.

Dhavan, Rajeev (2009) 'Obtaining Moral Consensus in a Law and Order Society', in Arvind Rajagopal (ed.), *The Indian Public Sphere: Readings in Media History*, Oxford: Oxford University Press, pp. 88–98.

Dickey, Sara (1993) 'The Politics of Adulation: Cinema and the Production of Politicians in South India', *Journal of Asian Studies*, 52/2: 340–72.

Dissanayake, Wimal and Malti, Sahai (1992) *Sholay: A Cultural Reading*, New Delhi: Wiley Eastern.

Diwakar (2006) 'Bollywood "Soft Touch" to Overpower China', *The Times of India*, at: <http://timesofindia.indiatimes.com/india/Bollywood-soft-touch-to-overpower-China/articleshow/1390088.cms.>; accessed 8 February 2010.

Dossani, Rafiq and Kenney, Martin (2003) *Went for Cost, Stayed for Quality?: Moving the Back Office to India*, Stanford, CA: Asia Pacific Research Center.

Dossani, Rafiq and Kenney, Martin (2007) 'The Next Wave of Globalization: Relocating Service Provision to India', *World Development*, 35/5: 772–91.

Dossani, Rafiq and Kenney, Martin (2009) 'Service Provision for the Global Economy: The Evolving Indian Experience', *Review of Policy Research*, 26/1–2: 77–104.

Drucker, Peter (1969) 'Knowledge Society', *New Society*, 13/343: 629–31.

Dudrah, Rajinder (2002a) 'Vilayati Bollwood: Popular Hindi Cinema-Going and Diasporic South Asian Identity in Birmingham (UK)', *Javnost*, 9/1: 19–36.

Dudrah, Rajinder (2002b) 'Zee Tv-Europe and the Construction of a Pan-European South Asian Identity', *Contemporary South Asia*, 11/2: 163–81.

Dudrah, Rajinder (2005) 'ZEE TV Diasporic Non-Terrestrial Television in Europe', *South Asian Popular Culture*, 3/1: 33–47.

Dutt, Amitava Krishna and Rao, J. Mohan (2000) 'Globalization and its Social Discontents: The Case of India', Center for Economic Policy Analysis (CEPA), *Working Paper Series I, 16*. New York: New School University.

Dwyer, Rachel (2000) '"Indian Values" and the Diaspora: Yash Chopra's Films of the 1990s', *West Coast Line* (autumn): 6–27.

Dwyer, Rachel and Patel, Divia (2002) *Cinema India: The Visual Culture of the Hindi Film*, London: Reaktion Books.

Eckert, Julia M. (2003) *The Shiv Sena and the Politics of Violence*, New Delhi: Oxford University Press.

Fernandes, Leela (2000) 'Nationalizing "The Global": Media Images, Cultural Politics and the Middle Class in India', *Media Culture and Society*, 22/5: 611–28.

Fernandes, Leela (2004). 'The Politics of Forgetting: Class Politics, State Power and the Restructuring of Urban Space in India', *Urban Studies*, 41/12: 2415–30.

Fernandes, Leela (2006) *India's New Middle Class: Democratic Politics in an Era of Democratic Reform*, Minneapolis, MN, and London: University of Minnesota Press.

Film Distributors Association UK (2005) 'Film Piracy in the UK: Who Gains and Who Loses from Film Theft', at: <http://www.launchingfilms.com/piracy/index.html>; accessed 15 November 2006.

Fleischman, Lana (1993) 'The Empire Strikes Back: The Influence of the United States Motion Picture Industry on Russian Copyright Law', *Cornell International Law Journal*, 26/1: 189.

Flew, Terry (2007) *Understanding Global Media*, Houndmills: Palgrave Macmillan.

Frank, Katherine (2011) *Indira: The Life of Indira Nehru Gandhi*, London: HarperCollins.

Freitag, Sandria B. (2001) 'Visions of the Nation: Theorizing the Nexus Between Creation, Consumption, and Participation in the Public Sphere,' in Rachel Dwyer and Christopher Pinney (eds), *Pleasure and the Nation: The History, Politics and Consumption of Public Culture in India*, New Delhi: Oxford University Press, pp. 35–75.

Friedberg, Anne (2000) 'The End of Cinema: Multi-media and Technological

Change', in Gledhill, Christine and Linda Williams (eds) *Reinventing Film Studies*, London: Arnold.

Friedlander, Peter, Jeffrey, Robin and Seth, Sanjay (2001) 'Subliminal Charge: How Hindi-Language Newspaper Expansion Affects India', *Media International Australia*, 100: 147–66.

Friedman, Milton (1993) *Why Government is the Problem*, Stanford, CA: Hoover Institution.

Gandhi, Mohandas (1942) *Harijan* (May), Ahmedabad.

Gangadhar, V. (2005) 'Bhai Power', *Spectrum* (16 January 2005), at: <http://www.tribuneindia.com/2005/20050116/spectrum/main1.htm>; accessed 10 November 2006.

Geetha, J. (2003) 'Bollywood Ending', *Sight and Sound*, 13/6: 31–2.

Gellner, Ernest (1998) *Nationalism*, London: Phoenix.

Gibson, Owen (2005) 'Bollywood Claims Scalp in Fight against Bootlegs', *Guardian Unlimited* (23 February 2005), at: <http://film.guardian.co.uk/News_Story/Guardian/0,,1423411,00.html>; accessed 4 September 2006.

Giddens, Anthony (2002) *Runaway World*, London: Routledge.

Gillespie, Marie (1995) *Television, Ethnicity and Cultural Change*, London: Routledge.

Gokulsing, K. Moti and Dissanayake, Wimal (1998) *Indian Popular Cinema: A Narrative of Cultural Change*, Stoke on Trent: Trentham Books.

Gold, Gerald and Attenborough, Richard (1983) *Gandhi: A Pictorial Biography*, New York: Newmarket Press.

Golding, Peter and Harris, Phil (eds) (1996) *Beyond Cultural Imperialism: Globalization, Communication and the New International Order*, London, Thousand Oaks, CA, and New Delhi: Sage.

Gopalan, Lalitha (2003) *Cinema of Interruptions: Action Genres in Contemporary Indian Cinema*, New Delhi: Oxford University Press.

Gopinath, K. (2009) 'Internet in India', in Arvind Rajagopal (ed), *The Indian Public Sphere: Readings in Media History*, Oxford: Oxford University Press, pp. 291–311.

Govil, Nitin (2007) 'Bollywood and the Frictions of Global Mobility', in Daya Thussu (ed.), *Media on the Move: Global Flow and Contra-Flow*, London: Routledge.

Greenspan, Anna (2004) *India and the IT Revolution: Networks of Global Culture*, Houndmills: Palgrave Macmillan.

Grieco, Joseph M. (1984) *Between Dependency and Autonomy: India's Experience with the International Computer Industry*, Berkeley and Los Angeles, CA: University of California Press.

Guardian (2010) 'US Embassy Cables: How India Can Help Stabilize Afghanistan', the *Guardian*, at: <http://www.guardian.co.uk>; accessed 16 December 2010.

Gupta, Shubhra (2001) 'Who Will Bell This Cat?', *BusinessLine Internet Edition* (12 November 2001), at: <http://www.hinduonnet.com/businessline/2001/11/12/stories/101287a6.htm>; accessed 4 September 2006.

Habermas, Jürgen (1989) *The Structural Transformation of the Public Sphere: An Inquiry in a Category of Bourgeois Society*, Cambridge: Polity.

Habermas, Jürgen (1996) 'The European Nation-State: On the Past and Future of Sovereignty and Citizenship', in Gopal Balakrishnan (ed.), *Mapping the Nation*, London: Verso, pp. 281–94.

Hall, Stuart (1980) 'Encoding/Decoding', in Stuart Hall et al. (eds), *Culture, Media, Language*, London: Hutchinson, pp. 128–38.

Haniffa, Aziz (2011) 'India Does Not Want To Be America's Ally', at: <http://www.rediff.com/news/slide-show/slide-show-1-india-does-not-want-to-be-americas-ally/20110210.htm>; accessed 10 February 2011.

Hansen, Thomas Blom and Jaffrelot, Christophe (2000) *The BJP and the Compulsions of Politics in India*, New Delhi: Oxford University Press.

Hariharan, K. (1999) 'Revisiting Sholay, a.k.a Flames of the Sun', *Asian Cinema*, 10/2: 151–4.

Hassam, Andrew and Paranjape, Makarand (eds) (2010) *Bollywood in Australia: Transnationalism and Cultural Production*, Perth: UWA Press, pp. 23–44.

Hayek, Friedrich August (1944) *The Road to Serfdom*, New York: Routledge.

Heeks, Richard (1996) *India's Software Industry: State Policy, Liberalization and Industrial Development*, New Delhi: Sage Publications.

Heitzman, James (1999) 'Corporate Strategy and Planning in the Science City', *Economic and Political Weekly*, 34/5: 7–11.

Hewitt, Vernon (2007) *Political Mobilization and Democracy in India: States of Emergency*, London and New York: Routledge.

Higson, Andrew (2000) 'The Limiting Imagination of National Cinema', in Mette Hjort and Scott Mackenzie (eds), *Cinema and Nation*, London and New York: Routledge, pp. 63–74.

Hindu Business Line (2003) 'Ribeiro Links Piracy to Funding of Terrorism', *Hindu Business Line Internet Edition* (25 November 2003), at: <http://www.thehindubusinessline.com/2003/11/25/stories/2003112501270200.htm>; accessed 18 November 2006.

Hobsbawm, Eric and Ranger, Terence (eds) (1983) *The Invention of Tradition*, Cambridge: Cambridge University Press.

Holden, Todd and Scrase, Timothy (eds) (2006) *Medi@sia: Global Media/tion in and out of Context*, London and New York: Routledge.

Hopkins, Antony (ed.) (2002) *Globalization in World History*, London: Random House.

Hughes, Stephen P. (2000) 'Policing Silent Film Exhibition in Colonial South India', in Ravi S. Vasudevan (ed.), *Making Meaning in Indian Cinema*, New Delhi: Oxford University Press, pp. 39–64.

IBEF (2011) 'India Brand Equity Foundation', at: <http://www.ibef.org/>; accessed 20 January 2011.

IIFA (2011) 'Indian International Film Academy', at: <http://www.iifa.com/web07/cntnt/iifa.htm>; accessed 20 January 2011.

Inden, Ronald (1999) 'Transnational Class, Erotic Arcadia and Commercial Utopia in Hindi Films', in Christine Brosius and Melissa Butcher (eds), *Image Journeys: Audio-Visual Media and Cultural Change in India*, New Delhi: Sage, pp. 41–68.

India Planning Commision (1981) *Evaluation Report on Satellite Instructional Television Experiment (SITE)*, PEO Study No. 119, New Delhi: Government of India.

Indian Express (2000) 'Cops Tighten Bollywood's Security Blanket', *Indian Express News Service* (19 December 2000), at: <http://www.expressindia.com/ie/daily/20001219/ina19064.html>; accessed 9 October 2006.

Industry Trust for IP Awareness Ltd. (2004) 'UK's Largest Ever DVD Anti Piracy Campaign Places Organised Crime And Terrorist Gangs In The Frame', Press Release (12 July 2004); available at: <http://www.copyrightaware.co.uk/about-the-industry-trust/press-releases.asp>; accessed: 15 March 2008.

Innis, Harold (1951) *The Bias of Communication*, Toronto: University of Toronto Press.

Innis, Harold (1952) *Changing Concepts of Time*, Toronto: University of Toronto Press.

Jacques, Martin (2009) *When China Rules the World: The Rise of the Middle Kingdom and the End of the Western World*, London: Allen Lane.

Jaikumar, Priya (2003) 'More Than Morality: The Indian Cinematograph Committee Interviews (1927)', *The Moving Image*, 3/1: 82–109.

Jaikumar, Priya (2006) *Cinema at the End of Empire: A Politics of Transition in Britain and India*, Durham, NC: Duke University Press.

Jain, Madhu (1990) 'The 80s Cinema: Triumph Trauma and Tears', *India Today* (15 January 1990): 44–9.

Jeffrey, Robin (2000) *India's Newspaper Revolution*, London: C Hurst.

Jeffrey, Robin (2002a) 'Communications and Capitalism in India 1750–2010', *South Asia: Journal of South Asian Studies*, XXV/2: 61–76.

Jeffrey, Robin (2002b) 'Grand Canyon, Shaky Bridge: Media Revolution and the Rise of "Hindu" Politics', *South Asia*, XXV/3: 281–300.

Jeffrey, Robin (2009) 'The Mahatma Didn't Like Movies and Why It Matters', in Arvind Rajagopal (ed.), *The Indian Public Sphere: Readings in Media History*, Oxford: Oxford University Press, pp. 171–87.

Jeganathan, P (1998) 'eelam.com: Place, Nation and Imagi-Nation in Cyberspace', *Public Culture*, 10/3: 515–28.

Jenkins, Henry (2004) 'The Cultural Logic of Media Convergence', *International Journal of Cultural Studies*, 7/1, pp. 33-43.

Jenkins, Henry (2006) *Convergence Culture: Where Old and New Media Collide*, New York: New York University Press.

Jinnah, Mohamed Ali (1984) *The Collected Works of Quaid-e-Azam Mohammad Ali Jinnah*, Karachi: East and West Pub. Co.

Juluri, Vamsee (2002) 'Music Television and the Invention of Youth Culture in India', *Television and New Media*, 3/4: 367–86.

Juluri, Vamsee (2003) *Becoming a Global Audience: Longing and Belonging in Indian Music Television*, New Delhi: Peter Lang.

Karim, Karim H. (ed.) (2003) *The Media and Diaspora*, London and New York: Routledge.

Kasbekar, Asha (1996) 'An Introduction to Indian Cinema', in J. Nelmes (ed.), *An Introduction to Film Studies*, London: Routledge, pp. 382–415.

Kaur, Ravinder (2002) 'Viewing the West Through Bollywood: A Celluloid Occident in the Making', *Contemporary South Asia*, 11/2: 199–209.

Kaur, Raminder (2005) 'Cruising on the Vilayati Bandwagon: Diasporic Representations and Reception of Popular Indian Movies', in Ravinder Kaur and Ajay Sinha (eds), *Bollyworld: Popular Indian Cinema through a Transnational Lens*, pp. 309–29.

Kaur, Ravinder and Sinha, Ajay (eds) (2005) *Bollyworld: Popular Indian Cinema through a Transnational Lens*, New Delhi: Sage.

Kazmi, F. (1999a) 'How Angry is the Angry Young Man?: "Rebellion" in Conventional Hindi Films', in Ashis Nandy (ed.), *The Secret Politics of Our Desires: Innocence, Culpability and Indian Popular Cinema*, New Delhi: Zed Books, pp. 134–56.

Kazmi, F. (1999b) *The Politics of India's Conventional Cinema: Imaging a Universe, Subverting a Multiverse*, New Delhi: Sage.

Kerrigan, Finola and Ozbilgin, Mustafa (2002) 'Art for the Masses or Art for the Few?: Ethical Issues of Film Marketing in the UK', *International Journal of Nonprofit and Voluntary Sector Marketing*, 7/2: 195–203.

Khan, Aamer Ahmed (2005a) 'How Piracy is Entrenched in Pakistan', *BBC Online*, 08/05/2005, <http://www.news.bbc.co.uk/2/hi/south_asia/4523089.stm>; accessed 4 July 2005.

Khan, Aamer Ahmed (2005b) 'Pakistan – Copyright Piracy Hub', *BBC Online*, 03/05/2005, <http://news.bbc.co.uk/2/hi/south_asia/4495679.stm>; accessed 4 July 2005.

Khan, N. S. (2003) 'Popularity of Hindi Films in Indonesia', at: <http://tamanbollywood.singcat.com/artikel/bollywood_in_indonesia.shtml>; accessed 3 October 2004.

Kim, Youna (ed.) (2008) *Media Consumption and Everyday Life in Asia*, New York: Routledge.

Kobayashi-Hillary (2005) *Outsourcing to India: The Offshore Advantage*, Berlin: Springer Verlag.

Kohli, Ritu (1993) *Political Ideas of M.S. Golwalkar: Hindutva, Nationalism, Secularism*, New Delhi: Deep & Deep Publications.

Kohli-Khandekar, Vanita (2006) *The Indian Media Business*, 2nd edn, New Delhi: Response Books.

Kohli-Khandekar, Vanita (2010) *The Indian Media Business*, 3rd edn, New Delhi: Response Books.

Koppikar, Smruti (1997) 'Murder In Mumbai', *India Today* (25 August): 26–32.

KPMG-CII (2005) *Indian Entertainment Industry Focus 2010: Dreams to Reality*, Mumbai and New Delhi: KPMG India and Confederation of Indian Industry, at: <http://www.kpmg.de/library/pdf/050331_Focus_Dreams_to_Reality_en.pdf>; accessed 25 April 2006.

Krishna, Gopal (1966) 'The Development of the Indian National Congress as a Mass Organisation 1918–1923', *Journal of Asian Studies*, 25/3: 413–30.

Kulkarni, Manu (2001) 'Asia's Technology future: Transforming Business or People?', *Economic and Political Weekly*, 36/24: 2122–4.

Kumar, Krishan (2005) *From Post-Industrial to Post-Modern Society: New Theories of the Contemporary World*, Oxford: Blackwell.

Lakhanpal, Gauri (2006) 'Combating Movie Piracy in Asia', *Financial Express*, at: <http://www.financialexpress.com/fe_full_story.php?content_id=136344>; accessed 4 September 2006.

Lal, K. (2000) *Institutional Environment and the Development of Information and Communication Technology in India*, Delhi: Institute of Economic Growth.

Lal, Vinay (1999) 'The Impossibility of the Outsider in the Modern Hindi Film', in Ashis Nandy (ed.), *The Secret Politics of Our Desires: Innocence, Culpability and Indian Popular Cinema*, New Delhi: Zed Books, pp. 228–59.

Larkin, Brian (1997) 'Indian Films and Nigerian Lovers: Media and the Creation of Parallel Modernities', *Africa*, 67/3: 406–40.

Larkin, Brian (2003) 'Itineraries of Indian Cinema: African Videos, Bollywood and Global Media', in Ella Shohat and Robert Stam (eds), *Multiculturalism, Postcoloniality and Transnational Media*, New Brunswick, NJ, and London: Rutgers University Press, pp. 170–92.

Leadbeater, Charles (2000) *Living on Thin Air: The New Economy*, New York: Penguin.

Lerner, Daniel (1958) *The Passing of Traditional Society*, London: Macmillan.

Levinson, Paul (1999) *Digital McLuhan: Guide to the Information Millenium*, London and New York: Routledge.

Levy, Mark (1989) *The VCR Age: Home Video and Mass Communication*, Newbury Park, London and New Delhi: Sage.

Liang, Lawrence (2006) 'Copyright, Cultural Production and Open Content Licensing', *Alternative Law Forum*, at: <http://www.altlawforum.org/PUBLICATIONS/document.2004-12-18.0245048957>; accessed 1 November 2006.

Liebes, Tamar and Katz, Elihu (1990) *The Export of Meaning: Cross Cultural Readings of Dallas*, Oxford: Oxford University Press.

Lutze, Lothar (1985) 'From Bharata to Bombay: Change in Continuity in Hindi Film Aesthetics', in Beatrix Pfleiderer and Lothar Lutze (eds), *The Hindi Film: Agent and Re-agent of Cultural Change*, New Delhi: Manohar, pp. 3–15.

McCartney, Matthew (2009) *Political Economy, Liberalisation and Growth in India 1991–2008*, London and New York: Routledge.

McGuire, John and Copland, Ian (eds) (2007) *Hindu Nationalism and Governance*, New Delhi: Oxford University Press.

McLuhan, Marshall (1962) *The Gutenberg Galaxy: The Making of Typographic Man*, Toronto: University of Toronto Press.

McLuhan, Marshall (1964) *Understanding Media: The Extensions of Man*, New York: McGraw Hill.

McLuhan, Marshall and Fiore, Quentin (1968) *War and Peace in the Global Village*, New York: Bantam.

McMillin, Divya C. (2001) 'Localizing the Global: Television and Hybrid Programming in India', *International Journal of Cultural Studies*, 4/1: 45–68.

McMillin, Divya C. (2002) 'Choosing Commercial Television's Identities in India: A Reception Analysis', *Continuum: Journal of Media and Cultural Studies*, 16/1: 123–36.

McMillin, Divya C. (2003) 'Marriages are Made on Television: Globalization and National Identity in India', in Lisa Parks and Shanti Kumar (eds), *Planet TV: A Global Television Reader*, New York and London: New York University Press, pp. 341–60.

Mabhubani, Kishore (2008) *The New Asian Hemisphere: The Irresistible Shift of Global Power to the East*, New York: Public Affairs.

Manchanda, Rita (2002) 'Militarised Hindu Nationalism and the Mass Media: Shaping a Hindutva Public Discourse', *South Asia*, XXV/3: 301–20.

Manchanda, Usha (1998) 'Invasion from the Skies', *Australian Studies in Journalism*, 7: 136–63.

Masuda, Yoneji (1980) *The Information Society as Post-Industrial Society*, Bethseda: World Future Society.

Mazarella, William (2003) *Shovelling Smoke: Advertising and Globalization in Contemporary India*, Durham, NC, and London: Duke University Press.

Mazumdar, Ranjani (2000) 'From Subjectification to Schizophrenia: The 'Angry Man' and the 'Psychotic' Hero of Bombay Cinema', in Ravi S. Vasudevan (ed.), *Making Meaning in Indian Cinema*, New Delhi: Oxford University Press, pp. 238–64.

Mehta, Nalin (2006) 'India as a New Media Capital: The Global and Regional Impact of Indian Television', paper presented at AusAID-Asia Pacific Research Futures Research Network Conference, Canberra, 25–6 September 2006; unpublished conference paper.

Mehta, Nalin (2007) *India on Television: How Satellite News Has Changed the Way We Think and Act*, New Delhi: HarperCollins.

Mishra, Samina (1999) 'Dish is Life: Cable Operators and the Neighbourhood', in Christine Brosius and Melissa Butcher (eds), *Image Journeys: Audio-Visual Media and Cultural Change in India,* New Delhi: Sage, pp. 261–78.

Mishra, Vijay (1985) 'Towards a Theoretical Critique of Bombay Cinema', *Screen*, 26/3–4: 133–46.

Mishra, Vijay (2002) *Bollywood Cinema: Temples of Desire*, London: Routledge.

Mitra, Ananda (2008) 'Bollyweb: Search for Bollywood on the Web and See What Happens!', in Anandam Kavoori and Aswin Punathambekar (eds), *Global Bollywood*, New York: New York University Press, pp. 268–81.

Moore, Christopher, 2005, 'Creative Choices: Changes to Australian Copyright Law and the Future of the Public Domain', *Media International Australia*, 114: 71–82.

Moran, Albert (ed.) (2009) *TV Formats Worldwide: Localizing Global Programs*, Bristol and Chicago, IL: Intellect.

Moran, Albert and Keane, Michael (2003) *Television Across Asia: TV Industries, Program Formats and Globalization*, London: Routledge.

Morley, David (1980) *The Nationwide Audience: Structure and Decoding*, London: British Film Institute.

Moullier, Bertrand (2007) *Whither Bollywood?: IP Rights, Innovation and Economic Growth in India's Film Industries*, Washington, DC: George Washington University Law School.

Mughda, Rai and Cottle, Simon (2008) 'Television News in India: Mediating Democracy and Difference', *International Communication Gazette*, 70/1: 76–96.

Nadeem, Shehzad (2011) *Dead Ringers: How Outsourcing is Changing the Way that Indians Understand Themselves*, Princeton, NJ: Princeton University Press.

Nair, K. S. and White, Shirley (eds) (1993) *Perspectives on Development Communication*, Thousand Oaks, CA: Sage.

Nandy, Ashis (ed.) (1999) *The Secret Politics of Our Desires: Innocence, Culpability and Indian Popular Cinema*, New Delhi, Zed Books.

Nandy, Ashis (2002) 'Telling the Story of Communal Conflicts in South Asia: Interim Report on a Personal Search for Defining Myths', *Ethnic and Racial Studies*, 25/1: 1–19.

Narula, Ranjan (2003) 'Battles In Bollywood: The Fine Line between Idea and Expression in India', at: <http://www.iprights.com/publications/articles/article.asp?articelID=208>; accessed 19 May 2006.

NASSCOM (2009) *The Software Industry in India 2009 Strategic Review*, New Delhi: National Association of Software and Service Companies.

NASSCOM (2011) *The IT BPO Sector in India: Strategic Review 2011*, New Delhi: National Association of Software and Service Companies.

NASSCOM and A. T. Kearney (2008) 'Location Roadmap For IT-BPO Growth: Assessment Of 50 Leading Cities', at: http://www.nasscom.in/>; accessed 24 July 2008.

Nayar, Pramod K. (2009) 'India Goes to the Blogs: Cyberspace, Identity, Community', in Moti Gokulsing and Wimal Dissanayake (eds), *Popular Culture in a Globalized India*, London: Routledge, pp. 207–22.

NCAER (1994) *The Consumer Classes*, New Delhi: National Council of Applied Economic Research.

Nederveen Pieterse, Jan (1995) 'Globalisation as Hybridization', in Mike Featherstone, Scott Lash and Roland Robertson (eds), *Global Modernities*, Thousand Oaks, CA: Sage, pp 45–68.

Nehru, Jawaharlal (1961) *The Discovery of India*, Bombay: Asia Publishing House.

Nilan, Pamela (2003) 'The Social Meanings of Media for Indonesian Youth', in Tim Scrase, Todd Holden and Scott Baum (eds), *Globalization, Culture and Equality in Asia*, Melbourne: Trans Pacific Press, pp. 168–80.

Nye, Joseph (2004) *Soft Power: The Means to Success in World Politics*, New York: Public Affairs.

Nye, Joseph (2005) 'Soft Power Matters in Asia', *Japan Times* (5 December 2005), at: <http://belfercenter.ksg.hardvard.edu/publication/1486/soft_power_matter sin_asia.html>; accessed 10 December 2009.

Nye, Joseph (2008) *The Powers to Lead: Soft Hard and Smart*, New York: Oxford University Press.

Obama, Barack (2010) 'Speech to the Indian Parliament', at: <http://indialawyers. wordpress.com/2010/11/08/obama-praises-gandhi-in-speech-to-indian-parliame nt/>; accessed 8 November 2010.

Ohm, Britta (1999) 'Doordarshan: Representing the Nation's State', in Christine Brosius and Melissa Butcher (eds), *Image Journeys: Audio-Visual Media and Cultural Change in India*. New Delhi: Sage, pp. 69–98.

Oomen, T. K. (2000) 'Conceptualising Nation and Nationality in South Asia', in S. L. Sharma and T. K. Oomen (eds), *Nation and National Identity in South Asia*, Hyderabad: Orient Longman.

O'Regan, Tom (1991) 'From Piracy to Sovereignty: International VCR Trends', *Continuum*, 4/2, at: <http://wwwmcc.murdoch.edu.au/ReadingRoom/4.2/ oregan.html>; accessed 12 May 2006.

Orsini, Francesca (2002) *The Hindi Public Sphere 1920–1940: Language and Literature in the Age of Nationalism*, New York: Oxford University Press.

Oza, Rupal (2006) *The Making of Neoliberal India*, New York: Routledge.

Padmanabhan, Anil (2005) 'Cinema Scope', *India Today International Edition* (28 February): 25–8.

Page, David and Crawley, William (2001) *Satellites Over South Asia: Broadcasting, Culture and the Public Interest*, New Delhi: Sage.

Page, David and Crawley, William (2005) 'The Transnational and the National: Changing Patterns of Cultural Influence in the South Asian TV Market', in J. K. Chalaby (ed.), *Transnational Television Worldwide: Towards a New Media Order*, London and New York: I.B. Tauris, pp. 128–55.

Pandian, M. S. S. (2000) 'Parasakthi: Life and Times of a DMK Film', in Ravi S. Vasudevan (ed.), *Making Meaning in Indian Cinema*, New Delhi: Oxford University Press, pp. 65–96.

Parel, Anthony (ed.) (1997) *Gandhi: Hind Swaraj and Other Writings*, Cambridge: Cambridge University Press.

Parthasarathy, Balaji (2004) 'India's Silicon Valley Or Silicon Valley's India? Socially Embedding The Computer Software Industry In Bangalore', *International Journal of Urban and Regional Research*, 28/3: 664–85.

Parthasarathy, Balaji (2010) 'The Computer Software Industry as a Vehicle of Late Industrialization: Lessons from the Indian Case', *Journal of the Asia Pacific Economy*, 15/3: 247–70.

Parthasarathy, Balaji and Aoyama, Yuko (2006) 'From Software Services to R&D Services: Local Entrepreneurship in the Software Industry in Bangalore, India', *Environment and Planning A*, 38: 1269–85.

Parthasarati, Ashok (2010) *Technology at the Core: Science and Technology with Indira Gandhi*, New Jersey: Prentice Hall.

Pendakur, Manjunath (1990) 'India', in J. Lent (ed.), *The Asian Film Industry*, Austin, TX: University of Texas Press, pp. 229–52.

Pendakur, Manjunath (2003) *Indian Popular Cinema: Industry, Ideology and Consciousness*, Cresskill: Hampton Press.

Pendakur, Manjunath and Radha Subramanyam (1996) 'Indian Cinema beyond National Borders', in John Sinclair, Elizabeth Jacka and Stuart Cunningham (eds), *New Patterns in Television: Peripheral Vision*, Oxford: Oxford University Press, pp. 67–100.

Pinkerton, Alasdair (2008) 'Radio and the Raj: broadcasting in British India (1920–1940)', *Journal of the Royal Asiatic Society of Great Britain & Ireland (Third Series)*, 18: 167–91.

Prabhakar, Jyoti (2006) 'Bollywood: Made in China', *Times News Network* (8 May 2006), at: <http://timesofindia.indiatimes.com/delhi-times/Bollywood-Made-in-China/articleshow/1521283.cms>; accessed 15 March 2008.

Prasad, M. Madhava (1998) *Ideology of the Hindi Film: A Historical Construction*, New Delhi: Oxford University Press.

Price Waterhouse Coopers (2008) *The Indian Entertainment and Media Industry: Sustaining Growth*, at: <http://www.pwc.com/extweb/pwcpublications.nsf/docid/BF27519CD3178AAACA2574210026EFAC/$file/ExecutiveSummary1.pdf>; accessed 20 September 2008.

Punathambekar, Aswin and Kavoori, Anandam P. (eds) (2008) *Global Bollywood*, New York and London: New York University Press.

Purewal, Navtej (2003) 'The Indo-Pak Border: Displacements, Aggressions and Transgressions, *Contemporary South Asia*, 12/4: 539–55.

Quah, Danny (2001) 'The Weightless Economy in Economic Development', in Matti Pohjola, (ed.), *Information Technology, Productivity and Economic Growth: International Evidence and Implications for Economic Development*, Oxford: Oxford University Press, pp. 72–98.

Rai, Amit (2009) *Untimely Bollywood: Globalization and India's New Media Assemblage*, Durham, NC: Duke University Press.

Rai, Mugdha and Cottle, Simon (2007) 'Global Mediations: On the Changing Ecology of Satellite Television News', *Global Media and Communication*, 3/1: 51–78.

Raj Isar, Yudhishthir (2010) 'Chindia: A Cultural Project?', *Global Media and Communication*, 6/3: 277–84.

Rajadhyaksha, Ashish (2000a). 'Realism, Modernism, and Post-Colonial Theory', in John Hill and Pamela Gibson (eds), *World Cinema: Critical Approaches*, Oxford: Oxford University Press, pp. 29–41.

Rajadhyaksha, Ashish (2000b) 'Viewership and Democracy in the Cinema', in Ravi S. Vasudevan (ed.), *Making Meaning in Indian Cinema*, New Delhi: Oxford University Press, pp. 267–96.

Rajadhyaksha, Ashish (2003) 'The "Bollywoodization" of the Indian Cinema: Cultural Nationalism in a Global Arena', *Inter-Asia Cultural Studies*, 4/1: 25–39.

Rajadhyaksha, Ashish and Willemen, Paul (1999) *Encyclopaedia of Indian Cinema*, London: BFI.

Rajagopal, Arvind (1993) 'The Rise of National Programming: The Case of Indian Television', *Media Culture and Society*, 15/1: 91–111.

Rajagopal, Arvind (2001) *Politics After Television: Hindu Nationalism and the Reshaping of the Public in India*, New Delhi: Sage.

Rajagopal, Arvind (ed.) (2009) *The Indian Public Sphere: Readings in Media History*, Oxford: Oxford University Press.

Rajan, Mira T. Sundara (2006) *Copyright and Creative Freedom*, London and New York: Routledge.

Raju, Zakir Hussain (2008) '"Bollywood in Bangladesh": Transcultural Consumption in Globalizing South Asia', in Youna Kim (ed.), *Media Consumption and Everyday Life in Asia*, London: Routledge, pp. 155–66.

Raman, Bhaskaran (2007) 'Experiences in Using WiFi for Rural Internet in India', *Communications Magazine*, 45/1: 104–10.

Ramesh, Jairam (2007) *Making Sense of Chindia: Reflections on China and India*, New Delhi: Indian Research Press.

Ranganathan, Maya (2010) 'Nationalism as a Marketing Tool by MNC Advertisements', in Maya Ranganathan and Usha Rodrigues (eds), *Indian Media in a Globalised World*, New Delhi: Sage, pp. 26–51.

Ranganathan, Maya and Rodrigues, Usha (2010) *Indian Media in a Globalised World*, New Delhi: Sage.

Rao, C.N.R. (2007) 'If IT is Going to Take Away Our Values: Burn Bangalore, Burn IT', *Outlook* (12 December): 108.

Rao, Sandhya (1999) 'The Urban–Rural Dichotomy of Doordarshan's Programming in "India: An Empirical Analysis"', *Gazette: Journal of International Communication*, 61/1: 23–37.

Ray, Manas (2000) 'Bollywood Down Under: Fiji-Indian Cultural History and Popular Assertion', in S. Cunningham and J. Sinclair (eds), *Floating Lives: The Media and Asian Diasporas*, St Lucia: University of Queensland Press, pp. 136–79.

Ray, P. K. and Ray S. (2010) 'Resource-Constrained Innovation for Emerging Economies: The Case of the Indian Telecommunications Industry', *IEEE Transactions on Engineering Management*, 57/1: 144–56.

Ray, Satyajit (1976) *Our Films, Their Films*. Hyderabad: Disha Books.

Reddy, B. Muralidhar (2003) 'Bollywood Reels in Pakistan', *The Hindu*, at: <http://www.hindu.com/thehindu/mag/2003/11/23/stories/2003112300220500.htm>; accessed 10 November 2004.

Robertson, Roland (1992) *Globalization: Social Theory and Global Culture*, London: Sage.

Robertson, Roland (1994) 'Globalization or Glocalization?', *Journal of International Communication*, 1/1: 33–52.

Rodrigues, Usha (2010) 'Public Service Broadcasting in India: Doordarshan's Legacy', in Maya Ranganathan and Usha Rodrigues, *Indian Media in A Globalised World*, New Delhi: Sage, pp. 181–205.

Roy, Abhijit (2008) 'Bringing Up TV: Popular Culture and the Developmental Modern in India', *South Asian Popular Culture*, 6/1: 29–43.

Said, Salim (1991) *Shadows on the Silver Screen: A Social History of Indonesian Film*, Jakarta: Lontar Foundation.

SARAI (2007) 'Welcome to Sarai', at: <http://www.sarai.net/>; accessed 1 February 2007.

Savarkar, V. D. (credited as 'A. Maratha') (1923) *Hindutva*, Nagpur: V.V. Kelkar.

Saxenian, AnnaLee (2001) 'Transnational Communities and the Evolution of Global Production Networks: The Cases of Taiwan, China and India', *East West Center Working Papers*, Economics Series, No. 37, Hawaii: East West Center.

Saxenian, AnnaLee (2005) 'From Brain Drain to Brain Circulation: Transnational Communities and Regional Upgrading in India and China', *Studies in Comparative International Development*, 40/2: 35–61.

Schaefer, David J. and Karan, Kavita (2010) 'Problematizing Chindia: Hybridity and Bollywoodization of Popular Indian Cinema in Global Film Flows', *Global Media and Communication*, 6/3: 309–16.

Schiller, Herbert (1976) *Communication and Cultural Domination*, White Planes: International Arts and Sciences Press.

Schlesinger, Philip (2000) 'The Sociological Scope of "National Cinema" in Mette Hjort and Scott Mackenzie (eds), *Cinema and Nation*, London and New York: Routledge, pp. 19–31.

Schramm, Wilbur (1964) *Mass Media and National Development: The Role of Information in Developing Societies*, Stanford, CA: Stanford University Press.

Scrase, Timothy and Ganguly-Scrase, Ruchira (2010) *Globalization and the Middle Classes in India: The Social and Cultural Impact of Neoliberal Reforms*, London: Routledge.

Seagrave, Kerry (2003) *Piracy in the Motion Picture Industry*, Jefferson, NC, and London: McFarland and Company.

Sengupta, Shuddhabrata (1999) 'Vision-Mixing: Marriage-Video-Film and the Video-walla's Images of Life', in Christine Brosius and Melissa Butcher (eds), *Image Journeys: Audio-Visual Media and Cultural Change in India*, New Delhi: Sage, pp. 279–307.

Sharma, S. L and T. K. Oommen (eds) (2000) *Nation and National Identity in South Asia*. Hyderabad: Orient Longman.

Shohat, Ella and Robert Stam (1996) 'From the Imperial Family to the Trans-national Imaginary: Media Spectatorship in the Age of Globalization', in Rob Wilson and Wimal Dissanayake (eds), *Global/Local Cultural Production and the Transnational Imaginary*, Durham, NC, and London: Duke University Press, pp. 145–70.

Sinclair, John and Harrison, Mark (2004) 'Globalization, Nation, and Television in Asia: The Cases of India and China', *Television and New Media,* 5/1: 41–54.

Singh, Manmohan (2007) 'PM's remarks at the Book Release Function of Dev Anand's Autobiography "Romancing With Life"' (September 26), Office of the Prime Minister of India, at: <http://pmindia.nic.in/speech/content4print. asp?id=586>; accessed 28 May 2009.

Singh, Manmohan (2011) 'PM Inaugurates 9th Pravasi Bharatiya Divas' (9 January), Office of the Prime Minister of India, at: <http://pmindia.nic.in/speech/content. asp?id=1003>; accessed 11 January 2011.

Singhal, Arvind, Doshi, J. K., Rogers, Everett and Rahman, S. Adnam (1988) 'The Diffusion of Television in India', *Media Asia*, 15/4: 222–9.

Singhvi, L. M. (2000) *Report of the High Level Committee on the Indian Diaspora*, New Delhi: Ministry of External Affairs, Foreign Secretary's Office, Government of India, at: <http://www.indiaday.org/singhvi.htm>; accessed 14 May 2004.

Sinha, Dipankar (2005) 'Development (without) Communication: Viewing Doordarshan Methodologically', *Journal of the Moving Image*, 4: 140–53.

Smith, Anthony (1999) *Myths and Memories of the Nation*, Oxford: Oxford University Press.

Sonwalkar, Prasun (2001) 'India: Makings Of Little Cultural/Media Imperialism?', *Gazette: Journal of International Communications*, 63/6: 505–19.

Soros, George (2002) *On Globalization*, Oxford: Public Affairs.

Sparks, Colin (2007) *Globalization, Development and the Mass Media*, London: Sage.

Sridharan, Eswaran (1996) *The Political Economy of Industrial Promotion: Indian, Brazilian, and Korean Electronics in Comparative Perspective 1969–1994*, London: Praeger.

Srinivas, S. V. (2000a) 'Is There a Public in the Cinema Hall?', at: <http://www. frameworkonline.com>; accessed 10 November 2000.

Srinivas, S. V. (2000b) 'Devotion and Defiance in Fan Activity', in Ravi S. Vasudevan (ed.), *Making Meaning in Indian Cinema*, New Delhi: Oxford University Press, pp. 297–317.

Srivastava, Sanjeev (2000) 'Underworld Scandal Rocks Bollywood', at: <http://news. bbc.co.uk/2/hi/south_asia/1072398.stm>; accessed 4 March 2002.

Srivastava, Sanjeev (2003) 'Analysis: Bollywood and the Mafia', at: <http://news.bbc. co.uk/1/hi/entertainment/3152662.stm1>; accessed 5 May 2008.

Stahlberg, Pers (2006) 'Brand India: The Storyline of a Superpower in the Making', *Media and Identity in Asia*, CD-ROM, Sarawak: Curtin University of Technology.

Stallmeyer, John C. (2011) *Building Bangalore: Architecture and Urban Transformation in India's Silicon Valley*, London and New York: Routledge.

Stiglitz, Joseph (2003) *Globalization and its Discontents*, New York: Penguin.

Stiglitz, Joseph (2010) *Freefall: Free Markets and the Sinking of the Global Economy*, New York: Penguin.

Straubhaar, Joseph (1991) 'Beyond Media Imperialism: Assymetrical Interdependence and Cultural Proximity', *Critical Studies in Mass Communication*, 8/1: 33–59.

Straubhaar, Joseph (2010) 'Chindia in the Context of Emerging Media and Cultural Powers', *Global Media and Communication*, 6/3: 253–62.

Stremlau, John (1996) 'Bangalore: India's Silicon City', *Monthly Labour Review*, 119: 21–47.

Subramanian, C. R. (1992) *India and the Computer: A Study of Planned Development*, New Delhi: Oxford University Press.

Suchitra (1995) 'What Moves Masses: Dandi March as Communication Strategy', *Economic and Political Weekly*, 30/14: 743–6.

Sumarno, M. and Achnas, N. T. (2002) 'In Two Worlds', in Aruna Vasudev, Latika Padgoankar and Rashmi Doraiswamy (eds), *Being and Becoming: The Cinemas of Asia*, New Delhi: Macmillan India, pp. 152–70.

Sundaram, Ravi (2010) *Pirate Modernity: Delhi's Media Urbanism*, Abingdon and New York: Routledge.

Swaraj, Sushma (2003) 'Keynote Address on Entertainment, Ethnic Media and the Diasporic Identity', Pravasi Bharatiya Divas, New Delhi, 2003, at: <http://www.indiaday.org/pbd1/pbd-sushmaswaraj.asp>; accessed 23 September 2009.

Taeube, Florian (2003) 'Proximity and Innovation: Evidence from the Indian Software Industry', paper presented at Clusters, Industrial Districts and Firms: The Challenge of Globalization Conference, September 12–13, 2003, Modena.

Taeube, Florian (2009) 'The Indian Software Industry: Cultural Factors Underpinning its Evolution' in Moti Gokulsing and Wimal Dissanayake (eds), *Popular Culture in a Globalized India*, London: Routledge, pp. 223–35.

Taeube, Florian and Sonderegger, Petra (2009) 'Cluster Lifecycle and Diaspora Effects: Evidence from the Indian IT Cluster in Bangalore', paper presented at the Copenhagen Business School Summer Conference 2009, Copenhagen.

Tharoor, Shashi (2008) 'Why Nations Should Pursue "Soft" Power', at: <http://www.ted.com/talks/shashi_tharoor.html>; accessed 15 September 2009.

Thomas, Pradip Ninan (1999) 'Trading the Nation: Multilateral Negotiations and the Fate of Communications in India', *Gazette: Journal of International Communication*, 61: 275–92.

Thomas, Pradip Ninan (2010) *Political Economy of Communications in India: The Good, The Bad and the Ugly*, New Delhi: Sage.

Thomas, Pradip Ninan and Servaes, Jan (eds) (2006) *Intellectual Property Rights and Communications in Asia: Conflicting Traditions*, New Delhi: Sage.

Thompson, Kenneth (2002) 'Border Crossings and Diasporic Identities: Media Use and Leisure Practices of an Ethnic Minority', *Qualitative Sociology*, 25/3: 409–18.

Thoraval, Yves (2000) *The Cinemas of India*, New Delhi: Macmillan India.

Thussu, Daya Kishan (1999) 'Privatizing the Airwaves: The Impact of Globalization on Broadcasting in India', *Media Culture and Society*, 21: 125–31.

Thussu, Daya Kishan (2000) 'Indian Media – from Colonial to Global?', *Imperium*, I, at: <http://www.imperiumjournal.com/>; accessed 2 April 2003.

Thussu, Daya Kishan (2005) 'The Transnationalization of Television: The Indian Experience', in J. K. Chalaby (ed.), *Transnational Television Worldwide: Towards a New Media Order*, London and New York, I.B. Tauris, pp. 156–72.

Thussu, Daya Kishan (ed.) (2007a) *Media on the Move: Global Flow and Contra-Flow*, London and New York: Routledge.

Thussu, Daya Kishan (2007b) 'The "Murdochization" of News: The Case of Star TV in India', *Media Culture and Society*, 29/4: 593–611.

Thussu, Daya Kishan (2008) 'The Globalization of Bollywood: The Hype and the Hope', in Anandam Kavorri and Aswin Punathambekar (eds), *Global Bollywood*, New York: New York University Press, pp. 97–114.

Time Magazine (1930) 'India: Pinch of Salt' (13 November). Reproduced at: <http://www.time.com/time/magazine/article/0,9171,738958,00.html>; accessed 14 January 2011.

Tomlinson, John (1991) *Cultural Imperialism: A Critical Introduction*, London: Continuum.

Trehan, Madhu (2010) *Tehelka as Metaphor: Prism Me a Lie, Tell Me a Truth*, New Delhi: Roli Books.

Turner, Graeme (2009) 'Television and the Nation: Does This Matter Anymore?', in Graeme Turner, and Jinna Tay (eds), *Television Studies After TV: Understanding Television in the Post-Broadcast Era*, London: Routledge, pp. 54–64.

Turner, Rachel S. (2011) *Neo-Liberal Ideology: History, Concepts and Policies*, Edinburgh: Edinburgh University Press.

Umchanda, Usha (1998) 'Invasion from the Skies', *Australian Studies in Journalism*, 7: 136–63.

UNESCO (2001) *Universal Declaration on Cultural Diversity*, Paris: UNESCO.

Valenti, Jack (2003) 'Testimony of Jack Valenti, President and CEO Motion Picture Association of America, before the SubCommittee on Courts, the Internet, and Intellectual Property', Committee on the Judiciary, US House of Representatives: 'International Copyright Piracy: Links to Organized Crime and Terrorism', (13 March) at: <http://www.kuro5hin.org/story/2003/3/14/234939/956>; accessed 26 July 2006.

Varma, P. K. (1998) *The Great Indian Middle Class*, New Delhi: Penguin.

Varma, P. K. (2006) *Being Indian: Inside The Real India*, London: Arrow Books.

Vasudevan, Ravi S. (2000a) 'The Politics of Cultural Address in a "Transitional" Cinema: A Case Study of Indian Popular Cinema', in Christine Gledhill and Linda Williams (eds), *Reinventing Film Studies*, London: Arnold, pp. 130–61.

Vasudevan, Ravi S. (ed.) (2000b) *Making Meaning in Indian Cinema*, New Delhi, Oxford University Press.

Vasudevan, Ravi S. (2003) 'Cinema in Urban Space', *Seminar*, 525, at: <http://www.india-seminar.com/2003/525/525%20ravi%20vasudevan.htm/>; accessed 18 April 2006.

Velayutham, Selvaraj (2008) *Tamil Cinema: The Cultural Politics of India's Other Film Industry*, London and New York: Routledge.

VHP (2011) 'Vishva Hindu Parishad' (official website 2011), at: <http://vhp.org/>; accessed 1 April 2011.

Voyce, Malcolm (2007) 'Shopping Malls in India: New Social Dividing Practices', *Economic and Political Weekly*, 42/22: 2055–62.

Wang, Shujen (2003) 'Recontextualizing Copyright: Piracy, Hollywood, the Sate and Globalization', *Cinema Journal*, 43/1: 25–43.

Whitaker, Mark (2004) 'TamilNet: Some Reflections on Popular Anthropology, Nationalism and the Internet', *Anthropological Quarterly*, 77/3: 469–98.

White, Amanda and Rughani, Pratip (2003) *ImagineAsia Evaluation Report*, BFI, at: <http://www.bfi.org.uk/about/imagineasia-evaluation/imagineasia-evaluation.pdf>; accessed 4 March 2004.

Willeman, Paul and Ashish Rajadhyaksha (eds) (1999 edn) *Encyclopaedia of Indian Cinema*, London: BFI.

Williams, Raymond (1974) *Television: Technology and Cultural Form,* London: Collins.

Wood, Denise (2009) 'Call Centre Conundrum', in Arvind Rajagopal (ed.), *The Indian Public Sphere: Readings in Indian Media History*, Oxford: Oxford University Press, pp. 313–19.

Yash Raj Films (2004a) 'Counterfeit Yash Raj Films' Titles Seized In Virginia, USA', at: <http://www.yashrajfilms.com/news/n_titlesvirginia.htm>; accessed 27 September 2011.

Yash Raj Films (2004b) 'Thousands of Pirated Indian Film CDs, DVDs Seized In Fairfax, Virginia', at: <http://www.yashrajfilms.com/news/n_piracy.htm>; accessed 27 September 2011.

Yash Raj Films (2005) 'Dutch Raids Uncover Bollywood Piracy In Europe', at: <http://www.yashrajfilms.com/News/NewsDetails.aspx?NewsID=a49ca8f2-ee97-479d-9474-84320f81a566>; accessed 27 September 2011.

Yash Raj Films (2006) 'Southall and Ealing Piracy Raids Successful', at: <http://www.yashrajfilms.com/News/NewsDetails.aspx?Typeid=&newsid=1a3f43da-9691-481d-bb60-4df2484f094b>; accessed 27 September 2011.

Yusufzai, Rahimullah (2001) 'In which Lollywood gives Bollywood Those Ones', *Himal South Asian*, at: <http://www.himalmag.com/march2001/analysis.html>; accessed 7 July 2006.

Zins, M. J. (1989) 'The Emergency 1975–77', in S. N. Jha Hasan, and R. Khan (eds), *The State, Political Process and Identity: Reflections on Modern India*, New Delhi: Oxford University Press, pp. 150–79.

Index